EMPOWERING THE NEW AMERICAN WORKER

MARKET-BASED SOLUTIONS FOR TODAY'S WORKFORCE

EDITED BY SCOTT LINCICOME

For Eve.

ISBN 978-1-952223-79-2 (print)
ISBN 978-1-952223-80-8 (digital)

Library of Congress Cataloging-in-Publication Data available.
Library of Congress Control Number: 2022951547.

Cover design and art direction by Jon Meyers.
Book design by Melina Yingling Enterline.
Printed in the United States of America.

Cato Institute
1000 Massachusetts Ave. NW
Washington, DC 20001
www.cato.org

CONTENTS

INTRODUCTION   1

POLICY SOLUTIONS   17

Ensuring a Sound Macroeconomic Foundation   19

Facilitating Personal Improvement   29
    Private-Sector Labor Regulation   31
    Higher Education   47
    Occupational Licensing   59
    Independent Work   71
    Entrepreneurship and Home Businesses   85
    Criminal Justice   95

Enabling Mobility and Independence   107
    Transportation   109
    Remote Work   125
    Employee Benefits   135
    Welfare Reform   149

Improving Living Standards   161
    Childcare   163
    K–12 Education   175
    Health Care   187
    Housing Affordability   205
    Homeownership   219
    Essential Goods   227

CONCLUSION   241

INTRODUCTION

BY SCOTT LINCICOME

Since the 2016 presidential election, politicians have become enamored with policies intended to help the American worker. President Donald Trump issued a 2020 "Pledge to America's Workers" in which he heralded past executive actions, such as those creating the American Workforce Policy Advisory Board and the National Council for the American Worker.[1] President Biden has since embraced similar rhetoric and policies, such as his "worker centric" trade policy and an infrastructure law with "Buy America" rules that "create[ ] jobs for American workers."[2] And almost everywhere you go in Washington these days, you find a politician, bureaucrat, or wonk lamenting the supposed plight of today's American worker and promising to fix it.

In some ways, this plight has been oversold. For example, inflation-adjusted median personal income in the United States increased by 61 percent between 1984 and 2019 (see Figure 1), while nonmanagement wages grew substantially as well.[3] According to the most recent calculations from economist Michael Strain, real wages increased between 1990 and 2022 by 50, 48, 38, and 39 percent at the 10th, 20th, 30th, and 50th (median) percentiles, respectively.[4]

FIGURE 1 Inflation-adjusted U.S. incomes have increased substantially since the 1980s

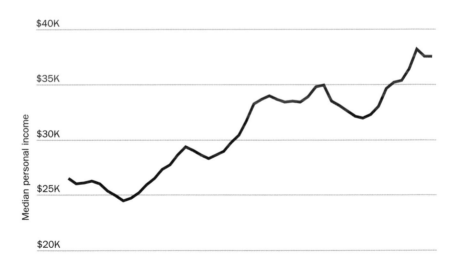

Source: "Real Median Personal Income in the United States," Federal Reserve Economic Data, Federal Reserve Bank of St. Louis, September 13, 2022.
Note: In 2021 dollars.

Meanwhile, recent economic analyses show that the supposed "hollowing out" of the middle class has occurred not because workers are falling into lower wage brackets but because they're generally moving up the income ladder (see Figure 2).[5]

The percentage of two-earner households in the United States also has barely budged over the last several decades and has actually declined a bit for American families since 1990 (see Figure 3)—contrary to the common narrative that an increasing number of working families have fallen into the "two earner trap."[6]

In 2022, in fact, economists have been far more worried about the labor market being too hot—as indicated by record-setting job openings, the "great resignation," and quickly rising private sector wages—than too cold.[7]

FIGURE 2 The share of high-income U.S. households has almost tripled since the 1960s

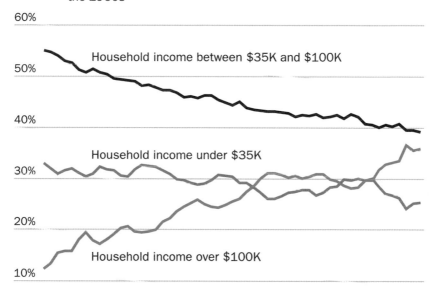

Source: Jessica Semega and Melissa Kollar, "Income in the United States: 2021," (U.S. Census Bureau, September 2022).
Note: Income figures are in 2021 dollars, adjusted using the R-CPI-U-RS. Household income is "total money income," defined by the Census Bureau as "the arithmetic sum of money wages and salaries, net income from self-employment, and income other than earnings," for all income recipients in the household.

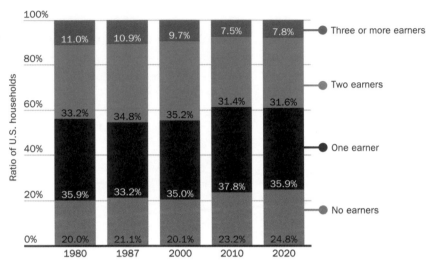

FIGURE 3 The number of two-earner U.S. households has remained steady since 1980

Source: "1981 to 2021 Annual Social and Economic Supplements," U.S. Census Bureau Current Population Survey, October 8, 2021.

Nevertheless, there are some real reasons for concern about the U.S. labor market and American workers' situation therein. Prior to the pandemic, various measures of "labor dynamism"—the natural market churn of workers moving from job to job or place to place—had been in a decades-long decline. Measures of business dynamism, especially new business formation (for workers-turned-entrepreneurs), exhibited similar trends. At the same time, certain segments of the workforce, such as less-educated prime-age men, were exiting the labor force altogether, and workers of all income and education levels have faced increasing costs of essential goods and services, such as housing and childcare. Thus, policymakers' attention to the American worker is both unsurprising and, perhaps, even necessary.[8]

Unfortunately, the most common proposals addressing the challenges facing American workers today—heavy on government intervention in labor, trade, or other markets—ignore several critical facts and might therefore make things worse for the vast majority of the workforce. First, the proposals tend to overlook the laundry list of current federal, state, and local policies that enrich politically powerful interest groups but in the process disempower and tax most American workers, while breeding broader economic sclerosis along the way. Second, they ignore the numerous free-market solutions than can boost workers' independence, mobility, wealth, resilience, and quality of life. Neither a major new government program nor a fundamental rethinking of free-market capitalism is needed—in fact, much the opposite.

Finally, and perhaps most importantly, most "pro-worker" policy proposals fundamentally misunderstand that today's American worker is far different from the cookie-cutter models—for example, a middle-aged, sole breadwinner male in a unionized, nine-to-five, assembly line job, or a single, college-educated, urbanite female—that those policies most often target. Some American workers conform to those stereotypes, but many more do not, because the "American worker" is actually a diverse group of distinct individuals across a wide range of industries and localities, each with his or her own goals, desires, and skills.

For instance, the vast majority of American workers, female and male, are today employed in industries other than manufacturing (see Figure 4), whose share of the workforce (today about 8 percent) has declined steadily since 1953 (about 32 percent).[9] And in 2021, the number of blue-collar, male-dominated (60 percent or more) nonmanufacturing jobs in the United States outnumbered nonsupervisory manufacturing jobs by a nearly four-to-one margin (see Figure 5).

Contrary to the conventional wisdom, moreover, the current U.S. manufacturing job situation is not due to a lack of demand for these workers (caused by globalization or automation, for example): in the first quarter of 2022, there were around 850,000 unfilled manufacturing job openings, and new research from Deloitte and the Manufacturing Institute estimates that this figure could hit 2.1 million by 2030.[10] There are plenty of manufacturing jobs—for those who want and can qualify for them.

FIGURE 4 Most American workers are employed in industries other than manufacturing

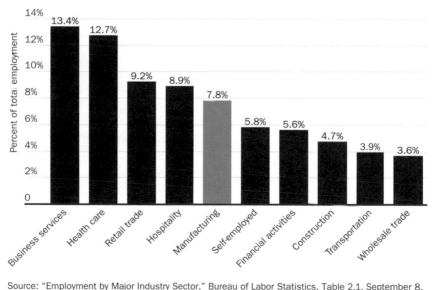

Source: "Employment by Major Industry Sector," Bureau of Labor Statistics, Table 2.1, September 8, 2022.

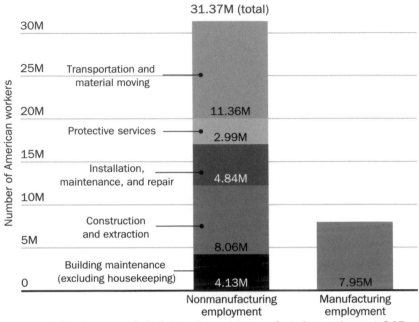

FIGURE 5 Four times as many American workers are employed in male-dominated, blue-collar service industries than in manufacturing

Ratio of nonmanufacturing employment to manufacturing employment: **3.95**

Source: "Labor Force Statistics from the Current Population Survey," Bureau of Labor Statistics, Table 11, January 20, 2022.
Note: Blue-collar is defined as a nonmanagement occupation. Male-dominated is defined as industries in which at least 60 percent of workers are male. Production occupations are used as a proxy for manufacturing employment.

Indeed, much of the current lack of manufacturing workers in America reflects the changing nature and demands of modern manufacturing work. Two new studies from the Federal Reserve system have found that the long-standing manufacturing wage premium over nonmanufacturing jobs has essentially disappeared, and "manufacturing companies are increasingly competing with other sectors for skilled labor."[11] Furthermore, many of the manufacturing jobs of tomorrow will actually be in services (e.g., industrial robot maintenance and repair) or require advanced skills and postsecondary education—far different from the routine assembly line jobs of the past that required only a high school degree.[12] As of 2021, more manufacturing workers above the age of 25 had an associate's degree or higher (45.1 percent) than had, at most, a high school degree (40.2 percent), continuing a trend of increasing education in the sector that dates back decades.[13]

This does not mean, of course, that all workers must aspire to attain a traditional four-year bachelor's degree, either. Today, online educational institutions—driven in part by the pandemic—have become increasingly popular and well-respected, while "Google has launched certificate programs that it says it will treat as the equivalent of four-year college for hiring purposes."[14] Noncollege pathways also are promising: store managers at Whole Foods can make well over $100,000 without a degree, and employer-led apprenticeship and retraining initiatives, such as Toyota's Federation for Advanced Manufacturing Education program, have successfully vaulted participants into a similar pay range.[15] And massive retailers including Amazon, Walmart, and Target employ millions of Americans and are constantly pushing the compensation envelope (and each other). Walmart announced in 2022 that first-year truck drivers will make up to $110,000, with both training and licensing paid by the company.[16] It thus pays more today—*much more* in some places—to move the proverbial "cheap T-shirt" in America than it does to manufacture it here.[17]

As a result of these college alternatives and other factors (e.g., rising student debt loads), the "wealth premium" (extra net worth) that American college graduates long enjoyed over their noncollege peers has shrunk dramatically in recent years, and the unemployment rate for young college graduates has actually exceeded the rate for all workers since 2018 (though young college grads still enjoy some, albeit shrinking, employment advantage over noncollege workers of the same age).[18] In short, college isn't for everyone, nor does it need to be.

The pandemic has also accelerated fundamental changes to workers' relationships with their workplace. According to the Census Bureau, 30 percent of employed adults reported in February 2022 that they worked remotely most or all of the time (up from 6 percent in 2019), and Pew Research Center reports that 61 percent of respondents working from home preferred that arrangement to going to their workplace (see Figure 6).[19] Contrary to conventional wisdom, these "teleworkable" jobs are available not merely to wealthy or college-educated workers but also to those with less education or income.

The growing prominence of remote and hybrid work has profound implications, not only for the traditional office and workweek but also for entire industries and communities in the United States. For example, remote work's rise has likely increased employment opportunities for disabled workers and those with small children or relatives needing long-term care. And research shows that telework has fueled significant changes in where people are moving and living while also boosting home prices.[20]

Remote work's post-pandemic durability reflects, at least in part, that many American workers, especially younger ones, value flexibility and lifestyle above higher wages or the office work routine. Barrero et al. (2022) have therefore shown that many employers have offered remote work options to temper wage increases because their workers value this new amenity more than a slightly larger paycheck.[21] Notoriously demanding investment banks, meanwhile, are begrudgingly bending to workers' desire for more flexibility.[22] And even in manufacturing,

FIGURE 6 Remote work has increased dramatically since 2019

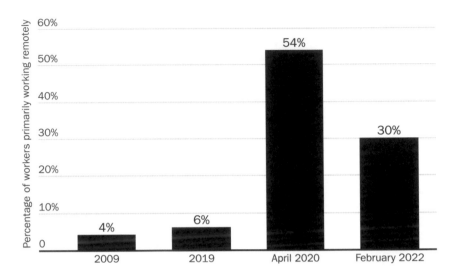

Sources: Patrick Coate, "Remote Work before, during, and after the Pandemic," National Council on Compensation Insurance, January 25, 2021; Lydia Saad and Ben Wigert, "Remote Work Persisting and Trending Permanent," Gallup, October 13, 2021; and Taylor Orth, "Many More Americans Prefer Working from Home than Currently do," Yougov, February 11, 2022.

prospective workers today increasingly value personal well-being, work flexibility, and geography above other employment attributes.[23]

More Americans are also going out on their own—and making good money doing so. Between 2017 and 2021, the share of workers categorized as "freelance" held steady at about 36 percent, but that share increasingly consisted of skilled workers—in computer programming, business consulting, marketing, information technology, and other services—while the percentage of temp workers declined.[24] In 2021, more than half of all freelancers in the United States provided skilled services or labor.[25] The number of new business applications, both "high propensity" (i.e., those likely to have employees and payrolls) and sole proprietorships, also increased substantially during the pandemic and has remained elevated (see Figure 7).

The self-employment trend is not, however, limited to part-time gig workers or white-collar knowledge workers. Commercial trucking, for example, recently saw a significant increase in drivers quitting large firms and becoming independent owner-operators, and large shares of new business applications have been in industries other than knowledge or gig work (see Figure 8).[26]

American workers' increased desire for flexibility and self-determination again looms large in these figures. Along with pursuing work they find "meaningful," freelancers surveyed by Upwork in late 2021 said control over their schedule

FIGURE 7 New business applications soared during the pandemic

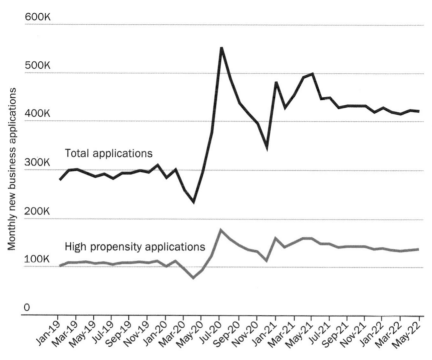

Source: "Monthly Business Applications (Seasonally Adjusted)," Business Formation Statistics, U.S. Census Bureau, September 14, 2022.

(78 percent) and location flexibility (73 percent) were key motivators.[27] Gig workers report much the same.[28]

Workers' personal lives also vary widely, and in ways that again often diverge from the caricatures drawn by many politicians. According to new research from the University of Texas, for example, approximately 70 percent of American mothers can today expect to be the primary breadwinner in their household for at least one year, and this trend is mostly about married moms, not unmarried ones: the share of primary-earning mothers who were married increased from 15 to 40 percent between 2000 and 2017.[29] A Center for American Progress study found that approximately 41 percent of working mothers in 2019 were sole or primary breadwinners, but these numbers varied widely by race, income, and locality.[30] Evidence is mixed, on the other hand, as to whether Americans want bigger families.[31]

At the same time, the pandemic may have changed long-standing views of the lives we *thought* workers wanted. The decades leading up to 2020 saw Americans moving to urban centers (especially on the coasts) and parents working away from home—situations that were assumed would continue indefinitely but that

FIGURE 8 Self-employment increased across a wide range of industries from 2019 to 2021

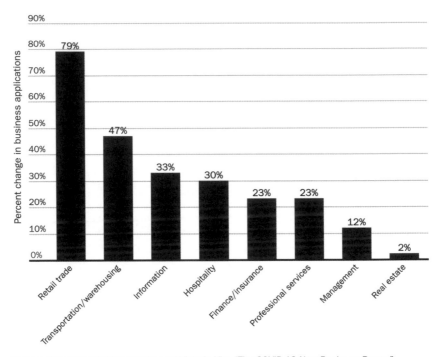

Source: Guillaume Vandenbroucke and Victoria Yin, "The COVID-19 New Business Boom," *Economic Synopses* 6 (2022): 2.
Note: "Accommodation and Food Services" was renamed "Hospitality" due to space constraints.

might now be changing.[32] Suddenly, Americans are moving back to the suburbs, and the country's hottest job markets are in small or midsize cities in the Sun Belt and Midwest.[33] Juggling childcare and children's schooling has required working parents to rearrange their schedules and work off-hours, which has strengthened their preferences for flexibility, remote work options, and starting their own businesses—preferences that are reflected in Figures 6–8.[34]

Finally, the American worker is increasingly globalized, contrary to the common assumption that protectionism and nativism are working class policies. According to the review of new Census Bureau data in Handley et al. (2021), American companies that engage in international goods trade constitute only 6 percent of all U.S. companies yet account for half of U.S. jobs.[35] These same goods traders support jobs not only in manufacturing but increasingly in services, such as management, retail, transportation, utilities, and wholesale trade. And they are increasingly responsible for job creation, accounting for more than half of all net new jobs in the United States since the Great Recession, which is due primarily to new business establishments (startups). Even in manufacturing, goods traders experienced net job creation since 2011, while nontrader manufacturers lost jobs overall. Leaving aside the numerous other benefits of trade and foreign investment for the economy, the data present a compelling case against worker-centric protectionism and for greater international engagement.

Overall, these trends argue for pro-worker policies that, instead of promoting a certain kind of American worker or presuming that the employment and lifestyle trends of today will last beyond tomorrow, maximize workers' autonomy and mobility between jobs or localities. Market-oriented policies that achieve these objectives not only would boost workers' freedom and resilience but also have been shown to boost their long-term wages and living standards. By contrast, supposedly pro-worker policies that end up reducing mobility, raising employers' costs, and pigeonholing workers into certain preordained jobs or workplace arrangements not only contradict recent trends but also significantly reduce workers' lifetime earnings, career advancement, and skills accumulation—thus harming a nation's overall labor productivity and economy more broadly (see Figure 9 and Figure 10).[36]

FIGURE 9 Fluid labor markets tend to make it easier to start and run a business

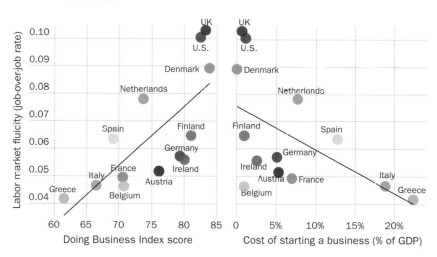

Source: Niklas Engbom, "Labor Market Fluidity and Human Capital Accumulation," National Bureau of Economic Research Working Paper no. 29698, January 2022, p. 38.
Note: Data for men between the ages of 25–54. Labor market fluidity calculated using the annual job-over-job rate, which is the frequency of workers' transitions from job to job. Doing Business Index and cost of starting a business scores are from the World Bank. Cost of starting a business is relative to gross national income per capita.

FIGURE 10 Fluid labor markets tend to have higher wage growth, employment levels, and productivity

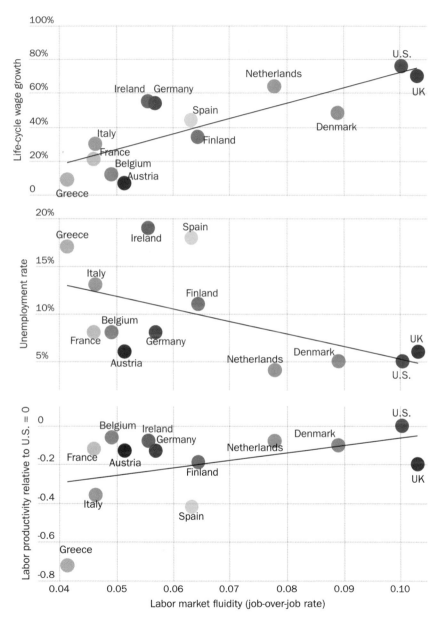

Source: Niklas Engbom, "Labor Market Fluidity and Human Capital Accumulation," National Bureau of Economic Research Working Paper no. 29698, January 2022, p. 28.
Note: Data for men between the ages of 25–54. Labor market fluidity calculated using the annual job-over-job rate, which is the frequency of workers' transitions from job to job.

Put simply, pro-*market* policies are very much pro-*worker* policies too.

This book identifies what Cato Institute scholars believe to be the most important market-oriented policies for the new American worker today, covering a broad array of issues including education, housing, remote work, health care, criminal justice, and licensing. These policies fall into four categories: policies to ensure a sound macroeconomic foundation that broadly improves workers' living standards and the long-term health of the economy; policies to facilitate workers' professional improvement or advancement; policies to promote worker mobility and independence; and policies to improve workers' access to, and to lower the cost of, essential goods and services. Each chapter will identify current problems facing American workers and their causes and then will suggest pro-market ways for federal, state, and local policymakers to fix them.

Combined, these policies will give individuals in the United States the freedom and resources they need to be the American worker *they want to be*—not the one a few policymakers think they *should* be—and to be happier and more prosperous in the process.

NOTES

1. "Pledge to America's Workers," Trump White House, May 26, 2022.

2. Joseph R. Biden, "Remarks by President Biden in Honor of Labor Unions," transcript of speech delivered at the White House, Washington, DC, September 8, 2021.

3. Scott Lincicome, "The Annoying Persistence of the Income Stagnation Myth," *The Dispatch*, October 7, 2020.

4. Michael Strain, "Have Wages Stagnated for Decades in the U.S.?," *Observator Finansowy,* National Bank of Poland, June 27, 2022.

5. Scott Lincicome, "Some Reasons for Optimism Regarding the 'Hollowing Out' of America's Middle Class," *Cato at Liberty* (blog), Cato Institute, August 20, 2020.

6. See Pew Research Center, "The Rise in Dual-Income Families," June 15, 2017; and Bureau of Labor Statistics, "Employment Characteristics of Families—2021," April 20, 2022.

7. Christopher Rugaber, "Why Fed Worries about the Strongest US Job Market in Decades," *US News and World Report*, April 22, 2022.

8. Scott Lincicome, "Not Ready for Prime Time," *The Dispatch*, November 4, 2021.

9. U.S. Bureau of Labor Statistics, "All Employees, Manufacturing [MANEMP]," FRED, Federal Reserve Bank of St. Louis, August 5, 2022.

10. See U.S. Bureau of Labor Statistics, "Job Openings: Manufacturing [JTS3000JOL]," FRED, Federal Reserve Bank of St. Louis, June 23, 2022; and Dani Romero, "Supply Chains: 'Nearshoring' Could Be the Answer to America's Logistics Problems, Deloitte Exec Says," *Yahoo Finance*, April 3, 2022.

11. See Kimberly Bayard et al., "Are Manufacturing Jobs Still Good Jobs? An Exploration of the Manufacturing Wage Premium," Federal Reserve Finance and Economics Discussion Series, March 2022. See also Joel Elvery and Julianne Dunn, "Manufacturing Wage Premiums Have Diverged between Production and Nonproduction Workers," Cleveland Fed Regional Policy Report, November 9, 2021; and Paul Wellener et al., "Competing for Talent: Recasting Perceptions of Manufacturing," Deloitte and the Manufacturing Institute, 2022.

12. Thomas Black, "Robot Subscription Services Let Companies Automate on the Cheap," *Bloomberg Businessweek*, March 31, 2022. See also Gary Winslett (@GaryWinslett), "It's the servitization of manufacturing and it's gonna be very cool," Twitter, April 3, 2022, 10:10 a.m.; and Josh Mitchell, "How Apprenticeship, Reimagined, Vaults Graduates into Middle Class," *Wall Street Journal,* October 19, 2020. See also Wellener et al., "Competing for Talent."

13. See Austen Hufford, "American Factories Demand White-Collar Education for Blue-Collar Work," *Wall Street Journal,* December 9, 2019. See also U.S. Census Bureau, "Educational Attainment of the Population 25 Years and Over, by Selected Characteristics: 2021," February 24, 2022.

14. Spencer Jakab, "The $670 Billion College-Industrial Complex Is under Threat from Online School," *Wall Street Journal,* June 25, 2021.

15. Catherine Clifford, "Whole Foods CEO John Mackey: Store Managers Could Be Making 'Well over $100,000,' without a College Degree," *CNBC*, November 5, 2020.

16. Melissa Repko, "Walmart Says It Is Raising Truckers' Pay and Starting a Training Program as It Grapples with a Driver Shortage," *CNBC*, April 7, 2022.

17. Scott Lincicome and Huan Zhu, "Amazon, Alabama, and Nostalgianomics," *Cato at Liberty* (blog), Cato Institute, April 21, 2021.

18. William R. Emmons, Ana H. Kent, and Lowell R. Ricketts, "Is College Still Worth It? The New Calculus of Falling Returns," *Federal Reserve Bank of St. Louis Review* 101, no. 4 (Fourth Quarter 2019): 297–329; Alexandre Tanzi, "Young US College Graduates Face Tougher Job Market than Average," *Bloomberg*, July 30, 2022; and "The Labor Market for Recent College Graduates: Unemployment," Federal Reserve Bank of New York, July 29, 2022.

19. Kim Parker, Juliana Menasce Horowitz, and Rachel Minkin, "COVID-19 Pandemic Continues to Reshape Work in America," Pew Research Center, February 16, 2022.

20. Adam Ozimek, "How Remote Work Is Shifting Population Growth across the U.S.," Economic Innovation Group, April 13, 2022; and John A. Mondragon and Johannes Wieland, "Housing Demand and Remote Work," National Bureau of Economic Research Working Paper no. 30041, May 2022.

21. Jose Maria Barrero et al., "The Shift to Remote Work Lessens Wage-Growth Pressures," Becker Friedman Institute Working Paper no. 2022-80, July 2022.

22. Lananh Nguyen, "Wall Street's Rigid Culture Bends to Demands for Flexibility at Work," *New York Times,* April 4, 2022.

23. Wellener et al., "Competing for Talent."

24. Kathryn Dill, "People Are Quitting Full-Time Jobs for Contract Work—and Making Six Figures," *Wall Street Journal*, March 15, 2022.

25. Adam Ozimek, "Freelance Forward Economist Report," Upwork, December 8, 2021.

26. Grace Dean, "There Isn't a Shortage of Truck Drivers—They Just Don't Want to Drive for Mega Carriers Anymore," *Business Insider*, April 3, 2022.

27. "Upwork Study Finds 59 Million Americans Freelancing amid Turbulent Labor Market," Upwork, December 8, 2021.

28. Laura Katsnelson and Felix Oberholzer-Gee, "Being the Boss: Gig Workers' Value of Flexible Work," Harvard Business School Working Paper no. 21-124, May 18, 2021.

29. Jennifer Glass, R. Kelly Raley, and Joanna Pepin, "Mothers Are the Primary Earners in Growing Numbers of Families with Children," Council on Contemporary Families, November 2, 2021.

30. Sarah Jane Glynn, "Breadwinning Mothers Are Critical to Families' Economic Security," Center for American Progress, March 29, 2021.

31. Scott Winship, "Is It Really Too Expensive to Raise a Family?," *The Dispatch,* April 30, 2021.

32. Kim Parker, Juliana Menasce Horowitz, and Rachel Minkin, "Americans Are Less Likely than before COVID-19 to Want to Live in Cities, More Likely to Prefer Suburbs," Pew Research Center, December 16, 2021. See also Aaron De Smet et al., "Married to the Job No More: Craving Flexibility, Parents Are Quitting to Get It," McKinsey and Company, December 3, 2021.

33. Arjun Ramani and Nicholas Bloom, "The Donut Effect of Covid-19 on Cities," National Bureau of Economic Research Working Paper no. 28876, May 2021; and Danny Dougherty, "Austin, Elkhart Top Rankings of Best U.S. Job Markets," *Wall Street Journal,* April 22, 2022.

34. Wendy Wang and Jenet Erickson, *Homeward Bound: The Work-Family Reset in Post-COVID America* (Charlottesville, VA: Institute for Family Studies: May 2021).

35. Kyle Handley, Fariha Kamal, and Wei Ouyang, "The Rise of Exporters and Importers in US Job Growth: Insights from Newly Released Data," *VoxEU*, February 14, 2022.

36. See Niklas Engbom, "Labor Market Fluidity and Human Capital Accumulation," National Bureau of Economic Research working paper no. 29698, January 2022. See also Fatih Karahan et al., "Do Job-to-Job Transitions Drive Wage Fluctuations over the Business Cycle?," *American Economic Review* 107, no. 5 (2017): 353–57.

POLICY SOLUTIONS

ENSURING A SOUND MACROECONOMIC FOUNDATION

BY JEFFREY MIRON AND PEDRO ALDIGHIERI

THE ISSUE: ECONOMIC GROWTH GENERATES BROAD-BASED PROSPERITY FOR ALL AMERICAN WORKERS

Since the late 18th century, the world has experienced massive economic growth.[1] Despite dire predictions that explosive population growth would impoverish the human species, real gross domestic product per capita (RGDPpc) has skyrocketed alongside population, albeit unevenly. Before that, living standards were mostly stagnant worldwide.[2] Economists call this unprecedented phenomenon—shown in Figure 1—the "hockey stick" of human prosperity.

FIGURE 1 Real GDP per capita has skyrocketed worldwide since the 19th century

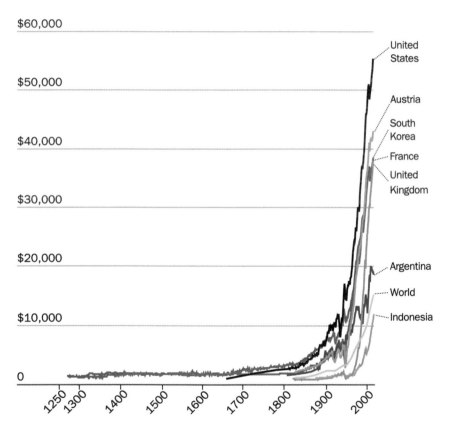

Source: "GDP Per Capita, 1 to 2018," Our World in Data, https://ourworldindata.org/grapher/maddison-data-gdp-per-capita-in-2011us-single-benchmark?country=IDN~ARG~KOR~FRA~GBR~AUT~USA~OWID_WRL.

But what does economic growth mean, and why should a "pro-worker" agenda focus on it? Real GDP measures the inflation-adjusted value of final goods and services produced in a given period. Since many things that people (and thus, workers) need and care about have a monetary value—food, clothing, health care, housing, travel, concert tickets, etc.—RGDPpc is a good proxy for standards of living. Fundamentally, RGDPpc growth measures how much more stuff we produce per person.

Problems with GDP measurement are well-known. GDP ignores illegal or non-monetary transactions, like selling drugs or cooking dinner at home. Government services have no market prices, so they are tallied by their costs, which might be higher or lower than society's willingness to pay for them. Adjusting for the ever-changing quality of goods and services is hard; sometimes a product gets more expensive, but also much better—in some cases, a product can get better *and* cheaper. A different limitation is that GDP rarely accounts for production of "bads," such as pollution or greenhouse gas emissions; in principle these should be subtracted from GDP, but measuring and valuing them is challenging. And GDP does not account for changes in leisure time, which also affect material well-being. In the 19th century, the average American laborer worked around 70 hours a week.[3] Currently, American workers toil less than half that amount—for a total of 1,791 hours a year, or 34.4 hours weekly.[4]

Nevertheless, RGDPpc is a useful measure. It is widely available, and approximate estimates go far back in time, allowing for comparisons across countries and over centuries. It also correlates with many nonmaterial things we care deeply about, such as life expectancy, education, child mortality, happiness, and more.[5]

Finally, RGDPpc gains have coincided with incredible increases in material well-being. Economists bypass problems with measures of standard of living across long time frames by looking at the real cost—often in labor-hours—of producing a constant-quality good. Nordhaus (1996), for example, looked at the cost of lighting (measured in lumens) across the centuries and finds that, roughly, "an hour's work today will buy 300,000 times as much illumination as could be bought in early Babylonia."[6] Similarly, Nordhaus found that the cost of computations, like adding or subtracting, has fallen by a factor of 73 trillion (7.3 x 10^{13}) relative to manual calculations, from 1850 through 2006.[7] This and other work suggest that trying to gauge costs by looking at adjusted prices usually understates, by orders of magnitude, how much the real costs of goods have fallen—and thus how real standards of living have increased—over the last two centuries of skyrocketing RGDPpc growth.

Establishing that economic growth reliably indicates better living standards and that RGDPpc has soared, however, is not enough to show that the average *worker* has benefited. RGDPpc says nothing about the distribution of incomes between or within countries; economic growth might accrue mainly to the richest, even as RGDPpc grows. Fortunately, this is not the case. Empirically, growth is good for the poor: incomes in the bottom quintile rise proportionally with average incomes. Furthermore, global inequality has been falling in the last several decades.[8] As shown in Figure 2, U.S. hourly manufacturing wage growth has far outpaced food price growth throughout the 20th century.

We can therefore safely assume that a rising RGDPpc tide will indeed lift all boats.

FIGURE 2 Manufacturing wage growth has outpaced food price growth in the United States

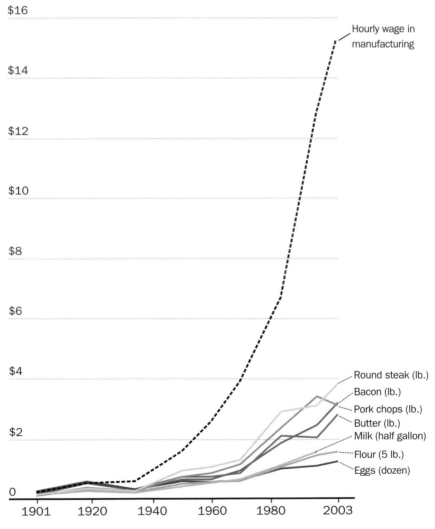

Source: "Wages in Manufacturing vs. Several Food Prices, USA, 1901 to 2003," Our World in Data, https://ourworldindata.org/grapher/wages-in-the-manufacturing-sector-vs-several-food-pricesusa.

THE POLICY SOLUTION: PRODUCTIVITY, NOT REDISTRIBUTION, IS KEY

We have seen that the world has witnessed incredible economic growth, and workers have undeniably benefited from it. What are the proximate causes of this unprecedented prosperity? Economic historians mainly point to the Industrial Revolution, but we are interested in how that period resulted in growth and income gains. In short, the answer lies in productivity, with technological change (new machines and tools, for example) and division of labor as its main drivers.

Nobel laureate Paul Krugman famously said that "productivity isn't everything, but, in the long run, it is almost everything." Productivity is the ability to produce more output with a given set of inputs. Exceptionally productive workers produce more per period than their counterparts, usually due to a combination of superior ability, experience, or effort. Economists often use the terms "productivity" or "technology" interchangeably to explain the output variation between firms and across time that is not accounted for by measurable inputs, such as labor-hours and physical capital (e.g., industrial robots).

Labor productivity is more narrowly defined as the real output produced by an hour of work. Growth in RGDPpc can *always* be traced back to labor productivity, since sustained economic growth cannot merely arise from adding more hours of labor per capita—one can only work so many hours a day.

Several factors can drive labor productivity. First, higher productivity comes from capital accumulation. More tools, machines, and facilities increase worker hourly output. Second, the division of labor and specialization further drive labor productivity. Specialization allows workers to learn their tasks faster, to become better at them, and to save time that would otherwise be spent changing between different tasks. Likewise, education and training increase labor productivity. Third, technological, scientific, and institutional progress improve the quality of capital, give birth to new management techniques, and allow for new modes of organization.

The increasing productivity of labor also explains why we should expect that at least part of the benefits from economic growth accrue to workers. From an employer's standpoint, the value of a worker comes from how much revenue that worker's extra labor-hours can produce. If labor productivity increases, the worker becomes more valuable to the employer. Of course, employers want to keep wages to a minimum, but they also want to maximize their profits. If they keep their workers' wages below their labor productivity, other employers can profitably poach those employees by offering higher wages. As firms compete for workers, we expect hourly wages to equal the productivity of adding an extra labor-hour in a competitive market.

When markets are not perfectly competitive, wages may stay below the competitive level. Yet the same principle applies: as labor productivity increases, the demand for labor goes up since workers can produce more valuable stuff, thus driving real wages up. Even a monopolist must compete with other industries, potential entrants, or with individuals' leisure time.

For this reason, evidence shows that productivity and pay are linked, even though the correlation between compensation and labor productivity varies across time and countries.[9] As long as labor productivity continues to increase, so will real wages over time.

In the long run, by contrast, there are hard limits to what government redistribution can achieve for wages and workers. As shown in Figure 1, the United States had a RGDPpc in 1800 of $2,545 (measured in 2011 dollars; this would be equal to $3,210 in 2021). If there had been no productivity growth since 1800, everyone would get an annual check for $3,210 under a perfectly egalitarian government—assuming (incorrectly) that the government could perfectly redistribute resources with no negative impact on GDP. Yet current U.S. guidelines set the poverty threshold for a single-person household at $12,880. In other words, the whole American population would be considered poor today under perfect equality by 1800s standards of living.[10]

By contrast, that $3,210 would place an individual below the sixth percentile of the U.S. market income distribution in 2021.[11] If we consider average yearly lifetime earnings, the percentile is likely to be even lower. Most people on the bottom of the income distribution are out of work, are inexperienced, or have suffered a negative income shock and will likely improve their earnings over time. Thus, over the very long run, government redistribution is mostly irrelevant to explain how standards of living change, except that redistribution might affect how productivity grows. To the extent that government redistribution reduces labor productivity and economic growth—for example, by discouraging human capital investments through taxes on labor income to fund the transfers—these adverse effects can compound over time to add to a massive cost, even for the poorest.

Increasing labor productivity is therefore the key to improve standards of living for workers in the long term. The trillion-dollar question then becomes: How do we explain and maximize productivity growth and technological progress? The answers are still up for debate and are beyond the scope of this chapter. Several factors might play a role, such as institutions, geography, culture, and even luck.[12]

Nevertheless, decades of economic history and analysis show that free markets and property rights play a crucial role in increasing productivity and standards of living.[13] Well-functioning markets are key to properly allocating labor and capital, putting scarce resources to good use.[14] Free exchange allows individuals to further their own interests while providing valuable services and goods to others, and property rights help ensure that individuals will be rightfully compensated for doing so. As a result, market discipline forces firms and individuals to relentlessly increase labor productivity and standards of living, if only to maximize profits. In a free market, firms that are unable to put labor resources to good use will eventually go out of business.

Policy-wise, this means that governments should strive to open markets to competition as much as possible—for example, by slashing trade barriers, dropping occupational licensing requirements, allowing for labor mobility (migration) within and between countries, lowering regulatory barriers to entry, and so on. Tax rates should be kept at relatively low and stable levels so as not to discourage investment, savings, and work. Governments must keep expenditure in check or risk runaway inflation. Finally, the rule of law and a predictable regulatory environment are crucial to foster long-term investments and to ensure that creditors can recoup their loans. Concretely, this translates to a fast, efficient, and predictable court system that is able to enforce laws and contracts.

CONCLUSION

Standards of living have grown tremendously during the past few centuries, even as world population has exploded. This is an unprecedented phenomenon in history: poverty had been the natural state of mankind until two centuries ago. These gains have accrued to the rich and poor alike. Poverty fell precipitously, and even global inequality has been falling in recent decades.[15] This growth is a result of the ability of human labor to produce ever-increasing value, largely enabled by free markets and property rights. Understanding this phenomenon and its causes should be a crucial feature of contemporary literacy, lest we throw away the tenets, values, and institutions that saved and improved so many lives in our recent history.

NOTES

1. "World GDP over the Last Two Millennia," Our World in Data.

2. "Malthusianism," Wikipedia, June 11, 2022; Paul R. Ehrlich, *The Population Bomb* (Cutchogue, NY: Buccaneer Books, 2007); "The Global Population Hockey Stick," Our World in Data, October 8, 2021; and Walter Scheidel, "Real Wages in Early Economies: Evidence for Living Standards from 1800 BCE to 1300 CE," *Journal of the Economic and Social History of the Orient* 53, no. 3 (2010): 425–62.

3. Robert Whaples, "The Shortening of the American Work Week: An Economic and Historical Analysis of Its Context, Causes, and Consequences," *Journal of Economic History* 51, no. 2 (June 1991): 454–57.

4. Organisation for Economic Co-operation and Development, "Hours Worked: Employment," August 17, 2022.

5. "Life Expectancy vs GDP per Capita, PPP," Gapminder; Markus Brückner and Mark Gradstein, "Income and Schooling," VoxEU CEPR, April 4, 2013; "Child Mortality vs GDP per Capita, 2016," Our World in Data, June 6, 2019; and Betsey Stevenson and Justin Wolfers, "Subjective Well-Being and Income: Is There Any Evidence of Satiation?," Brookings Institution.

6. William D. Nordhaus, "Do Real-Output and Real-Wage Measures Capture Reality? The History of Lighting Suggests Not," in Timothy F. Breshanan and Robert J. Gordon, eds., *The Economics of New Goods* (Chicago: University of Chicago Press, 1996), pp. 27–70; and "Lumen (Unit)," Wikipedia, June 24, 2022.

7. William D. Nordhaus, "Two Centuries of Productivity Growth in Computing," *Journal of Economic History* 67, no. 1 (March 2007): 128–59.

8. David Dollar and Aart Kraay, "Growth Is Good for the Poor," *Journal of Economic Growth* 7, no. 3 (September 2002): 195–225; and Max Roser, "Global Income Inequality," Our World in Data, 2013.

9. Jacob Greenspon, Anna Stansbury, and Lawrence H. Summers, "Productivity and Pay: A Comparison of the US and Canada," VoxEU CEPR, February 15, 2022; and Michael R. Strain, "The Link between Wages and Productivity Is Strong," in Melissa S. Kearney and Amy Ganz, eds., *Expanding Economic Opportunity for More Americans* (Washington: Aspen Institute, February 2019), pp. 168–79.

10. "U.S. Federal Poverty Guidelines Used to Determine Financial Eligibility for Certain Federal Programs," U.S. Department of Health and Human Services, Office of the Assistant Secretary for Planning and Evaluation, February 1, 2021.

11. PK, "Income Percentile Calculator for the United States," *Don't Quit Your Day Job* (DQDJY)(blog).

12. Jared Diamond, *Guns, Germs, and Steel: The Fates of Human Societies* (New York: W. W. Norton & Company, 1999); Luigi Guiso, Paola Sapienza, and Luigi Zingales, "Does Culture Affect Economic Outcomes?," *Journal of Economic Perspectives* 20, no. 2 (Spring 2006): 23–48; Daron Acemoglu, Simon Johnson, and James A. Robinson, "The Colonial Origins of Comparative Development: An Empirical Investigation," *American Economic Review* 91, no. 5 (December 2001): 1369–401; and Paul Krugman, "History versus Expectations," *Quarterly Journal of Economics* 106, no. 2 (May 1991): 651–67.

13. Timothy Besley and Maitreesh Ghatak, "Property Rights and Economic Development," Suntory and Toyota International Centres for Economics and Related Disciplines discussion paper EOPP/2009/6, London School of Economics and Political Science, 2009.

14. Philippe Aghion, Peter Howitt, and David Mayer-Foulkes, "The Effect of Financial Development on Convergence: Theory and Evidence," *Quarterly Journal of Economics* 120, no. 1 (February 2005): 173–222; and Diego Restuccia and Richard Rogereson, "The Causes and Costs of Misallocation," *Journal of Economic Perspectives* 31, no. 3 (Summer 2017): 151–74.

15. Max Roser, "Extreme Poverty: How Far Have We Come, How Far Do We Still Have to Go?," Our World in Data, November 22, 2021.

FACILITATING PERSONAL IMPROVEMENT

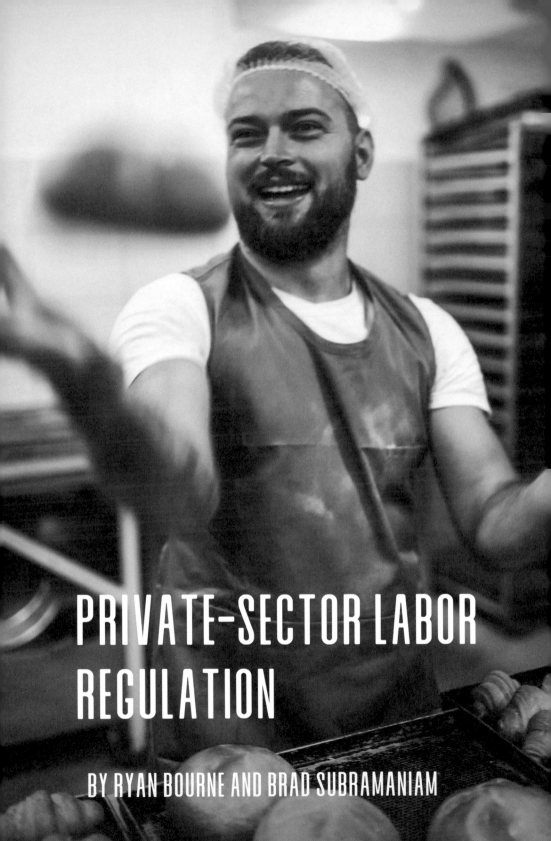

PRIVATE-SECTOR LABOR REGULATION

BY RYAN BOURNE AND BRAD SUBRAMANIAM

THE ISSUE: FEDERAL, STATE, AND LOCAL LABOR REGULATIONS THAT ARE INTENDED TO HELP WORKERS OFTEN END UP HURTING MANY OF THEM, CONSTRAINING OPPORTUNITIES OR SLASHING PAY OR PERKS

Many government policies regulate private-sector work agreements. These rules are based on the widely held view that regulation to help workers is needed because labor markets reflect unequal bargaining power between employers and employees.

Most labor regulations tend to assume an adversarial relationship between workers and management, rather than jobs being mutually beneficial agreements reflecting the negotiated preferences of workers and firms in meeting a business's collaborative goals. As regulation has proliferated, it has often sought to impose one-size-fits-all constraints on workers and firms. The practical effect is not merely needless tension between workers and their employers but also a watering down of both workers' freedom to contract their labor and employers' flexibility to run their enterprises. This constrains jobs from reflecting the particular wants, needs, and circumstances of employees and employers.

The ways in which governments restrict the freedom of businesses to contract or adjust their workforces are legion. For example, anti-discrimination laws protect certain demographic classes from being fired or treated differently by employers based on their sex, gender, race, age, religion, or national origin.[1] Freedom to contract has been limited by federal and state minimum wage laws, overtime pay regulation, scheduling laws, restrictions on independent contracting, and states refusing to enforce noncompete clauses. Congress and other levels of government also mandate a range of employer-provided benefits that were previously voluntary, including family leave, medical coverage, and pregnancy benefits through the Family and Medical Leave Act.

Most such laws and regulations are simply assumed to benefit American workers, but economics tells us that they can reduce the availability of jobs and change the composition of workers' remuneration in ways that many workers might dislike. At best, these laws help some workers enjoy more security or higher pay or benefits—but they do so at the expense of others, who often suffer heavily. For example, the bulk of research on increasing minimum wage rates finds that they raise hourly pay for most affected workers but that they lower overall employment levels or hours worked. This can reduce job prospects for young and unskilled workers.[2]

There are two broad reasons to be worried about existing and possible new government policy barriers to hiring, firing, or freely negotiated contractual arrangements in the jobs market.

First, cross-country evidence suggests that restrictive labor market regulations raise the structural level of unemployment, particularly for demographic groups with the weakest attachment to the labor market, such as young and low-skilled workers. That is, there is a long-term shift in employment that places these workers at a serious, even permanent, disadvantage. Countries in the European Union have even more labor regulation than the United States, and the EU tends to have both lower employment rates and higher unemployment rates (see Table 1). These differences are particularly hard on young workers. Prior to the pandemic, for men and women, the EU saw youth unemployment rates (15–24-year-olds) of 15.3 percent and 14.8 percent. This compares to just 9.4 percent and 7.3 percent in the United States.[3]

TABLE 1 European Union countries with more labor regulation have higher unemployment than the less-regulated United States

	Employment to population rate, percent (2019)					
	Men			Women		
Age	European Union	United States	Difference	European Union	United States	Difference
15–24	36.1	51.3	−15.2	31.3	51.1	−19.8
25–54	86.3	86.4	−0.1	74.4	73.7	1
55–64	66	69.8	−3.8	52.6	58	−5.4
65+	8.1	24	−15.9	3.9	15.9	−12
15–64 Total	73.9	76.5	−2.6	63.1	66.3	−3.2
Total	59.9	66.6	−6.7	47.7	55.4	−7.7

	Unemployment rate, percent (2019)					
	Men			Women		
Age	European Union	United States	Difference	European Union	United States	Difference
15–24	15.3	9.4	5.9	14.8	7.3	7.5
25–54	5.8	3	2.8	6.8	3.1	3.7
55–64	5.1	2.5	2.6	5	2.7	2.3
65+	1.8	2.9	−1.1	1.8	3.1	−1.3
15–64 Total	6.5	3.8	2.7	7.1	3.6	3.5
Total	6.4	3.7	2.7	7	3.6	3.4

Source: "Employment Outlook 2021," Organisation for Economic Co-operation and Development (OECD), July 2021.

Second, the United States has already experienced a decline in the mobility of its labor market in recent decades, with a reduction in the movement of both jobs and workers across states, demographic groups, and industries prior to the pandemic. This lack of job fluidity has had worrisome effects for productivity and wages and, again, was especially acute for younger and less-educated workers.[4] While some of this trend is driven by the effects of an aging population, it is worsened by policies that make it more difficult to hire workers.

Indeed, Engbom (2022) found that lower job-to-job mobility (fewer transitions between jobs) across Organisation of Economic Co-operation and Development (OECD) countries resulted in 20 percent lower wage growth across a worker's lifecycle, alongside a 9 percent fall in aggregate productivity, when compared with the United States (see Figure 1).[5] This is consistent with prior research that found a strong link between job transitions and higher wages.[6]

Importantly, Engbom found that as policies and regulations raise the cost of doing business or hiring workers, job-to-job fluidity declines (see Figure 2). This linkage and its effects have continued since the pandemic began. In Europe, labor

FIGURE 1 Wage growth increases as labor market fluidity increases

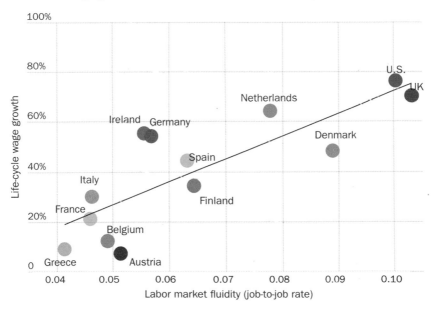

Source: Niklas Engbom, "Labor Market Fluidity and Human Capital Accumulation," National Bureau of Economic Research Working Paper no. 29698, January 2022, p. 28.
Note: Data are for men aged 25–54. Labor market fluidity is calculated using the annual job-over-job rate, which is the frequency of workers' transitions from job to job.

FIGURE 2 Nations that make it easier to start and run a business tend to have more fluid labor markets

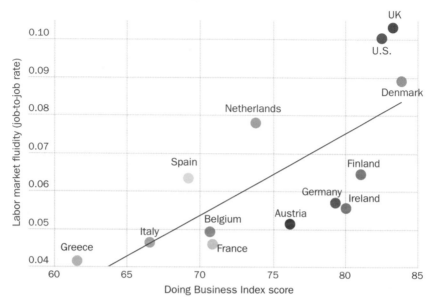

Source: Niklas Engbom, "Labor Market Fluidity and Human Capital Accumulation," National Bureau of Economic Research Working Paper no. 29698, January 2022, p. 38.
Note: Data are for men aged 25–54. Labor market fluidity is calculated using the annual job-over-job rate, which is the frequency of workers' transitions from job to job. The Doing Business Index and cost of starting a business scores are from the World Bank. Cost of starting a business is relative to gross national income per capita.

laws and pandemic policies have discouraged separations and restricted competition, and according to the OECD, job-to-job transitions are less frequent as a result. Workers across Europe, in turn, have experienced fewer working hours, weaker wage growth, *much* higher involuntary part-time work, and higher overall unemployment than their American counterparts.[7]

Although burdensome laws that have existed for decades cannot logically explain *recent* labor fluidity declines, undoing them could permanently raise the level of U.S. dynamism and improve productivity levels, much to American workers' long-term benefits.

These findings are especially pertinent today because there is political momentum—mainly from the left but also from certain parts of the right—for expanding U.S. labor regulation in a more static, "European" direction. For example, recent proposed legislation has sought to do the following: introduce a $15 federal minimum wage; expand government interventions into collective bargaining agreements; prohibit noncompete contract provisions; shoehorn gig economy and other independent workers into traditional employee-employer regulatory frameworks; and mandate benefits such as paid leave. These policies not only risk eliminating jobs, schedules, and compensation packages that many American workers desire but could also reduce the nation's job mobility, making it less productive and poorer. The prospect of legislated stasis is of particular concern today, as the pandemic induced significant structural shifts in both the types and locations of American firms, workers, and jobs based on changing tastes and ambitions.[8]

Indeed, there is substantial evidence that many policies that are intended to help American workers have actually harmed many, if not most, of them. These policies include discrimination laws, minimum wage laws, overtime laws, predictive scheduling laws, "ban the box" regulations, forced unionization, and other labor market regulations.

Discrimination laws. The Age Discrimination in Employment Act (ADEA), enacted in 1967, seeks to protect workers aged 40 and older from being forced out of jobs, discriminated against in hiring, or treated differently for promotions and pay due to their age. All states except South Dakota supplement this with their own age discrimination laws, with some state laws being stronger than the federal statute.

While these laws might dissuade firms from firing or overlooking older workers simply because of their age, they also create legal and financial risks for employers hiring older workers in the first place. For example, those most likely to sue (older males in high-status professional jobs) could extract greater severance packages from companies. The threat of litigation makes older workers less attractive to hire, on average, particularly because it is more difficult to prove discrimination in the hiring process than after termination.

Research shows that this risk is real and significant. Most notably, Lahey (2006) found that white male workers over the age of 50 in states with strong age discrimination laws were less likely to be fired but also less likely to be hired; they also worked fewer weeks per year and were more likely to be retired than in other states.[9] She concluded that these laws make companies "afraid to fire older workers," as expected but that the laws also induced firms to seek to avoid this litigation "by not employing older workers in the first place." Neumark and Button (2013) found similarly that the Great Recession harmed older workers more in states with strong age discrimination protections.[10] While some scholars contest these empirical findings, there's enough evidence to suggest that age discrimination laws may protect certain insiders who already have jobs to the detriment of older workers seeking them.[11]

There's also evidence showing that other, more contentious, discrimination laws might have even bigger effects on the hiring prospects for those affected, since most older workers are likely to voluntarily leave the labor market sooner than these other groups anyway. For example, the Americans with Disabilities Act of 1990 (ADA) offers similar employment protections for the disabled. Older research by Acemoglu and Angrist (1998) found that "the ADA had a negative effect on the employment of disabled men of all working ages and disabled women under age 40" due to reduced hiring.[12] These effects were stronger in states that had seen more ADA-related discrimination charges.

Minimum wage laws. All levels of American governments interfere directly in pay setting for low-wage workers. There is a federal statutory minimum wage of $7.25 per hour; 30 states have higher minimums, and some cities and localities go even further. New York City, for example, has a $15 minimum wage, while Seattle has the highest in the country, $17.27 per hour, for most employers. Given these laws, the average effective minimum wage across the United States was already almost $12 per hour back in 2019.

Minimum wage hikes are arguably the most studied policy issue in economics. As a result, one can find varied results about the impact on jobs, depending on the level of the minimum wage hike, the scale of the increase, the length of the time period examined, and the industry or population under the microscope. Overall, most of the literature finds that raising the minimum wage creates "disemployment" effects—that is, less employment or fewer hours worked. Raising the cost of labor, in other words, tends to result in fewer people being employed over time, primarily through reduced hiring.[13] These effects are especially pronounced for young and unskilled workers.[14]

Larger minimum wage hikes tend to have bigger negative effects on employment than smaller ones.[15] Studies that look at the aggregate impact on low-paid workers also tend to find bigger negative employment effects, whereas those that cherry-pick certain industries, such as restaurants, find smaller results.[16]

Past federal minimum wage increases hit hardest in states where the local minimum wage did not exceed the federal wage floor. Research from Clemens and Wither (2014) found that the 2009 hike even lowered the income growth of the target workers in these states. The increase in hourly pay was offset by "employment declines, increased probabilities of working without pay (i.e., an 'internship' effect), and lost wage growth associated with reductions in experience accumulation."[17]

Newer research shows that not all employers will cut employment, hiring, or worker hours in light of minimum wage increases. Yet other ways they might adjust to these cost increases may also hurt some workers. Fast-food outlets, restaurants, and childcare providers, for example, have been found to pass a portion of the minimum wage cost increase onto consumers through higher prices.[18] These price hikes can reduce some of the benefit of a higher wage rate if they occur on goods or services that minimum wage workers purchase.

Evidence also suggests that employers sometimes cut other nonpay benefits at higher minimum wages, including the generosity of health insurance benefits, workplace amenities, or other perks.[19] International research finds that firms facing higher minimum wages seek other ways to manage their labor costs, such as offering workers less predictable schedules.[20]

Some companies react to minimum wage hikes by seeking ways to improve the productivity of their workforces. This is often not costless for workers either. It might require replacing inexperienced low-skilled employees with more experienced, higher productivity employees; making longer-term investments in labor-saving machines; or pushing existing workers harder. These all either reduce opportunities for low-skilled workers in the longer term or make workers' experience at work less pleasant.

None of this is to deny that minimum wage increases benefit the workers who are fortunate enough to keep their jobs and hours. But policymakers must acknowledge that these laws come with big trade-offs and that the costs are often borne by young or unskilled workers who are looking for entry-level positions, are regarded as more dispensable by employers, and have the most to lose from fewer employment opportunities. Neumark and Nizalova (2007) found that workers who were paid high minimum wages when they were younger worked less and earned less even in their late 20s. This effect was especially strong for black Americans.[21]

Overtime laws. Employees covered under the federal Fair Labor Standards Act, which goes back to 1938, must receive 1.5 times their regular pay for any hours worked over 40 per week. Numerous exemptions to this federal requirement exist, including for salaried workers who have "executive, administrative, or professional" duties and have an annual base salary of more than $35,568.

Originally envisaged to stop exploitation and even to boost employment (by sharing work between more workers), these laws have harmed workers in important ways. A 2020 Institute for Labor Economics study shows that because overtime regulations increase compliance costs and create additional financial constraints on how employers might operate most cost-effectively, they reduce net employment and hours worked.[22]

To manage the additional costs and restraints that overtime laws bring, moreover, some companies avoid paying overtime rates by adjusting base pay or redefining work roles for workers earning near the exemption thresholds. Research has found that there are 89 percent more salaried "managerial" positions around the threshold, with position titles including "coffee cart managers" and "lead reservationists," suggesting there is substantive "overtime avoidance."[23]

Thus, overtime laws might help some workers get modestly higher wages but at the cost of less-efficient schedules for them and fewer jobs or hours for others.

Predictive scheduling laws. Predictive scheduling laws generally force employers to disclose anticipated schedules for employees in advance (usually within two weeks' notice) and strictly limit an employer's ability to change those schedules. Some versions include mandatory rest periods between employee shifts and require overtime pay if a business changes an employee's schedule after the notice period has passed. Although these laws were initially adopted to provide more certain schedules for workers in the retail and restaurant industry, where fast-shifting demand can lead to sudden changes in the need for staff, they have been expanded in many jurisdictions to cover other industries.

Although predictive scheduling laws are still in their infancy, Oregon has recently become the first state with a blanket regulation and is joined by several major cities, including the San Francisco metropolitan area, Chicago, Philadelphia, and New York.[24] Overall, the result has been a messy web of regulations for businesses to navigate and draconian penalties on employers for perceived violations.

Because predictive scheduling laws raise costs on employers who change a worker's schedule, managers have unsurprisingly found it more difficult to calibrate staffing levels with staffing needs. Thus, to avoid making large losses at quiet times, businesses have cut the number of workers on shifts that are expected to have uncertain demand. In fact, research published by the Institute for the Study of Free Enterprise in 2022 suggests that these laws have corresponded with a 9.2 percentage point increase in part-time workers from 2014 to 2020 in the retail and restaurant industry.[25] Workers themselves attributed more than two-thirds of this increase in part-time employment to involuntary causes such as an "inability to find full-time work" or "unfavorable business conditions," rather than noneconomic reasons such as "childcare issues" or "family obligations." More evidence suggests that businesses affected by these laws respond by offering less flexibility with employee schedule changes, scheduling fewer employees per shift, and offering fewer jobs overall.[26]

"Ban the box" regulations. Ban the box regulations (BTBs) are intended to expand work opportunities for ex-convicts by delaying the point at which employers can ask job applicants about their criminal history. These BTB statutes, which started in the 1990s, are now widespread. Four-fifths of the U.S. population currently reside in a jurisdiction with some form of these laws, and other expansions are in the works.[27]

As discussed in the Criminal Justice chapter, boosting the employment prospects of Americans with criminal records is a worthwhile objective, given the barriers they currently face in the labor market. Unfortunately, however, BTBs appear to be harming many vulnerable American workers. In particular, employers left without a straightforward method to determine an applicant's criminal history frequently turn to other proxies, such as screening for race or ethnicity, to minimize the risk of hiring a former inmate. Thus, Doleac and Hansen (2016) showed that low-skilled black and Hispanic men are less likely to be employed in jurisdictions with a BTB law.[28] White job applicants are significantly more likely to receive a callback than black job applicants after the passage of BTBs.[29] These laws also can lead employers to lobby for and utilize other means of screening applicants with criminal records, such as occupational licensing.[30]

Forced unionization. The National Labor Relations Act (NLRA), which has been in effect since the 1930s, makes it unlawful for an employer not to bargain with a union that has majority worker support, while also granting that union the sole representation rights for all employees. This exclusive representation provision means that governments are forcing certain employees to be represented by a union to collectively bargain for them, even when the individual worker may not desire such representation.

The act is explicitly based on the idea that employees face an inequality of bargaining power with employers, something that the law seeks to correct by providing collective bargaining opportunities from independent unions—that is, unions that have no connection with the company's management. As such, the law entrenches an adversarial labor model. It explicitly bans individual company unions in which a firm might deal with its own union worker representatives who might better enhance the collaborative prospects of labor and management. The act also promotes union security, the principle under which workers who are represented by a union can be forced to join or pay dues to it, to ensure the union's survival.

Clearly, the NLRA has become less problematic over the decades, as union membership has declined to just 6.1 percent of private-sector workers, down from 36 percent in 1953. These days, 28 states also have right-to-work laws, which prohibit employees from negotiating contracts in which nonunion members are forced to pay for the costs of union representation. The development of the gig economy and other flexible forms of work further makes the law an anachronism in the modern economy.

However, 22 states still lack right-to-work laws; the NLRA's regulatory burdens are still significant; and many policymakers are working to expand the law's scope through reinterpretation or new legislation. For example, some appointees at the National Labor Relations Board (the federal agency tasked with enforcing labor law) broaden the conception of "concerted action" to prevent employers from fully responding to employees' unwelcome speech or workplace histrionics.[31] A proposed Protecting the Right to Organize Act, meanwhile, would abolish state right-to-work laws and attempt to redefine gig workers and independent contractors as employees, ensnaring them within applicable state and federal labor laws. At other times, progressive groups have pushed for the criminalization of employers who might have unwittingly sidestepped vague labor rules, and previous Democratic administrations have attempted to make companies liable for breaches of labor and employment law committed by their franchisees or contractors.[32]

All these factors increase risks for employers, dampening their propensity to hire and encouraging them to locate in right-to-work states or even other countries.[33] Furthermore, most analyses of private-sector unions and collective bargaining arrangements find that, although unionization can generate a short-term wage premium for union-covered workers, a union presence reduces job growth at the firm level.[34] Unionized firms also tend to struggle with maintaining investments in capital or research and development, thus harming productivity and lowering wages in the longer term.[35] The presence of a union also changes the composition of the employed workforce, with older and higher-paid workers tending to leave the firm as younger and lower-paid workers join.[36] More recently, Kini (2022) showed that unionization can also harm consumers, for example by increasing prices or decreasing product quality.[37] Laws and regulations that encourage or mandate a big union presence thus tend to reduce job opportunities, on net, while favoring insiders at the expense of all other workers.

Other labor market regulations. Governments regulate labor markets in other ways that also harm American workers. For example, as analyzed in the Employee Benefits chapter, government-mandated benefits enforce certain types of benefits for workers, distorting worker remuneration in a variety of ways. The federal Davis–Bacon Act commits federal construction projects to pay prevailing wages for workers, often meaning union rates at significantly higher cost, to the detriment of minorities and taxpayers. As discussed in the Independent Work chapter, restrictions on contract or gig work, such as those in California's Assembly Bill 5, reduce workers' scheduling flexibility and hours and reduce employment in the knowledge economy.

THE POLICY SOLUTIONS: DEREGULATE LABOR MARKETS TO IMPROVE AMERICAN WORKERS' EMPLOYMENT PROSPECTS

Given the demonstrable benefits of labor market mobility for American workers and the problems caused by various labor regulations, policymakers should return to respecting Americans' freedom of contract and employers' right to employ at will—that is, being able to terminate work relationships for any reason. Doing so will ensure that the labor market is as dynamic as possible, provides the greatest opportunities for higher wages and levels of employment, and meets the widely varying needs and desires of *all* American workers.

Having freedom of contract as the lodestar of labor law would require repealing many of the labor regulations that currently prohibit agreements or decisions that employers and employees might reach in free negotiation. Doing so would inevitably be disruptive, and even harmful, for some workers in the short term, but government interference in the labor market brings net economic harm, while benefiting some insiders at the expense of far more outsiders (who tend to be young and unskilled workers with the most to lose). Many of these regulations, moreover, hurt many of the same workers they are allegedly intended to help, in turn preventing better employer-employee job matching and thus worsening productivity.

In terms of specifics, age-based discrimination laws should be repealed, and other discrimination laws should be reassessed due to their potential unintended consequences. Policymakers also should scrap minimum wage laws entirely, or—

where doing so is politically impossible—hold the dollar value of minimum wages constant (so they become less significant in real terms over time) and resist any large federal minimum wage increases, which would particularly harm people in lower-wage, rural areas and many young or low-skilled Americans. Policymakers should repeal overtime and scheduling mandates, which reduce workers' job security, hours, and, often, their preferred work arrangements, while also making businesses less productive. They should also water down the worst aspects of the anachronistic, adversarial National Labor Relations Act or repeal it entirely: in general, federal law should neither encourage nor prevent employers and employees from agreeing to unionize their firms' workforces as they see fit.

Finally, state and local BTB laws, which risk stifling mutually beneficial job matching between businesses and workers *without* criminal records, should be repealed and new laws should be avoided. Instead, as discussed in the Criminal Justice chapter, governments should pursue expungement to improve employment outcomes for Americans with criminal histories. Companies that have voluntarily instituted BTB, such as Walmart, Target, and Koch Industries, can of course maintain those policies. This would avoid the unintended consequences created by BTB mandates because these firms do not desire to know applicants' criminal histories (and thus will not use racial or other proxies to determine them).

Labor-related regulations detailed in other chapters, such as those on independent work and occupational licensing, should also be reformed as recommended there.

ACTION PLAN

Although intended to help American workers, many labor laws and regulations often hurt them and create unnecessary hurdles to employers and employees as they attempt to develop mutually beneficial workplace relationships. Congress should therefore

- repeal the federal minimum wage, overtime, and other provisions of the Fair Labor Standards Act;
- repeal the Family and Medical Leave Act;
- repeal federal age discrimination law, such as the Age Discrimination in Employment Act, including its ban on the practice of automatic retirement ages at private workplaces;
- repeal, in whole or large part, the Americans with Disabilities Act, in particular its coverage of disabilities beyond traditional categories such as deafness, blindness, and paraplegia;
- repeal the National Labor Relations Act; and
- reject proposals for a $15 federal minimum wage, newly strengthened collective bargaining rights for trade unions, attempts to redefine independent

workers as employees, as well as the push for using antitrust powers to counteract labor market power.

State and local governments, meanwhile, should

- repeal minimum wage laws;
- repeal state age discrimination laws;
- repeal BTB legislation;
- avoid or repeal laws that require workers to join a labor union; and
- avoid or repeal laws that seek to regulate the gig economy or independent contractors as the equivalent of employees.

NOTES

1. "At-Will Employment–Overview," National Conference of State Legislatures, April 15, 2008.

2. David Neumark and Peter Shirley, "Myth or Measurement: What Does the New Minimum Wage Research Say about Minimum Wages and Job Loss in the United States?," National Bureau of Economic Research Working Paper no. 28388, March 2022.

3. "Youth Unemployment Rate," OECD Data, Organisation for Economic Co-operation and Development, April 2022.

4. Steven J. Davis and John Haltiwanger, "Labor Market Fluidity and Economic Performance," National Bureau of Economic Research Working paper no. 20479, September 2014; and Raven S. Molloy et al., "Understanding Declining Fluidity in the U.S. Labor Market," *Brookings Papers on Economic Activity* (Spring 2016): 183–237.

5. Niklas Engbom, "Labor Market Fluidity and Human Capital Accumulation," National Bureau of Economic Research Working Paper no. 29698, January 2022.

6. Fatih Karahan et al., "Do Job-to-Job Transitions Drive Wage Fluctuations over the Business Cycle?," *American Economic Review* 107, no. 5 (May 2017): 353–57.

7. Tom Fairless, "Europeans Are Working Even Less, and Not by Choice," *Wall Street Journal*, July 15, 2022.

8. John Haltiwanger, "Spatial and Sectoral Reallocation of Firms, Workers and Jobs in the Pandemic and Recovery," Asian Bureau of Finance and Economic Research, May 2022.

9. Joanna Lahey, "State Age Protection Laws and the Age Discrimination in Employment Act," National Bureau of Economic Research Working Paper no. 12048, February 2006.

10. David Neumark and Patrick Button, "Did Age Discrimination Protections Help Older Workers Weather the Great Recession?," National Bureau of Economic Research Working Paper no. 19216, June 2013.

11. David Neumark, "Strengthen Age Discrimination Protections to Help Confront the Challenge of Population Aging," Brookings Economic Studies Program, Brookings Institution, November 2020.

12. Daron Acemoglu and Joshua Angrist, "Consequences of Employment Protection? The Case of the Americans with Disabilities Act," National Bureau of Economic Research Working Paper no. 6670, July 1998.

13. Jonathan Meer and Jeremy West, "Effects of the Minimum Wage on Employment Dynamics," National Bureau of Economic Research Working Paper no. 19262, January 2015.

14. Neumark and Shirley, "Myth or Measurement."

15. Jeffrey Clemens and Michael R. Strain, "The Heterogeneous Effects of Large and Small Minimum Wage Changes: Evidence over the Short and Medium Run Using a Pre-Analysis Plan," National Bureau of Economic Research Working Paper no. 29264, September 2021.

16. Ekaterina Jardim et al., "Minimum Wage Increases, Wages, and Low-Wage Employment: Evidence from Seattle," National Bureau of Economic Research Working Paper no. 23532, June 2017.

17. Jeffrey Clemens and Michael Wither, "The Minimum Wage and the Great Recession: Evidence of Effects on the Employment and Income Trajectories of Low-Skilled Workers," National Bureau of Economic Research Working Paper no. 20724, December 2014.

18. Orley Ashenfelter and Štěpán Jurajda, "Wages, Minimum Wages, and Price Pass-Through: The Case of McDonald's Restaurants," Princeton University Industrial Relations Section Working Paper no. 646, January 2021; Sylvia Allegretto and Michael Reich, "Are Local Minimum Wages Absorbed by Price Increases? Estimates from Internet-Based Restaurant Menus," *ILR Review* 71, no. 1 (2018): 35–63; and Jennifer J. Otten et al., "Responding to an Increased Minimum Wage: A Mixed Methods Study of Child Care Businesses during the Implementation of Seattle's Minimum Wage Ordinance," *Early Childhood Education and Care* 16, no. 1 (2018): 538.

19. Jeffrey Clemens, "How Do Firms Respond to Minimum Wage Increases? Understanding the Relevance of Non-employment Margins," *Journal of Economic Perspectives* 35, no. 1 (Winter 2021): 51–72; and Christine Eibner et al., "Panel Paper: Do Minimum Wage Changes Affect Employer-Sponsored Insurance Coverage in the Post-ACA Era?," Association for Public Policy Analysis and Management, 39th Annual Research Conference, November 4, 2017.

20. Nikhil Datta, Giulia Giupponi, and Stephen Machin, "Zero Hours Contracts and Labour Market Policy," *Economic Policy* 34, no. 99 (July 2019): 369–427.

21. David Neumark and Olena Nizalova, "Minimum Wage Effects in the Longer Run," *Journal of Human Resources* 42, no. 2 (Spring 2007): 435–52.

22. Ronald L. Oaxaca and Galiya Sagyndykova, "The Effect of Overtime Regulations on Employment," Institute for Labor Economics (IZA) World of Labor, December 2020.

23. Lauren Cohen, Umit G. Gurun, and N. Bugra Ozel, "Too Many Managers: Strategic Use of Titles to Avoid Overtime Payments," SSRN, November 16, 2020.

24. Dan Whitehead, "Predictive Scheduling Laws: What They Cover and How to Comply," Workforce.com, May 18, 2021.

25. Aaron Yelowitz, "Predictive Scheduling Laws Do Not Promote Full-Time Work," Institute for the Study of Free Enterprise Working Paper no. 46, January 2022.

26. Aaron Yelowitz and Lloyd Corder, "Weighing Priorities for Part-Time Workers: An Early Evaluation of San Francisco's Formula Retail Scheduling Ordinance," Employment Policies Institute, May 2016; and "Inflexible Scheduling: How Employees, Employers, and Consumers Are Hurt by Predictive Scheduling Laws," American Consumer Center for Citizen Research, October 15, 2019.

27. Beth Avery and Han Lu, "Ban the Box: U.S. Cities, Counties, and States Adopt Fair Hiring Policies," National Employment Law Project, October 1, 2021.

28. Jennifer L. Doleac and Benjamin Hansen, "Does 'Ban the Box' Help or Hurt Low-Skilled Workers? Statistical Discrimination and Employment Outcomes When Criminal Histories Are Hidden," National Bureau of Economic Research Working Paper no. 22469, July 2016.

29. Amanda Y. Agan and Sonja B. Starr, "Ban the Box, Criminal Records, and Statistical Discrimination: A Field Experiment," University of Michigan Law and Economics Research Paper no. 16-012, June 14, 2016.

30. Peter Van Doren, "Ban the Box and Statistical Discrimination," *Cato at Liberty* (blog), Cato Institute, June 4, 2019.

31. Walter Olson, "A Federal Right to Online Drama in the Workplace?," *Cato at Liberty* (blog), July 1, 2022.

32. Walter Olson, "Labor Law: Feds Call Off Their War on Franchising and Subcontracting," *Cato at Liberty* (blog), Cato Institute, January 13, 2020.

33. See, for instance: Joe Deaux, "U.S. Steel Bets on a New Technology—and the South—to Survive," *Bloomberg*, May 6, 2022.

34. John T. Addison and Clive R. Belfield, "Unions and Employment Growth: The One Constant?," Institute for Labor Economics (IZA) Discussion Paper no. 479, April 2002.

35. Barry T. Hirsch, "Unions, Dynamism, and Economic Performance," Institute for Labor Economics (IZA) Discussion Paper no. 5342, December 6, 2010.

36. Brigham R. Frandsen, "The Surprising Impacts of Unionization: Evidence from Matched Employer-Employee Data," *Journal of Labor Economics* 39, no. 4 (October 2021): 861–94.

37. Omesh Kini et al., "Labor Unions and Product Quality Failures," *Management Science* 68, no. 7 (July 2022): 5403–5440.

38. Ryan Bourne, "The Case against a $15 Federal Minimum Wage: Q&A," Cato Institute, February 25, 2021.

HIGHER EDUCATION

BY NEAL MCCLUSKEY

THE ISSUE: U.S. HIGHER EDUCATION POLICY HAS PROVEN TO BE COUNTERPRODUCTIVE FOR MANY AMERICAN WORKERS, PRODUCING BALLOONING COLLEGE PRICES, LEADING EMPLOYERS TO DEMAND CREDENTIALS THEY DON'T NEED, AND FAILING TO PROVIDE COMMENSURATE INCREASES IN KNOWLEDGE OR SKILLS

Public policy has typically tasked elementary and secondary schools with producing "college- and career-ready" graduates, but with emphasis heavily on the former. It is in college that we have come to expect students to obtain specific skills and knowledge—human capital— for employment. But for many American workers, the higher education system has proven itself to be counterproductive, issuing too many empty degrees at prices that are too high and at rates that have put too many workers on a relentless credential treadmill. These burdens can weigh not only on prospective American workers but also on their employed parents who help shoulder the costs of education.

Going to college may now seem commonplace, but it is a relatively recent development. The share of the U.S. population aged 25 and over with a bachelor's degree did not hit 5 percent until about 1950, did not reach double digits until around 1970, and is still well under half, as Figure 1 shows.

For most of American history, colleges offered little practical instruction, focusing on religion and associated subjects, such as Greek, Latin, and philosophy. The federal government tried to change this by expanding higher education's reach in the 19th century via land grants, which produced funding to expand public colleges and the teaching of more practical subjects, such as agriculture and mining. These initiatives, however, did not greatly increase college attendance.[1]

What most spurred college enrollment appears to have been not an increasing need for skills and abilities that could most efficiently be transmitted via formal postsecondary schooling—a majority of Americans aged 25 and older had not completed *high school* until around 1965—but government subsidies.[2]

The first noticeable kink in Figure 1 is after 1940, corresponding with the passage of the Servicemen's Readjustment Act of 1944 (colloquially known as the G.I. Bill), which furnished billions of dollars to send newly returned World War II veterans to college. The bill's primary goal was to keep servicemen from flooding the labor market, not to increase their knowledge and skills. Within seven years, 2.3 million veterans had enrolled in college, versus total college enrollment in 1939–1940 of only 1.5 million.[3] Federal aid accelerated after the Soviet launch of Sputnik in 1957, which threw Americans into a panic over a

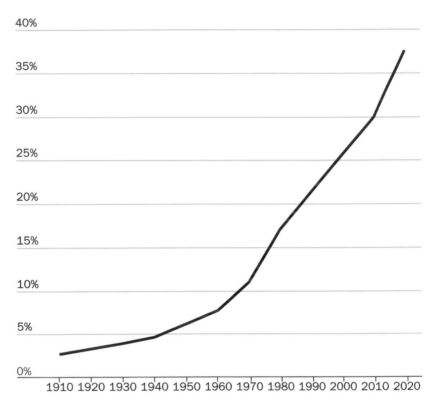

FIGURE 1 The percent of the U.S. population aged 25 or older with a bachelor's degree has risen 14-fold since 1910

Source: "Table 104.10: Rates of High School Completion and Bachelor's Degree Attainment among Persons Age 25 and Over, by Race/Ethnicity and Sex: Selected Years, 1910 through 2021," Digest of Education Statistics, National Center for Education Statistics, U.S.

perceived technological inferiority and led to the National Defense Education Act. One of the law's components was the first federal student loan program—G.I. Bill money was essentially a grant—in which Washington gave colleges money to lend to students (as opposed to federal loans going to students and only reaching schools when students choose them).

Next, President Lyndon Johnson made college a major part of the "Great Society," with the Higher Education Act of 1965 creating new grant and loan programs. Over the next several years, such programs were expanded, including creation of Pell Grants in 1972 and Sallie Mae, a government-sponsored enterprise that provided funds to lenders at low interest rates. Creation of state guarantee agencies, intended to cover all principal and interest on defaulted loans for lenders, was also encouraged by the federal government, which in the Higher

Education Act Amendments of 1976 said that it would cover any of those agencies' losses.[4] Through the early 1980s, the government repeatedly expanded aid, including creating non-means-tested Parent Loan for Undergraduate Student (PLUS) loans and extending loans to students who were financially independent of their parents. In 2006, the federal government created PLUS loans for graduate students that the students themselves could take out.

Concurrent with the establishment of federal subsidy infusions, the inflation-adjusted cost of tuition, fees, and room and board began to skyrocket, from $9,209 in 1980–1981 to $25,281 in 2019–2020, as Figure 2 shows.

FIGURE 2 As federal subsidies for higher education have increased, education-related expenses for undergraduates have skyrocketed

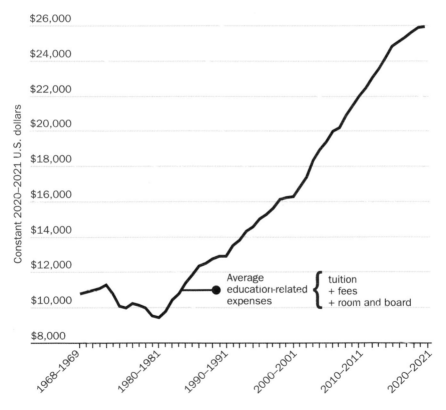

Source: "Table 330.10: Average Undergraduate Tuition, Fees, Room, and Board Rates Charged for Full-Time Students in Degree-Granting Postsecondary Institutions, by Level and Control of Institution: Selected Years, 1963–64 through 2020–21," Digest of Education Statistics, National Center for Education Statistics, U.S. Department of Education, 2022.

Aid and prices are clearly connected. For starters, basic economics says that more money chasing the same level of goods or services—in this case college seats—leads to inflation, but that is just part of the explanation for higher education's *hyper*inflation. Another driver is that third-party (read: taxpayer) money enables customers to demand more from providers, including increased entertainment, such as recreation programs, concerts, and waterparks; better food; and more comfortable accommodations.[5] Third-party payment has also rendered students less sensitive to resulting price increases. Prospective students' price insensitivity enables college employees to demand higher salaries, lower workloads, nicer offices, and other rewards. Thus, Lucca et al. (2019) found that a one-dollar increase in federal subsidized and unsubsidized loan maximums leads to college tuition price increases of about 60 and 20 cents, respectively.[6]

Unfortunately, President Biden's executive action on student debt announced in August 2022 would likely put further upward pressure on prices. Under the plan, the president would unilaterally cancel $10,000 to $20,000 (the higher amount is for borrowers who also had Pell Grants) of federal student loan debt for anyone making less than $125,000 individually or $250,000 for a household and would make income-driven repayment options much more generous for borrowers, including by reducing the share of income that determines borrowers' monthly payments before eventually getting their remaining balances forgiven. Both actions, if ultimately implemented, would decrease borrowers' sensitivity to tuition increases, essentially telling colleges to raise prices further and students to worry less about paying because the U.S. taxpayer will pick up the (now even larger) tab.[7]

Perhaps such inflation would be tolerable if it translated into proportionately greater human capital, but the data do not indicate that this is happening. Literacy assessments, for example, indicate *declining* human capital per degree. The National Assessment of Adult Literacy (NAAL), administered in 1992 and 2003, tested adults' ability to comprehend prose such as newspaper articles, documents such as tax forms, and mathematical reasoning.[8] From the first to the second administration of the test, the share of adults who topped out schooling with a bachelor's degree and were proficient prose and document readers dropped from 40 to 31 percent and 37 to 25 percent, respectively. For quantitative literacy, the share was unchanged. Advanced degree holders dropped from 51 to 41 percent prose proficient, 45 to 31 percent document proficient, and 39 to 36 percent quantitative proficient reasoning, although the last change was not statistically significant.

The Program for the International Assessment of Adult Competencies, administered in 2012/14 and 2017, is not directly comparable to NAAL, but it does identify literacy levels, with level 3 and above considered "proficient." For households with members aged 16 to 65 years old, in the 2012/14 administration, 68 percent of test takers with more than a high school education scored in the third literacy level or above. In 2017, only 64 percent did.[9] In numeracy, the drop was from 57 to 53 percent. Given such results, why the continued pressure to increase college enrollment and potentially burden students and their parents with a high-dollar, low-value degree?

Among several reasons, a diploma is increasingly needed to get hired even when job responsibilities have not markedly changed. In 2017, researchers with the Harvard Business School compared more than 26 million want ads and current occupants in middle-skill jobs. It revealed significant credential inflation.[10] The most striking instance was supervisors of production workers, with 67 percent of job postings calling for a bachelor's degree but only 16 percent of current occupants possessing one. Other yawning gaps were 47 percentage points for executive secretaries and executive administrative assistants and 44 points for supervisors of construction trade and extraction workers.

Do employers see degreed workers as superior? In many ways, no. Harvard Business School data show that employers less often judge workers without degrees but with experience as likely to need upfront training to reach full productivity, to need supervisor oversight, to be absent, and to turnover. Employers do, though, tend to believe that someone with a degree will end up being more productive and reach that level more quickly.

Of course, the cost of attaining a degree is usually not borne by an employer, so there is little cost to requiring one. And pickings are easy, with a glut of bachelor's degrees. Data from the Federal Reserve Bank of New York show that roughly a third of all four-year degree holders are in jobs that do not require their credential. And this is not just for new graduates, indicating that many degree holders are in career underemployment.[11]

Governments also spur demand and credential inflation by increasingly requiring their employees to have degrees. This includes public schools that employ millions of teachers. As of 1937, only five states required teachers to have four years of college for initial certification, while six required only high school graduation, and eight had no specific educational requirement. By 1986, the Carnegie Task Force on Teaching and the Holmes Group—an assemblage of education deans at leading research universities—was proposing that all teachers have an undergraduate education in specific subjects and master's degrees in education to enter the profession.[12]

Today, an advanced degree is not typically required to become a teacher, but teachers ordinarily rise on district salary scales by possessing one, and some states require that teachers obtain master's degrees within a certain number of years of licensure—*despite* research typically finding no positive impact on student achievement.[13]

States further fuel demand for college degrees by making them a condition for licensure in many private-sector jobs.[14] As discussed in the Occupational Licensing chapter, the last few decades have experienced major increases in the number of occupations and share of the American workforce that is subject to licensing. In the 1950s, around 5 percent of workers were subject to licensing laws, which jumped to 18 percent by the 1980s and 29 percent by the mid-2000s.[15] Many state licensing regulations today require college degrees for occupations, such as athletic trainers and auctioneers, that clearly do not need them.[16]

Even quintessential occupations needing specialized, advanced degrees and licenses to operate, such as doctors and lawyers, only started to see such requirements relatively recently. Many famous lawyers—Thomas Jefferson and Abraham Lincoln leap to mind, but more recently U.S. Supreme Court Justice Robert H. Jackson—practiced law without law degrees, largely learning independently and on the job with established attorneys.[17] Medical education slowly transformed from an apprenticeship model to an academic one, and states did not start to regulate length or content of training until the late 19th century.[18]

The federal government also restricts supply by making it difficult for innovative education providers, such as online institutions or competency-based degree programs that give credit for what students already know, to enter the higher education market.[19] For an institution to enroll students using federal aid, which is so widespread that almost all colleges must enroll such students to be competitive, it must be approved by an accreditor that is recognized by the U.S. Department of Education. Those accreditors tend to be focused on inputs and residential, four-year models, making it difficult for innovative, nontraditional options to enter the market and thrive.

Washington has also targeted the most dynamic higher education sector—for-profit schools—for extra regulatory scrutiny. For-profit institutions have typically been much quicker than traditional colleges to adapt to changing workforce needs and shape the modes, times, and places of their offerings for working adults. The sector does produce some poor outcomes, including a relatively high default rate of 11.2 percent versus 5.2 percent for borrowers who attended nonprofit private colleges and 7.0 percent for public college attendees.[20] But it also works with students with the greatest obstacles to success—for example, older ones from disadvantaged groups—and the schools do not receive the state and local subsidies of public institutions or the favored tax treatment of not-for-profit private schools that enable them to bring in substantial revenue from sources other than students.[21]

Regulatory restrictions not only deny students educational options that might be better suited to their skills, lifestyles, or interests but also insulate traditional colleges from having to compete on price, quality, or convenience.

Finally, while the postsecondary education system is primarily to blame for degree pressure and expense, the country's secondary education system also contributes to the problem. As discussed in the K–12 Education chapter, career and technical education has long been sidelined as states and districts have made college attendance the ultimate goal of public schooling, and students interested in gaining specific workforce skills have found themselves marginalized and without robust options. Providing more freedom to choose alternatives to college prep would do a lot to avoid higher education problems.

THE POLICY SOLUTIONS: REDUCE FEDERAL SUBSIDIES FOR HIGHER EDUCATION; REFORM OCCUPATIONAL LICENSING REQUIREMENTS; DECREASE REGULATORY BURDENS TO INCREASE INNOVATIVE SUPPLY; AND PROVIDE NONCOLLEGE OPTIONS FOR K–12 STUDENTS

College education is more expensive and in demand than it should be, due largely to government policies that subsidize demand and restrict supply. The right prescription for reform is to move postsecondary education closer to a free market, in which tuition prices more closely reflect a degree's value to the American worker who holds it and in which alternatives to degree programs can compete.

Foremost, the federal government must reduce student aid to release price and credential inflationary pressure. Ideally, Washington would phase out all aid programs, because any subsidy distorts demand, leading to overconsumption and price increases. It also decreases consumers' incentives to vet providers for cost and quality––a critical consideration given recent research showing the return on investment of most graduate degrees to be modest or even negative.[22] Finally, the Constitution gives the federal government only specific, enumerated powers, and authority to fund student aid is not among them.

Unfortunately, wholesale removal of federal subsidies is unlikely in the near term. Smaller reforms, however, are possible. In particular, Congress should eliminate all federal aid programs that are not means-tested and should increase the minimum academic requirements needed to obtain remaining loans or grants. Doing so would help federal subsidies target only needy students with good college completion prospects while tempering tuition inflation, unmanageable debt, and credentialism.

Federal, state, and local governments also should reduce formal education requirements for private- and public-sector workers wherever possible. As discussed in the Occupational Licensing chapter, states should eliminate many occupational licenses altogether and remove unnecessary credential requirements for those that remain. For many jobs, passage of an examination —written, practical, or both—is a better means of assessing competence than a degree. As long as a person can do a job, it should not matter how they attain the requisite knowledge and skills.

President Donald Trump moved in the right direction for federal workers in 2020, signing an executive order calling on the Office of Personnel Management to examine all federal jobs and eliminate unnecessary credential requirements.[23]

The state of Maryland recently did much the same, eliminating college degree requirements for thousands of state government jobs.[24] Other states and localities should follow suit.

Next, the federal government should stop restricting and distorting the supply of more diverse and innovative higher education services by freeing colleges from rigid accreditation requirements to enroll students who use reformed federal aid programs. Roughly along the lines laid out in the Higher Education Reform and Opportunity Act of 2019, the federal government could allow aid to be used at institutions that are accredited by states or state-recognized accreditors, including apprenticeship programs, competency-based programs, and short-term degrees.[25]

The federal government also should treat for-profit schools the same as putatively nonprofit ones, in contrast with proposed "gainful employment" regulations that clumsily differentiate between programs focused on a graduate getting a job, which are most often offered by for-profit institutions, such as medical technician training programs, and those focused more on academic subjects in typically not-for-profit institutions.[26] In reality, almost everyone who goes to college does so to improve their employment prospects. In a 2014 New America survey, 91 percent of young people either planning to go to college or recently matriculated cited "to improve my employment opportunities" as a "very important" or "important" reason for enrolling.[27] It was the top reason cited.

In general, the market should decide the success or failure of all higher education institutions—for-profit, nonprofit, online, brick-and-mortar, etc.—not regulations, subsidies, and politics.

Finally, states should redirect funding from state colleges to students or, preferably, taxpayers. And, as discussed in the K–12 Education chapter, states and localities should greatly expand options before college. Preferably, this should be done through school choice programs that enable funding to follow students to educational options, including private, of their choosing. Short of that, public schools should offer more robust career and technical education options. Preparation to enter the workforce should be possible for many people without any formal postsecondary education.

ACTION PLAN

Federal higher education policy has largely been driven by one simplistic notion: education is good, so more must be better. Moreover, much that has been done in the name of "education" does not supply in-demand skills and knowledge. Subsidies have been largely self-defeating, fueling higher prices and diploma demand.

Congress should repeal all student loan and grant programs. If it does not go that far, it should

- eliminate parent and grad PLUS loans, which are not means-tested (the former fuels indebtedness for many families that cannot afford it, while graduate students should be able to obtain private loans to study in-demand fields);
- eliminate all unsubsidized loans, which are not means-tested and are only unsubsidized in that the government charges interest while a borrower is in school and for six months after graduation;
- increase the minimum academic requirements to obtain a federal loan or grant—perhaps a 2.5 grade point average on a 4.0 scale in core classes and minimum ACT or SAT scores of 20 and 1060, the national means—which would protect potential borrowers who are academically unprepared from taking on unmanageable debt and would help cool credential inflation;
- allow remaining loans and other aid to follow students to schools with various kinds of accreditation, including by state-recognized accreditors; and
- treat all postsecondary options equally, avoiding gainful employment rules or applying them to all institutions and programs.

State and local governments should

- remove college degree requirements from public-sector job offerings for which specific college-level learning is not needed or in which competency-based assessments can be used;
- remove credential requirements from occupational licenses in which competency-based assessments can be used, or for which there is no clear college-level learning needed;
- reduce direct state and local subsidies for public colleges, either giving them to students or, ideally, reducing taxes; and
- as is discussed in more detail in the K–12 Education chapter, implement education choice programs, such as education savings accounts, and create more robust career and technical education programs in public schools.

NOTES

1. Richard Vedder, "The Morrill Land-Grant Act: Fact and Fiction," in Todd J. Zywicki and Neal P. McCluskey, eds., *Unprofitable Schooling: Examining Causes of, and Fixes for, America's Broken Ivory Tower* (Washington: Cato Institute, 2019), pp. 37–38.

2. "Table 104.10: Rates of High School Completion and Bachelor's Degree Attainment among Persons Age 25 and Over, by Race/Ethnicity and Sex: Selected Years, 1910 through 2021," Digest of Education Statistics, National Center for Education Statistics, U.S. Department of Education, National Center for Education Statistics, 2022.

3. Servicemen's Readjustment Act of 1944, Pub. L. No. 78-346, 58 Stat. 284 (1944); and "Table 301.20: Historical Summary of Faculty, Enrollment, Degrees Conferred, and Finances in Degree-Granting Postsecondary Institutions: Selected Years, 1869–70 through 2018–19," Digest of Education Statistics, National Center for Education Statistics, U.S. Department of Education, 2021.

4. Josh Mitchell, *The Debt Trap: How Student Loans Became a National Catastrophe* (New York: Simon and Schuster, 2021), pp. 17–44.

5. See Brian Jacob, Brian McCall, and Kevin Stange, "College as Country Club: Do Colleges Cater to Students' Preferences for Consumption?," *Journal of Labor Economics* 36, no. 2 (April 2018): 309–48.

6. David O. Lucca, Taylor Nadauld, and Karen Shen, "Credit Supply and the Rise in College Tuition: Evidence from the Expansion in Federal Student Aid Programs," *Review of Financial Studies* 32, no. 2 (February 2019): 423–66.

7. "President Biden Announces Student Loan Relief for Borrowers Who Need It Most," White House fact sheet, August 24, 2022.

8. Mark Kutner, Elizabeth Greenberg, and Justin Baer, "National Assessment of Adult Literacy (NAAL): A First Look at the Literacy of America's Adults in the 21st Century," Institute of Education Sciences, U.S. Department of Education, NCES 2006-470, 2006.

9. "Highlights of the 2017 U.S. PIAAC Results," National Center for Education Statistics, U.S. Department of Education, NCES 2020-777.

10. Joseph B. Fuller and Manjari Raman, "Dismissed by Degrees: How Degree Inflation Is Undermining U.S. Competitiveness and Hurting America's Middle Class," Harvard Business School, December 13, 2017.

11. "The Labor Market for Recent College Graduates: Underemployment," Federal Reserve Bank of New York, February 12, 2021.

12. David L. Angus and Jeffrey Mirel, "Professionalism and the Public Good: A Brief History of Teacher Certification," Thomas B. Fordham Foundation, January 2001, pp. 17–34.

13. Janie Sullivan, "What States Require a Master's Degree for Teachers?," Career Trend, December, 2, 2018; and see Helen F. Ladd and Lucy C. Sorensen, "Do Master's Degrees Matter? Advanced Degrees, Career Paths, and the Effectiveness of Teachers," National Center for Analysis of Longitudinal Data in Education Research Working Paper no. 136, August 2015.

14. Suzanne Hultin, "The National Occupational Licensing Database," National Conference of State Legislatures, March 1, 2022.

15. Morris M. Kleiner and Alan B. Krueger, "The Prevalence and Effect of Occupational Licensing," National Bureau of Economic Research Working Paper no. 14308, September 2008.

16. See Occupational Licensing chapter

17. Justice Robert H. Jackson had a certificate from Albany Law School but not a degree, having gained most of his training "reading law" with a practicing attorney. Tobias T. Gibson, "Robert Jackson," First Amendment Encyclopedia, Middle Tennessee State University, 2009.

18. Eugène Custers and Olle ten Cate, "The History of Medical Education in Europe and the United States, with Respect to Time and Proficiency," *Academic Medicine* 93, no. 35 (March 2018): S49–S54.

19. Michael B. Horn and Alana Dunagan, "Innovation and Quality Assurance in Higher Education," Christensen Institute, June 2018.

20. "Official Cohort Default Rates for Schools," Federal Student Aid, U.S. Department of Education, FY 2018.

21. "Characteristics of Postsecondary Students," National Center for Education Statistics, May 2022.

22. Preston Cooper, "Is Grad School Worth It? A Comprehensive Return on Investment Analysis," Foundation for Research on Equal Opportunity, February 24, 2022.

23. Kery Murakami, "Skills over Degrees in Federal Hiring," *Inside Higher Ed,* June 29, 2020.

24. Tyler Cowen, "Maryland Takes a Stand against the College Credential," *Bloomberg,* March 17, 2022.

25. Higher Education Reform and Opportunity Act of 2019, S. 2339, 116th Cong. (2019).

26. Scott Jaschik, "A Plan to Renew Gainful Employment," *Inside Higher Ed*, February 10, 2022.

27. Rachel Fishman, "2015 College Decisions Survey, Part 1: Deciding to Go to College," New America, p. 4.

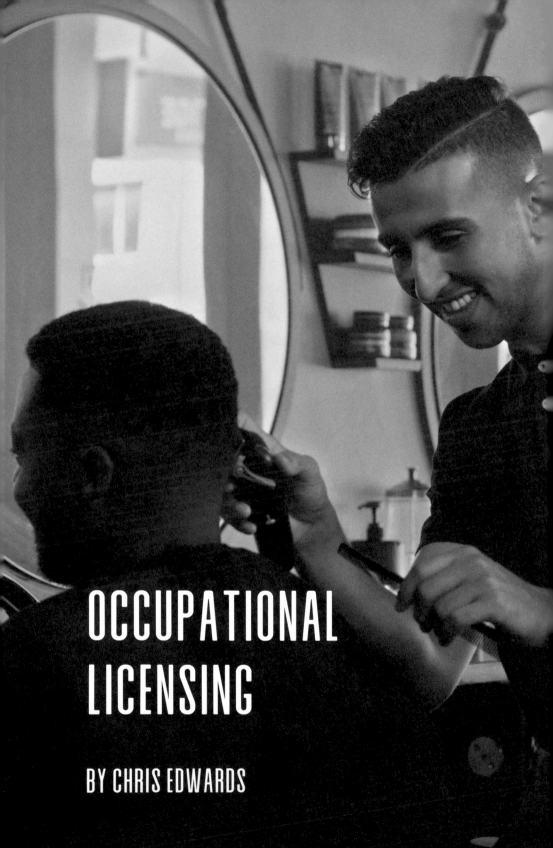

OCCUPATIONAL LICENSING

BY CHRIS EDWARDS

THE ISSUE: THE DRAMATIC INCREASE IN OCCUPATIONAL LICENSING RESTRICTIONS NEEDLESSLY DISCOURAGES WORK AND MOBILITY

The United States' relatively free and flexible labor markets support worker opportunities and boost lifetime earnings and economic growth.[1] However, one type of regulatory barrier, occupational licensing, has increased over the last several decades to affect more than one-fifth of the workforce, raising costs and undermining worker choices in the process.

State governments bar individuals from entering many occupations unless they fulfill specific educational, training, and testing requirements. Occupational licensing requirements vary by state, but they typically cover dozens of professions ranging from doctors and lawyers to cosmetologists, manicurists, barbers, preschool teachers, athletic trainers, makeup artists, security alarm installers, taxidermists, sports coaches, travel agents, bartenders, animal trainers, tree trimmers, tour guides, interior designers, auctioneers, massage therapists, and many others.[2]

The share of U.S. jobs requiring an occupational license increased from 5 percent in the 1950s to 22 percent in 2021.[3] Other estimates put today's share even higher.[4] Figure 1 shows the share of workers with a license by industry. The number of occupations requiring a license in at least one state rose from about 30 in 1920 to about 1,100 today.[5] The share of workers needing licenses ranges from 14 percent in Georgia to 27 percent in Nevada.[6]

The increase in mandatory licensing has reduced workforce mobility and created barriers to work and advancement. The barriers particularly harm young people starting their careers, people with low incomes, people switching occupations, people moving between states, veterans or military spouses, and people with a criminal record.

Kleiner (2015), for example, estimated that "the restrictions from occupational licensing can result in up to 2.85 million fewer jobs nationwide, with an annual cost to consumers of $203 billion."[7] Similarly, a 2018 Federal Trade Commission report found that while occupational licensing supports health and safety in some cases, it also reduces labor supply, restrains competition, and raises prices.[8] Kleiner and Soltas (2019) examined license variation among the states and found that shifting an occupation from unlicensed to licensed reduces employment in the licensed occupation by 29 percent.[9] The economists also discovered that licensing requirements delay the entry of younger workers into the relevant occupations far beyond the amount of time needed to meet any relevant education requirements. Kleiner and Xu (2020) found that licensing has significant negative effects on occupational mobility when switching both in to and out of licensed occupations, accounting for "at least 7.7 percent of the total decline in occupational mobility over the past two decades."[10] Such barriers also discourage hiring

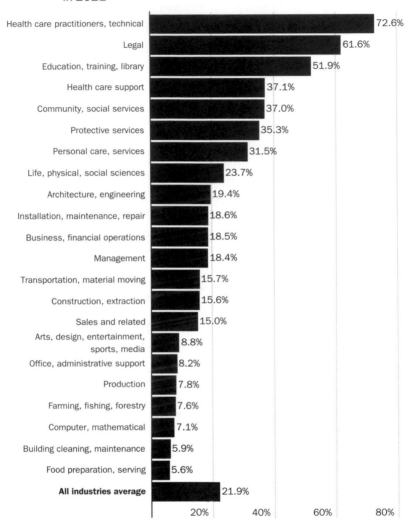

FIGURE 1 An increasingly large share of U.S. occupations required a license in 2021

Occupation	Percentage
Health care practitioners, technical	72.6%
Legal	61.6%
Education, training, library	51.9%
Health care support	37.1%
Community, social services	37.0%
Protective services	35.3%
Personal care, services	31.5%
Life, physical, social sciences	23.7%
Architecture, engineering	19.4%
Installation, maintenance, repair	18.6%
Business, financial operations	18.5%
Management	18.4%
Transportation, material moving	15.7%
Construction, extraction	15.6%
Sales and related	15.0%
Arts, design, entertainment, sports, media	8.8%
Office, administrative support	8.2%
Production	7.8%
Farming, fishing, forestry	7.6%
Computer, mathematical	7.1%
Building cleaning, maintenance	5.9%
Food preparation, serving	5.6%
All industries average	21.9%

Source: "Certification and Licensing Status of the Employed by Occupation, 2021 Annual Averages," Labor Force Statistics from the Current Population Service, U.S. Bureau of Labor Statistics, January 20, 2022.

across state lines, and thus limit workers' interstate mobility.[11] As Figure 2 shows, states with licensing requirements for more occupations (i.e., high licensing states) experience fewer job-to-job (i.e., directly from another employer) hires than do states with fewer licensing burdens.

Recent federal administrations have rightly been critical of licensing. A 2015 report by Obama administration economists concluded, "There is evidence

FIGURE 2 Fewer workers change jobs in high licensing states

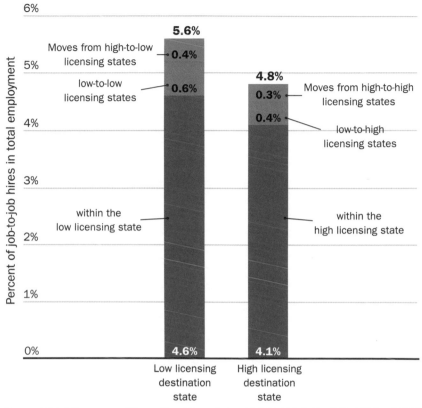

Source: Mikkel Hermansen, "Occupational Licensing and Job Mobility in the United States," OECD Economics Department Working Paper no. 1585, December 17, 2019, p. 23.
Note: Job-to-job hire rates in states with low and high licensing, weighted average percentage of employment, second quarter 2012 to first quarter 2018.

licensing requirements raise the price of goods and services, restrict employment opportunities, and make it more difficult for workers to take their skills across state lines."[12] The Trump administration also prioritized licensing reform, and its Federal Trade Commission continued several Obama-era actions targeting onerous state licensing regimes.[13] And the Biden's administration's *Economic Report of the President* for 2022 found that "occupational licensing can make it more difficult for workers to enter fields or move to places where their human capital would be more productive by increasing the cost of mobility in terms of fees for obtaining a license or time to complete required training or other licensing requirements."[14]

Many licensed occupations are found in small businesses, so licensing restrictions are restrictions on entrepreneurship, particularly for disadvantaged individuals. Slivinski (2015) found that those states that require licenses for a larger number of occupations with typically moderate incomes have lower rates of low-income entrepreneurship.[15] The Institute for Justice (IJ) calculated in 2017 that lower-income occupational licenses require, on average, nearly a year of education or experience, one exam, and more than $260 in fees.[16] Such burdens are disproportionately heavy for individuals who are unemployed, living paycheck-to-paycheck, or raising a child alone.

Military spouses are also disproportionately affected by state licensing rules, given the type of work they often do and their families' frequent interstate travel.[17] Also, veterans with specialized military training often find themselves ineligible for a license to do the same work as a civilian.[18] And, as discussed in the Criminal Justice chapter, licensing rules often bar individuals with a criminal record from applying, thus thwarting worthwhile "prison entrepreneurship" programs intended to rehabilitate inmates and decrease recidivism.[19] Only a few states earn good grades in this regard, despite the entrepreneurship programs' efficacy. States with heavier occupational licensing burdens have been found to have higher recidivism rates than those with lower barriers to entry, while states with the fewest barriers actually saw recidivism rates decline.[20]

Just as importantly, the usual consumer protection rationales for licensing have proven to be weak. Kleiner (2015) reviewed the academic literature and found that there "is little evidence to show that the licensing of many different occupations has improved the quality of services received by consumers."[21] Similarly, the 2015 Obama administration report concluded that "most research does not find that licensing improves quality or public health and safety."[22] More recent research shows much the same: Blair and Fisher (2022), for example, reviewed 21 million online transactions in the $500 billion home services market and found that "licensing a task reduces service provider surplus and platform surplus without increasing consumer surplus"—thus confirming previous studies of licensing's lack of benefits for consumers on digital platforms.[23] And looking internationally, a 2020 report by the Organisation for Economic Co-operation and Development found that "there is very little empirical evidence of a positive link between the stringency of regulations and the quality of services."[24]

That there are large differences in state licensing requirements and covered occupations is a strong indication that many licenses are unnecessary or overly burdensome. Athletic trainers, for example, are not licensed in California, but in Nevada they must have a college degree, pass an exam, and pay $666 for an initial license and $150 for annual renewals.[25] Auctioneers are not licensed in about half the states, but in North Carolina they must have a college degree, pass an exam, and pay $450 for an initial license and $250 for annual renewals. Heating, ventilation, and air conditioning (HVAC) contractors are not licensed in more than a dozen states, but in Nevada they must pass an exam and pay $1,135 for an initial license and $600 for biennial renewals.

Such large interstate differences suggest that rules are not based on analyses of health or safety but rather reflect differences in state and local politics. Current members of professions often sit on state regulatory boards, and they tend to favor increasing licensing requirements to limit entry and reduce competition. They also often lobby for new restrictions and against reform of current ones. For example, a 2022 IJ study shows that occupational licensing is usually initiated by industry groups, not consumers.[26] Numerous states use "sunrise reviews" when considering imposing new occupational licenses. The Institute for Justice studied 494 such reviews in 15 states from 1985 to 2017 and found that industry groups initiated 83 percent of the reviews, generally in the hopes of prompting lawmakers to impose licensing. For example, the "Maine Association of Wetland Scientists sought licensure of soil scientists and the Vermont Alarm and Signal Association sought licensure of burglar alarm installers."[27]

Sunrise reviews are a good idea when they are performed by independent experts, as they inform policymakers about the downsides of licensing. Just 20 percent of the independent reviews that IJ examined recommended adding new licensing rules.[28] Thus, the good news is that experts usually find that the costs of licensing are higher than the benefits.

The bad news, however, is that state legislatures often ignore the experts, as new licensing rules were enacted after 41 percent of the sunrise reviews. For example, lactation consultants often get voluntarily certified to signal their professional skills, but Georgia legislators mandated licensing in 2016, even though a state sunrise review recommended against it. The law required about two years of college courses and more than 300 hours of supervised clinical work. It threatened to put hundreds of current lactation consultants out of work and make them pay to get recertified, even though many had years of experience and voluntary certification. The Georgia law is currently on hold due to litigation.

Other examples of new licensing, even after state reviews recommended against, include: athletic trainers in Florida, Hawaii, and Washington; hearing aid dispensers in Colorado; HVAC technicians in South Carolina and West Virginia; landscape architects in Colorado, Vermont, and Virginia; massage therapists in Colorado, Georgia, and Virginia; motor vehicle salespeople in West Virginia; nutritionists in Hawaii; plumbers in South Carolina and West Virginia; tattooists in Minnesota and Virginia; and timekeepers in mixed martial arts in Hawaii.[29] Unfortunately, licensing is often "driven by special interests, not the public interest," concluded the 2022 IJ study.[30]

THE POLICY SOLUTIONS: REPEAL UNNECESSARY LICENSES; EMBRACE INTERSTATE LICENSE RECOGNITION; REDUCE LICENSING BURDENS FOR HIGHLY MOBILE OR DISADVANTAGED GROUPS; AND LOWER LICENSING FEES

In response to growing evidence of licensing's downsides, labor experts across the political spectrum have called for reforms to liberalize occupational licensing rules, and many states are pursuing such proposals. The best reform option for many occupations is full repeal of the state licensing requirement, particularly when licensing is unrelated to health and safety or is unnecessary. A simple way to determine if a licensing requirement is needed is to examine the experience of other states. States should lean toward repealing licensing of an occupation when numerous other states do not require it. In 2020, for example, Florida repealed licensing for interior designers, nail technicians, hair braiders, and boxing announcers.[31] Florida knew that repealing licensing for interior designers made sense because most states do not license that occupation.

Another reform approach is for states to perform cost-benefit analyses on all current licensing requirements and to repeal those that do not generate overall net benefits. Such analyses can be part of periodic "sunset reviews" performed by independent examiners on a rotating basis. For example, Utah recently added a requirement for a detailed examination of existing license requirements every 10 years.[32]

A further reform option is to replace compulsory licensing with voluntary (and superior) market mechanisms. For example, many occupations, such as those in information technology, eschew licensing and instead rely on workers gaining qualifications through voluntary certification. Such certifications encourage skill accumulation and signal worker abilities, but they do not pose a hard, artificial barrier to employment since they are voluntary. They also apply universally and thus do not restrict workers' interstate mobility.

Short of repealing licensing requirements, state policymakers should support worker mobility by opening their workforces to individuals licensed in other states.[33] If a person is licensed as, say, a nurse in one state, that individual should not face the costs of retaking courses and tests after moving. As discussed in the Health Care chapter, the need for greater interstate mobility was evident during the pandemic, as states facing surging hospital demands needed temporary help from doctors and nurses licensed elsewhere (and thus those states temporarily waived various licensing requirements).

One way to improve interstate mobility is through "compacts" among states, which recognize members' licenses for particular occupations. The Nurse Licensure Compact, for example, allows nurses in more than 30 states to practice in other states that are compact members.[34] Other multistate compacts exist for physical therapists, psychologists, and emergency medical services personnel.[35] A broader and likely better approach to interstate licensing reform is universal recognition, which was first passed by Arizona in 2019.[36] Governor Doug Ducey (R-AZ) championed the reforms, noting, "Plumbers, barbers, nurses, you don't lose your skills simply because you pack up a U-Haul truck and move to Arizona."[37] The law allows for expedited licensing approval for Arizona residents who hold similar licenses from other states. After the Arizona reform, 17 other states have enacted similar reforms, thus allowing greater interstate worker mobility.[38]

Other reforms can reduce the harms of licensing, especially for disadvantaged groups. One popular reform in recent years has been for states to direct licensing boards to grant a license to a veteran with equivalent military training, education, and experience. Other states have waived civilian training requirements and allow veterans to sit for licensure exams based on military training and experience alone. However, not all states have adopted these reforms; reformer states have omitted certain professions; and the reformed process can remain costly and time-consuming.[39]

States have also loosened licensing rules for military spouses, who often move frequently during their careers. About "35 percent of military spouses are employed in professions that demand a license, and those same families are 10 times more likely to move across state lines within the previous year than their civilian counterparts."[40] Reforms for military spouses are a good step, but spouses of other mobile professionals face similar problems and deserve relief as well.

Policymakers should also rethink licensing prohibitions related to past criminal activity. In about half the states, "applicants can be denied a license due to any kind of criminal conviction, regardless of whether it is relevant to the license sought or how long ago it occurred."[41] As detailed in the Criminal Justice chapter, individuals with criminal records are more likely to be unemployed or underemployed. It is in everyone's interest that they reboot their lives in a productive manner: finding employment is "a critical aspect of reducing recidivism" for ex-convicts, and licensing liberalization can support that goal.[42]

As discussed in the Health Care chapter, states also should liberalize scope-of-practice rules to narrow the services that only licensed professionals are allowed to provide. For example, expanding scope-of-practice rules for nurse practitioners or dental hygienists to perform some services currently performed by doctors or dentists, respectively, could reduce costs in the health care system and lower prices for consumers. Finally, if repeal and other reforms are not politically possible for certain occupations, states should at least cut the costs of obtaining and renewing licenses.

ACTION PLAN

Licensing may be appropriate in some technical professions where there are substantial health and safety concerns, but for most occupations such restrictions are unnecessary and harmful for American workers and the economy more broadly. Most often, market mechanisms, such as voluntary certification, can address any consumer protection concerns.

Every American has the right to "life, liberty, and the pursuit of happiness." Freedom to use one's labor in a chosen occupation is central to that pursuit. As such, policymakers should reject attempts to impose new licensing rules, and they should reduce existing requirements to maximize worker freedom in the marketplace.

State governments should

- not impose any new occupational licensing rules but rather rely on market-based mechanisms such as voluntary certification;
- review all current occupational licensing rules and repeal those that fail a cost-benefit test or that most other states do not require;
- establish independent "sunset reviews" for all licenses;
- where licensing is appropriate, work to increase interstate acceptance of licenses and reduce the costs of compliance, preferably through universal recognition;
- liberalize licensing rules related to past convictions, where appropriate, to encourage ex-convicts reentering the workforce;
- loosen licensing rules for veterans with equivalent military training, as well as for military spouses and other American workers who often move frequently during their careers; and
- liberalize scope-of-practice rules to narrow the services that only licensed professionals are allowed to provide.

NOTES

1. For instance, see Niklas Engbom, "Labor Market Fluidity and Human Capital Accumulation," National Bureau of Economic Research Working Paper no. 29698, January 2022.

2. Licensing can take numerous forms. A "title" law requires individuals to take steps to use a title such as "interior designer," whereas a "practice" law requires individuals to take steps such as training to offer the services that are included under the license rules. For background on licensing, see "Professional Certifications and Occupational Licenses: Evidence from the Current Population Survey," Monthly Labor Review, U.S. Bureau of Labor Statistics, June 2019.

3. The figure for 2021 is from "Labor Force Statistics from the Current Population Survey: Data on Certifications and Licenses," U.S. Bureau of Labor Statistics, January 20, 2022. The 1950s figure is from Morris M. Kleiner and Evgeny S. Vorotnikov, "At What Co$t? State and National Estimates of the Economic Costs of Occupational Licensing," Institute for Justice, November 2018.

4. "Options to Enhance Occupational License Portability," Federal Trade Commission, Economic Liberty, September 24, 2018.

5. U.S. Department of the Treasury Office of Economic Policy, Council of Economic Advisers, and U.S. Department of Labor, "Occupational Licensing: A Framework for Policymakers," White House, July 2015.

6. Kleiner and Vorotnikov, "At What Co$t?"

7. Morris M. Kleiner, "Reforming Occupational Licensing Policies," Hamilton Project Discussion Paper no. 2015-01, March 2015, p. 6.

8. Karen A. Goldman, "Options to Enhance Occupational Licensing Portability," Federal Trade Commission Policy Perspectives, September 2018.

9. Morris M. Kleiner and Evan J. Soltas, "A Welfare Analysis of Occupational Licensing in U.S. States," National Bureau of Economic Research Working Paper no. 26383, October 2019.

10. Morris M. Kleiner and Ming Xu, "Occupational Licensing and Labor Market Fluidity," Cato Institute Research Briefs in Economic Policy no. 239, November 4, 2020.

11. Mikkel Hermansen, "Occupational Licensing Has a Sizeable Impact on Job Mobility in the US," VoxEU, Centre for Economic Policy Research, March 15, 2020.

12. "Occupational Licensing: A Framework for Policymakers," p. 3.

13. Michelle Cottle, "The Onerous, Arbitrary, Unaccountable World of Occupational Licensing," The Atlantic, August 13, 2017; and "Options to Enhance Occupational License Portability."

14. Economic Report of the President (Washington: Government Publishing Office, April 2022), p. 153.

15. Stephen Slivinski, "Bootstraps Tangled in Red Tape," Goldwater Institute, February 10, 2015.

16. Kleiner and Vorotnikov, "At What Co$t?," pp. 8–13.

17. Shoshana Weissman and C. Jarrett Dieterle, "Bipartisan Help for Military Spouses," Wall Street Journal, May 8, 2019.

18. Amanda Winters, Rachael Stephens, and Jennifer Schultz, "Barriers to Work: Veterans and Military Spouses," National Conference of State Legislatures, July 17, 2018.

19. W. Sherman Rogers, "Occupational Licensing: Quality Control or Enterprise Killer? Problems That Arise When People Must Get the Government's Permission to Work," Journal of Business, Entrepreneurship, and the Law 10, no. 2 (June 2017): 145–202.

20. Nick Sibilla, "Barred from Working," Institute for Justice, August 2020; and Stephen Slivinski, "Turning Shackles into Bootstraps: Why Occupational Licensing Reform Is the Missing Piece of Criminal Justice Reform," Center for the Study of Economic Liberty at Arizona State University Policy Report no. 2016-01, November 7, 2016.

21. Kleiner, "Reforming Occupational Licensing Policies."

22. "Occupational Licensing: A Framework for Policymakers."

23. Peter Q. Blair and Mischa Fisher, "Does Occupational Licensing Reduce Value Creation on Digital Platforms?," National Bureau of Economic Research Working Paper no. 30388, August 2022, pp. 1 and 6–7.

24. Christina von Rueden and Indre Bambalaite, "Measuring Occupational Entry Regulations: A New OECD Approach," OECD Economics Department Working Paper no. 1606, March 2020, p. 13.

25. These examples come from the "National Occupational Licensing Database," National Conference of State Legislatures, March 1, 2022.

26. Kathy Sanchez, Elyse Smith Pohl, and Lisa Knepper, "Too Many Licenses?," Institute for Justice, February 2022.

27. Sanchez, Pohl, and Knepper, "Too Many Licenses?," p. 22.

28. Sanchez, Pohl, and Knepper, "Too Many Licenses?," table 9.

29. Sanchez, Pohl, and Knepper, "Too Many Licenses?," table 10.

30. Sanchez, Pohl, and Knepper, "Too Many Licenses?," p. 3.

31. "Governor Ron DeSantis Signs 'The Occupational Freedom and Opportunity Act' to Remove Unnecessary Barriers to Employment," Office of Florida Governor Ron DeSantis, June 30, 2020.

32. National Conference of State Legislatures, "Occupational Licensing Final Report: Assessing State Policies and Practices," December 2020, p. 62. The report was completed in conjunction with the National Governors Association and the Council on State Governments.

33. Iris Hentze and Zach Herman, "State Efforts to Improve Occupational Licensing Mobility," National Conference of State Legislatures, March 19, 2021.

34. "Licensure Compacts," National Council of State Boards of Nursing.

35. "Occupational Licensing Final Report," p. 51.

36. Jeffrey Singer and Michael Tanner, "Arizona Leads the Way in Licensing Reform," *Arizona Capitol Times,* October 29, 2020. This was law HB 2569.

37. Rich Ehisen, "Occupational Licensing Reform Gains Steam in Statehouses," State Net Capitol Journal, February 8, 2021.

38. "State Reforms for Universal License Recognition," Institute for Justice.

39. Winters, Stephens, and Schultz, "Barriers to Work: Veterans and Military Spouses."

40. Rich Ehisen, "Occupational Licensing Reform Gains Steam in Statehouses," State Net Capitol Journal, February 8, 2021.

41. "Occupational Licensing: A Framework for Policymakers," p. 5.

42. "Occupational Licensing Final Report," p. 68.

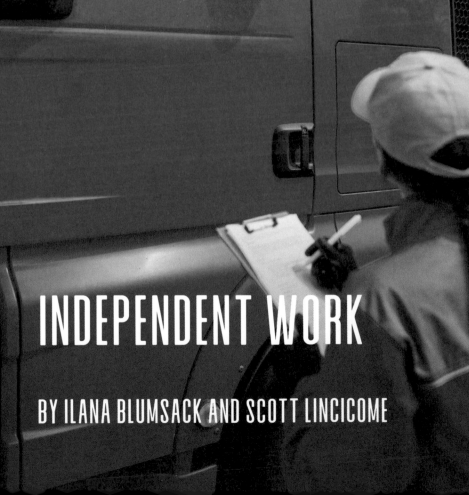

INDEPENDENT WORK

BY ILANA BLUMSACK AND SCOTT LINCICOME

THE ISSUE: GOVERNMENT POLICIES DISCOURAGE OR EVEN PROHIBIT INDEPENDENT WORK, WHICH IS INCREASINGLY PREVALENT AND OFTEN PREFERRED BY AMERICAN WORKERS OVER TRADITIONAL ARRANGEMENTS

Almost all political discussions about the American worker address traditional employees, who work for a single employer providing regular compensation in exchange for controlling how, where, and when the employees' work will be completed. Yet the U.S. freelancing platform Upwork estimated that at some point in 2021, about 36 percent of the American workforce engaged in independent work—in which individuals take on short-term, specific assignments from multiple clients, relatively free from the clients' control or direction.[1] These numbers swelled during the pandemic: the more than 50 million independent American workers in 2021 represented a 25 percent increase from 2019 (see Figure 1).[2]

FIGURE 1 The United States gained almost 13 million independent workers in 2021

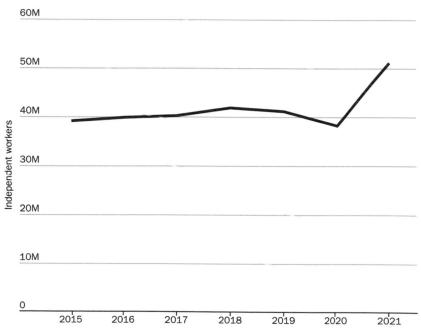

Source: "11th Annual State of Independence: The Great Realization," MBO Partners, December 2021.
Note: Includes those who engage in full-time, part-time, and occasional independent work.

While independent work often conjures images of supposedly "exploited" Uber drivers and DoorDash deliverers, the reality is far different. The IRS reports, for example, that only about 8.6 percent of all independent workers are employed in gig work (i.e., online platforms that enable on-demand services for the consumer and a flexible work arrangement for the provider), and the most common occupations for independent workers are in marketing, communications, and computer programming.[3] Freelance or contract work, moreover, is undertaken in almost every industry.

Much of this work is also high-paying: the *Wall Street Journal* reported in 2022 that many skilled freelancers make six-figure incomes, while Ravenelle and Kowalski (2022) found that these workers can command a $1,000 per day "minimum wage" on various global freelance platforms.[4] Yet policies seeking to discipline or even eliminate gig work usually affect these jobs too.

Furthermore, most Americans enter independent work arrangements because they prefer them to the more structured and controlled form of traditional employment, not because they have no other choice. A 2021 Upwork survey, for example, found that over 70 percent of both full-time and part-time independent workers see increased flexibility as the major reason for engaging in independent work.[5] A separate 2021 survey from MBO Partners showed that nearly 90 percent of respondents were happier in independent work than in traditional jobs and that roughly three-quarters of independent workers are satisfied with their work, intend to remain in independent work, and are optimistic about their career future (see Figure 2). By contrast, just 11 percent of these independent workers wanted to find full-time traditional employment.[6]

This preference extends to oft-maligned gig work. According to a 2021 Pew Research Center survey, for example, almost 80 percent of gig platform workers rated their experiences positively, with almost half citing schedule flexibility as a major reason for doing the work. Only 28 percent of respondents said they performed gig work because there were few other job opportunities available where they live.[7] And an examination by Chen et al. (2019) of more than a million U.S. Uber drivers over an eight-month period found that drivers valued the flexibility the arrangement provided—in both the timing and amount of work—at $150 per week (or 40 percent of expected earnings). Chen et al. also found that drivers would need a 50 percent raise to work for a less flexible taxicab company.[8]

Beyond the simple preference among many Americans for independent work are its significant economic benefits, which include boosting entrepreneurship, dynamism, and growth. Barrios et al. (2022) showed, for example, that the entrance of new gig economy platforms in different cities increased both new business registrations and new business loans in those places by roughly 5 percent, with the effect most pronounced in economically depressed areas.[9] Independent work also proved to be critical during the pandemic when, due to government restrictions or structural economic shifts, certain traditional employment options

FIGURE 2 Most independent workers viewed their work positively in 2021

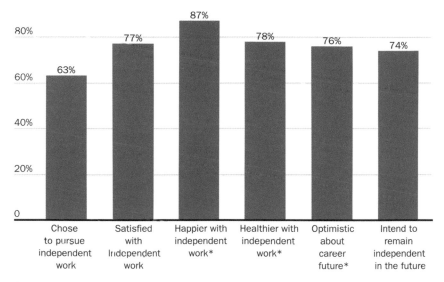

Source: "11th Annual State of Independence: The Great Realization," MBO Partners, December 2021.
Note: Questions were asked of full-time, part-time, and occasional independent workers.
* Denotes a question asked of full-time independent workers only.

disappeared. Much of the substantial uptick in new business formations in 2020–2021, in fact, can be attributed to increasing numbers of independent workers, both individuals selling goods on e-commerce platforms and traditional freelance workers in service sectors.[10] And as noted in the Introduction, this increase has not been limited to white-collar professionals: for example, the number of new independent truck drivers increased from 43,953 in 2018 to more than 109,000 in 2021, with an estimated 70 percent of these being single-driver operations.[11]

Finally, independent work has been a boon for consumers—both businesses and individuals—beyond simply the benefits arising from new competition (more and more innovative choices, lower prices, etc.). Research shows, for example, that ridesharing services such as Uber and Lyft have reduced drunk driving and drinking-related car crashes as more people choose to take a rideshare home rather than risk driving under the influence.[12] Meanwhile, food delivery services such as DoorDash and Uber Eats greatly assisted restaurants in weathering lockdowns imposed during the COVID-19 pandemic, as customers turned to food delivery when dine-in services were not allowed.[13] And recently, new gig platforms such as Bite Ninja have helped restaurants navigate shortages of drive-thru workers.[14] Beyond gig work, a 2021 Mercatus Center survey found that 57 percent of tech startup executives report that independent workers are an essential part of the function of their businesses.[15]

Despite these trends, many current and proposed laws restrict or even prohibit independent work, and politicians routinely demonize it. In 2019, for example, California enacted Assembly Bill 5 (AB 5), which expands the definition of "employee" to encompass many independent workers. Under the law, an independent worker must be free from the control of the entity for which the work is performed; perform work that is different from the hiring entity's usual business; and already work in the same trade, occupation, or business as the work being performed for the hiring entity (known as the "ABC test"). If these conditions are not met, the government considers a worker to be an employee.[16] A similar proposal that passed the U.S. House of Representatives in 2021—the Protecting the Right to Organize Act—would employ this test nationally to determine the status of independent workers.[17]

Although AB 5 garners most of the media attention, California is hardly the first state to utilize the ABC test. Massachusetts has employed it since 2005, but gig workers like Uber and Lyft drivers have thus far been treated as independent workers. Such an exemption may not hold: the state attorney general has challenged the rule, arguing that gig workers should be treated as employees under the commonwealth's statute, and the lawsuit is pending in a Massachusetts court as of August 2022.[18] In addition to California and Massachusetts, four states—Connecticut, Nebraska, New Jersey, and Vermont—restricted independent work in a similar fashion as of April 2021, while nearly 20 others utilized the ABC test to determine unemployment insurance eligibility.[19] Also, AB 5–style legislation has been proposed in Virginia, Washington State, and New York.[20]

These laws have serious consequences for workers and companies—not merely those in the gig economy. Forcibly reclassifying independent workers as traditional employees would subject their work to various labor regulations, often to the workers' detriment. For example, the Affordable Care Act requires that all companies with at least 50 full-time employees (defined as working at least 30 hours per week) provide health insurance to these workers and their families or face steep penalties.[21] According to a 2021 Trump White House Council of Economic Advisors report, studies have shown that this employer mandate can impose significant costs, particularly when it comes to smaller firms. The cost of providing government-mandated health coverage, including the higher administrative costs that smaller firms face, suppresses employees' wages and discourages small firms from adding jobs so as to avoid the mandate entirely.[22] As noted in the Private-Sector Labor Regulation and Employee Benefits chapters, moreover, other regulations dictating employee hours, schedules, and content eliminate the freedom and flexibility that independent workers desire, while accompanying wage and non-health benefit requirements would make them even more costly to hire for employers, potentially resulting in less work or pricing the workers out of the market.[23]

Given these and other legal requirements, a 2019 Barclays study estimated that classifying a rideshare driver as an employee would cost Uber an additional $3,625 per driver (approximately $3.6 billion overall using Uber's data on its number of U.S. drivers), and in 2020 Uber estimated reclassification would force the company to terminate more than 900,000 drivers nationally.[24] And following the passage of AB 5, Vox terminated 200 freelance writers in California for similar reasons.[25] As discussed in the Private-Sector Labor Regulation and Employee Benefits chapters, moreover, expanding labor regulations to cover independent workers also would likely diminish labor market fluidity and dynamism, which has been found to boost workers' lifetime earnings and productivity.

The additional costs associated with bills such as AB 5 would disproportionately harm smaller companies and startups that often rely on independent workers or lack the resources to offshore or automate certain core functions—thus benefiting large corporations and fueling the very market concentration that many AB 5 supporters claim to oppose.[26] These laws also would likely eliminate many common and widely accepted forms of independent work. For example, a freelance writer who contracts to write articles for online magazines would be considered an employee because the work is in line with the publications' usual business. A freelance fashion photographer would also be an employee because requirements to work at certain times (e.g., during a runway show) mean that the worker is not free from the hiring entity's control.

To assuage some of these concerns, and as a result of public outcry from independent workers themselves, California significantly reduced the scope of AB 5 to exempt more than 110 occupations, including photographers and writers, and ballot initiative Proposition 22 exempted gig economy workers.[27] However, many other common professions, such as the popular owner-operator model in domestic freight trucking, remain imperiled.[28] In fact, when court rulings applied AB 5 to commercial trucking in July 2022, potentially eliminating 70,000 independent truck owner-operators in California, hundreds of truckers protested their reclassification as employees and temporarily blockaded the Port of Oakland, one of the busiest shipping hubs in the country.[29]

These realities undermine proponents' most common justifications for new restrictions on independent work and reveal serious misunderstandings about it. First, they ignore that majorities of independent workers are satisfied with their incomes and work arrangements. For example, 58 percent of full-time independent workers reported they made more money than if they had been engaged in traditional employment, and 68 percent consider their work more secure than traditional employment (see Figure 3).[30] In Massachusetts, 83 percent of rideshare drivers want to remain independent workers, despite efforts to reclassify them as employees.[31]

Second, new restrictions on independent work would eliminate a critical lifeline for workers facing unemployment or other sudden declines in income. For example, a study of over 45,000 individuals from the United States, United Kingdom, and Italy found that respondents were more likely to migrate from

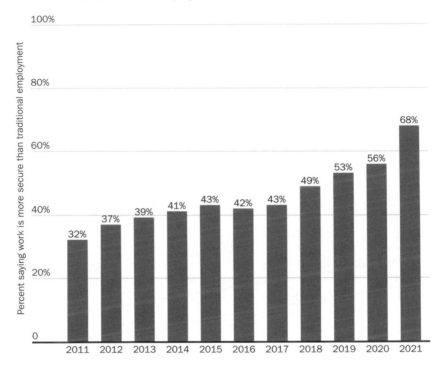

FIGURE 3 Independent workers increasingly say their work is more secure than traditional employment

Sources: "11th Annual State of Independence: The Great Realization," MBO Partners, December 2021; "The State of Independence in America 2020: A Decade of Independence: Trends that Matter," MBO Partners, December 2020; and "The State of Independence in America: 2019: The Changing Nature of the American Workforce," MBO Partners, June 2019.
Note: Responses are from full-time independent workers only.

unemployment to independent work, rather than from traditional employment to independent work.[32] The gig economy plays a similar role: Huang et al. (2020) found that a 1 percent increase in unemployment in a particular U.S. county led to a 21.8 percent increase in gig economy employment among county residents.[33] Eliminating this option via regulation could therefore harm many American workers who are trying to get back on their feet following an unexpected disruption in employment or a broader economic downturn.

Third, proponents of independent work regulations ignore that health, retirement, and other benefits are available to independent workers outside their workplaces. Health insurance, for example, may be obtained through a spouse, private markets, or government programs (although this can be improved, as discussed in the following section). Several retirement account options, such as a SIMPLE IRA or a 401(k), are also available to many independent workers. In fact, over 90 percent of independent workers have health insurance, and roughly two-thirds have a retirement savings account—figures similar to those of the general American workforce (see Figure 4).[34]

Fourth, concerns about independent workers' hours, wages, and benefits ignore that many independent workers do not work full-time in the field at issue and instead use the arrangement as a "side hustle" to pay for school or to pursue their passions. In fact, a survey by Brannon and Wolf (2021) of independent workers in Michigan, Ohio, and Pennsylvania found that more than 80 percent of respondents used part-time independent work to supplement a main source of income.[35] A 2021 report by MBO Partners found that roughly two-thirds of independent workers are either part-time or occasional independent workers.[36] And according to the Bernhardt et al. (2022) review of California taxpayers, independent work accounts for only 10.6 percent of earnings for the median worker with both traditional and independent work income.[37] Restrictions on independent work could deny these individuals an important source of extra income or the ability to follow their dreams in music, art, and other fields.

FIGURE 4 Most independent workers had a health insurance and retirement account in 2019

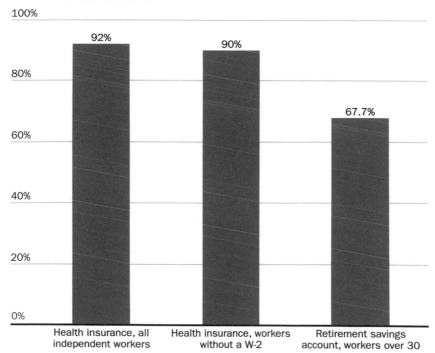

Source: Ike Brannon and Samuel Wolf, "An Empirical Snapshot of the Gig Economy," *Regulation* 44, no. 4 (Fall 2021): 4–8.
Note: Survey of 1,082 part-time and full-time independent workers in Michigan, Ohio, and Pennsylvania.

Beyond outright restrictions on independent work, federal tax laws can otherwise discourage it. For example, independent workers often overpay taxes or face monetary penalties because federal law requires most self-employed individuals to submit estimated quarterly tax payments or face penalties, even if they are owed a refund. More than one-third of independent workers were unaware of the need to file quarterly tax estimates in 2018 and thus faced hundreds of dollars in IRS penalties.[38] Many independent workers are also confounded by, or unaware of, various deductions to lower their tax burden. An independent worker must undertake almost twice as many steps to file taxes as a comparable traditional worker, and a recent survey found that only half of independent workers were aware of the tax deductions for which they may be eligible.[39] These rules can not only impose financial hardship on current independent workers but also make independent work less attractive to others considering it.

Starting in 2022, taxes became even more complicated and cumbersome for many independent workers and the online platforms that they utilize. In particular, federal tax reporting and filing (through form 1099-K) is now required for online sales of goods and services through a third-party payment service after a seller receives just $600 in gross annual payments (including fees, taxes, and even canceled orders), up from the previous $20,000 or 200 transactions minimum.[40] Seven states (California, Maryland, Massachusetts, Mississippi, Missouri, Vermont, and Virginia) and the District of Columbia have the same $600 reporting requirement for state taxes, while several other states have similar requirements with different, but still low, thresholds.[41] Freelancers, consultants, and gig platform workers will likely receive a different form, 1099-NEC, that has a similar reporting requirement.

Thus, for example, a working mom who uses Etsy and similar websites to sell artwork in her spare time will now receive a 1099-K tax form from each site at which she received more than $600 during a calendar year, even though she could hardly be considered employed in the gig economy and had numerous expenses (materials, marketing, etc.) that would—if she were aware and keeping track of them—reduce her final tax liability. Individuals simply reselling their own property would also receive these forms, even if they sold at a loss (and thus owe no taxes).[42] Given how many Americans use third-party sales sites to supplement their incomes, this change will likely increase tax reporting and compliance burdens for millions of people, discouraging them from engaging in independent work.

THE POLICY SOLUTIONS: AVOID OR REPEAL NEW LAWS RESTRICTING INDEPENDENT WORK AND EASE TAX BURDENS ON INDEPENDENT WORKERS

Policymakers should allow independent workers to remain independent rather than forcing millions of Americans into unwanted employee arrangements. Unfortunately, many jurisdictions are following California and doing the opposite, despite independent work's unique benefits and many Americans' desire to pursue it. To preserve workers' flexibility and independence, all such laws should be repealed—not merely riddled with new exceptions—and new proposals should be rejected.

Policymakers should also look to ease tax burdens on independent workers. First, to simplify tax compliance, Congress should enact a standard business deduction (SBD) that independent workers could use instead of reporting individual business expenses (such as an Uber driver's car maintenance)—a process that can be particularly cumbersome for many types of independent work. The standard business deduction would operate like the standard deduction for income and would be a percentage of an independent worker's income. Proponents of such a reform, such as University of North Carolina at Chapel Hill law professor Kathleen DeLaney Thomas and the Tax Foundation, suggest that the deduction should be 60 percent of income, while the remaining 40 percent would be taxable, a level that is comparable to average profit levels. Much like employee income taxes, independent workers could choose to continue to itemize business expenses instead of using the SBD.[43]

Second, Congress should allow companies to voluntarily withhold taxes from independent workers' wages, as is already the case for traditional employees. Companies could estimate an independent worker's income from their platform using the 1099 tax forms and, utilizing the new SBD, then withhold appropriate taxes on the remaining wages. (Proposals differ on the "appropriate" level of taxes withheld—based on workers' estimates or a simpler flat rate—but this detail need not be determined here.) Voluntary withholding would further simplify the tax code and do away with quarterly estimated payments--and penalties—for workers who choose to opt-in to the system and work primarily for companies, not individuals. Thus, for example, a wedding photographer hired by an engaged couple might not have taxes withheld, but a fashion photographer hired by a magazine could opt for withholding.[44]

Third, Congress and the states also should repeal the new $600 minimum for 1099-K reporting, which is unnecessary and burdensome (for workers, companies, and the IRS). Rather than return to the previous $20,000 or 200 transactions thresholds, which may have missed significant taxable income, policymakers could choose a middle ground—low enough to capture taxable income from individuals frequently engaging in independent work but high enough to exempt occasional sellers and hobbyists from needless paperwork. For example, both the National Taxpayers Union and congressional Democrats' Cut Red Tape for Online Sales Act have suggested setting the threshold at $5,000.[45] Congress should also reinstate a set number of transactions needed to trigger 1099-K reporting but lower the threshold to 25 or 50 transactions, thus again only subjecting those who are routinely engaged in the gig economy to IRS filing requirements.

Finally, many policy recommendations in other chapters would also benefit independent workers. For example, expanding the size and scope of health savings accounts as the Health Care chapter proposes would help independent workers, especially those who lack health insurance or health care savings, and might also encourage current "job-locked" employees to venture out on their own. Tax-advantaged universal savings accounts, as recommended in the Employee Benefits chapter, would help independent workers save for potential lulls in new business (or for any other reason). The Occupational Licensing chapter explains that eliminating and reforming licensure would increase access to, and support the viability of, many independent work professions that are currently restricted by law, such as freelance hair braiders, florists, and tour guides. And standardizing income tax and tax nexus requirements, as discussed in the Remote Work chapter, would benefit independent workers who sell their services or goods across state lines (or engage in interstate travel to do so).

ACTION PLAN

Given millions of Americans' clear preference for independent work and the economic benefits of these arrangements, legislators at both the state level and federal level should reduce regulatory and tax burdens on both independent workers and gig platforms.

Congress should

- refrain from passing legislation like the Protecting the Right to Organize Act or any other bill that expands the definition of an "employee" to include common independent work arrangements;
- enact an SBD of 60 percent of an independent worker's earnings, thus simplifying tax filing and compliance (workers could elect not to claim the deduction and could then continue to utilize the existing itemized tax system);
- allow companies and independent workers to agree to withhold a portion of the workers' earnings from the 1099 form as an estimated tax payment to further simplify tax filing and compliance;

- repeal the new $600 minimum for 1099-K reporting, replacing it with a significantly higher (e.g., $5,000 or 25 transactions) threshold for tax reporting; and
- allow independent workers to open and contribute tax-free funds to large health savings accounts and universal savings accounts, as the Health Care and Employee Benefits chapters respectively propose.

State governments should

- repeal laws that expand the definition of "employee," such as California's AB 5, or refrain from implementing such laws; and
- repeal minimum 1099-K reporting requirements and match them to the new federal standard recommended above.

Governments should also implement the reforms recommended in the other chapters, such as the Occupational Licensing and Remote Work chapters, which includes recommendations that would further benefit independent workers.

NOTES

1. Adam Ozimek, "Freelance Forward Economist Report," Upwork, December 2021.

2. "11th Annual State of Independence: The Great Realization," MBO Partners, December 2021.

3. Brett Collins et al., "Is Gig Work Replacing Traditional Employment? Evidence from Two Decades of Tax Returns," SOI Working Paper, March 25, 2019; Gordon Burtch, Seth Carnahan, and Brent N. Greenwood, "Can You Gig It? An Empirical Examination of the Gig Economy and Entrepreneurial Activity," *Management Science* 64, no. 12 (2018): 5497–520; and Ike Brannon and Samuel Wolf, "An Empirical Snapshot of the Gig Economy," *Regulation* 44, no. 4 (Fall 2021): 4–8.

4. See Kathryn Dill, "People Are Quitting Full-Time Jobs for Contract Work—and Making Six Figures," *Wall Street Journal,* March 15, 2022; and see Alexandrea J. Ravenelle and Ken Cai Kowalski, "Working at the Nexus of Global Markets and Gig Work," in *Economies, Institutions and Territories* (London: Routledge, 2022).

5. Liya Palagashvili, "Consequences of Restricting Independent Work and the Gig Economy," Mercatus Center Policy Brief, November 2022.

6. "11th Annual State of Independence: The Great Realization."

7. Monica Anderson et al., "How Gig Platform Workers View Their Jobs," in *The State of Gig Work in 2021* (Washington: Pew Research Center, December 2021).

8. M. Keith Chen et al., "The Value of Flexible Work: Evidence from Uber Drivers," *Journal of Political Economy* 27, no. 6 (2019): 2735–94.

9. John M. Barrios, Yael V. Hochberg, and Hanyi Yi, "Launching with a Parachute: The Gig Economy and New Business Formation," *Journal of Financial Economics* 144, no. 1 (2022): 22–43.

10. Adam Ozimek, "Work Marketplaces and Dynamism," Upwork, August 27, 2021.

11. Lyndon Finney, "Surging Ahead: Number of New Trucking Companies Shattering Records," *The Trucker,* February 24, 2022.

12. Cara Murez, "More Evidence Uber, Lyft Are Reducing Drunk Driving Crashes," *U.S. News and World Report*, June 28, 2022.

13. Kate Conger, "A Pandemic Lifeline for Restaurants, Delivery Is 'Here to Stay,'" *New York Times*, July 2, 2021.

14. Kerry Breen, Joe Enoch, and Vicky Nguyen, "Future of Fast Food: New Technology Allows Drive-Thru Workers to Work from Home," *TODAY*, April 1, 2022.

15. Palagashvili, "Consequences of Restricting Independent Work."

16. Brannon and Wolf, "An Empirical Snapshot of the Gig Economy."

17. Palagashvili, "Consequences of Restricting Independent Work."

18. Jeffrey Fritz and Joshua Nadreau, "Dispute over Gig Drivers' Independent Contractor Status Being Fought on All Fronts in Massachusetts," JDSupra, January 28, 2022.

19. Jon O. Shimabukuro, "Worker Classification: Employee Status under the National Labor Relations Act, the Fair Labor Standards Act, and the ABC Test," Congressional Research Service, R46765, April 20, 2021.

20. Stephanie Ferguson, "ABC Test Introduced in Virginia State Legislature," U.S. Chamber of Commerce, January 30, 2020; Rebecca Smith, "Washington State Considers ABC Test for Employee Status," National Employment Law Project, January 28, 2019; and Annie McDonough, "After Prop 22, New York Is Still Split on Gig Worker Reforms," *City & State New York,* January 15, 2021.

21. "Employer Mandate," Cigna, August 19, 2022.

22. "Economic Report Card for the Affordable Care Act's Employer Mandate," White House Council of Economic Advisors, January 11, 2021.

23. Palagashvili, "Consequences of Restricting Independent Work."

24. Palagashvili, "Consequences of Restricting Independent Work"; and authors' calculation based on "A First Step toward a New Model for Independent Platform Work," Uber, August 10, 2020.

25. Palagashvili, "Consequences of Restricting Independent Work."

26. Palagashvili, "Consequences of Restricting Independent Work."

27. Suhauna Hussain, "Freelance Journalists File Suit Alleging AB5 Is Unconstitutional," *Los Angeles Times*, December 17, 2019; and Brannon and Wolf, "An Empirical Snapshot of the Gig Economy."

28. See Finney, "Surging Ahead." See also John Kingston, "Supreme Court Rejects California Trucking Association's Appeal," *Freightwaves*, June 30, 2022.

29. Dominic Pino, "Truckers Protesting California's AB5 Block Port of Oakland," *National Review*, July 20, 2022.

30. "11th Annual State of Independence: The Great Realization."

31. Fritz and Nadreau, "Dispute over Gig Drivers' Independent Contractor Status."

32. Palagashvili, "Consequences of Restricting Independent Work."

33. Ni Huang et al., "Unemployment and Participation in the Gig Economy," *Information Systems Research* 31, no. 2 (June 2020): 431–48.

34. Brannon and Wolf, "An Empirical Snapshot of the Gig Economy."

35. Brannon and Wolf, "An Empirical Snapshot of the Gig Economy."

36. "11th Annual State of Independence: The Great Realization."

37. Annette Bernhardt et al., "Independent Contracting, Self-Employment, and Gig Work: Evidence from California Tax Data," National Bureau of Economic Research Working Paper no. 30327, August 2022.

38. Kathleen DeLaney Thomas, "Taxing the Gig Economy," *University of Pennsylvania Law Review* 166 (2018): 1415–73.

39. Garrett Watson, "Improving the Federal Tax System for Gig Economy Participants," Tax Foundation, October 18, 2019; and Thomas, "Taxing the Gig Economy."

40. Maurie Backman, "Yes, Side Hustle Income Is Taxable. Here's What to Know If You Made $600 or More in 2021," *Stevens Point Journal* (Stevens Point, WI), March 14, 2022.

41. "What Do I Need to Know about My 1099-K Tax Form?," Etsy Help Center.

42. See, for example, "What Do I Need to Know about My 1099-K Tax Form?"; Susan Tompor, "Gig Workers to Get Hit with Big Tax Surprise Next Year," *Detroit Free Press*, September 23, 2021; and Andrew Wilford and Andrew Moylan, "Congress Needs to Act to Provide Relief to Taxpayers (and the IRS) from Burdensome 1099-K Requirement," National Taxpayers Union Foundation Issue Brief, March 8, 2022.

43. Thomas, "Taxing the Gig Economy"; and Watson, "Improving the Federal Tax System for Gig Economy Participants."

44. Thomas, "Taxing the Gig Economy."

45. See Wilford and Moylan, "Congress Needs to Act"; and "Lawmakers Push to Increase 1099-K Reporting Threshold," Grant Thornton, March 29, 2022.

ENTREPRENEURSHIP AND HOME BUSINESSES

BY CHRIS EDWARDS

THE ISSUE: STATE AND LOCAL RULES CAN DISCOURAGE HOME-BASED BUSINESSES, WHICH ARE A PIPELINE FOR AMERICAN ENTREPRENEURSHIP

The pandemic has created lasting changes to the economy. More people are working from home, video calls are replacing business travel, and workers are switching jobs to find a better work-life balance. Another development is that home-based entrepreneurship is booming. The pandemic alerted people to the advantages of running a business from their homes, and new internet platforms are making it more feasible than ever. The number of arts and crafts businesses selling on Etsy.com, for example, jumped from 2.6 million in 2019 to 7.5 million in 2021 (see Figure 1).[1]

Overall, the Small Business Administration (SBA) estimates that about half of America's 30 million or so businesses are home-based.[2] These include accountants, daycare providers, repair persons, musicians, tutors, food producers, yoga teachers, contractors, caterers, wedding planners, dog groomers, haircutters, massage therapists, lawn-care specialists, software writers, and bloggers. Many great companies were launched from homes and garages, including Amazon, Apple, and Hewlett-Packard.

As the pandemic gripped the nation, the share of Americans working from home almost doubled in 2020 to 42 percent.[3] Since then, what started as a necessity has turned into a strong preference for many Americans who prefer to live and work at home. Indeed, home-based businesses provide many economic and lifestyle advantages over traditional work. They can provide a primary household income, supplemental income, or backup source of income while allowing people to care for children or elderly parents or to avoid the cost and hassle of a daily commute. According to a 2022 Institute for Justice (IJ) survey of 1,902 home-based entrepreneurs, over half of home-based entrepreneurs are women—a larger share than among all U.S. small businesses—and 31 percent of respondents listed having a disability as one reason for starting their business at home.[4] Other than earning income, the top reasons individuals surveyed said they launched their home business were: to be their own boss, to have a more flexible schedule, to work at something enjoyable, and to have a better work-life balance.

Home businesses also have benefits for local communities. They reduce automobile pollution and congestion. Neighborhood customers of home businesses, such as daycares and tutoring services, gain from the convenience. Home businesses can also "bring goods and services into areas whose needs are not being met because they are far from commercial centers."[5]

Finally, home-based businesses are critical for entrepreneurship and innovation. Without locating at home, some businesses would not be viable if entrepreneurs had to foot the costs of commercial rent, commuting, and perhaps childcare. This

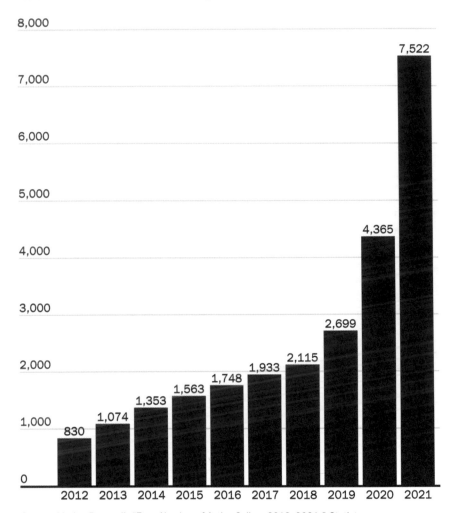

FIGURE 1 The number of active Etsy sellers has soared in recent years

Source: Marina Pasquali, "Etsy: Number of Active Sellers 2012–2021," Statista.com.

dynamic is evident in the booming cottage food industry (home food production for retail sale),[6] which—as the *New York Times* recently examined—has benefited from new internet food platforms:

> Several days a week, Juliet Achan moves around the kitchen of her apartment in Greenpoint, Brooklyn, stirring up dishes from her Surinamese background: fragrant batches of goat curry, root vegetable soup and her own take on chicken chow mein. She packages the meals, and they are picked up for

delivery to customers who order through an app called WoodSpoon. "Joining WoodSpoon has made a huge difference during the pandemic, giving me the flexibility to work safely from home and supplement my income," Ms. Achan said.[7]

Homes have also been important for the American craft beer industry, which exploded after home brewing was federally legalized in 1978 and state beer distribution laws were relaxed starting in the 1980s. The number of breweries in America has grown from less than 100 in 1980 to more than 8,300 today.[8] Craft brewing is a $22 billion industry today that grew out of a previously illegal home-based activity.[9]

There is no better place for low-cost product experimentation than an entrepreneur's home. Homes are low-cost incubators to test business ideas before larger investments are made. Startups are risky and have high failure rates, so entrepreneurs need early, low-cost feedback from consumers. Food entrepreneurs, for example, want to test recipes with consumers but may not be able to initially afford commercial kitchen space. Home production can give entrepreneurs the confidence, skills, and capital they need to later open a brick-and-mortar location.

Despite home businesses' many benefits, they often face significant legal barriers. First, local governments impose zoning rules that can ban, restrict, or raise costs for home businesses in residential neighborhoods. Such restrictions accumulated during the 20th century, but changes in culture and technology should prompt state and local policymakers to rethink yesterday's restrictive rules.

Early in the nation's history, most Americans worked from their homes (not only as farmers but also as doctors, lawyers, blacksmiths, retailers, and so on), but this changed with the rise of large-scale industry in the 19th century. Twentieth-century governments then solidified the separation with single-use, or "Euclidean," zoning, which split cities into residential, commercial, and industrial zones.[10] The purpose of such zoning was to "address the possibility that nonresidential uses will inflict negative externalities on residential neighborhoods."[11] Businesses were assumed to impose noise, congestion, and other problems that conflict with residential lifestyles.

However, 20th-century zoning was usually based not on analyses of actual externalities but on blunt rules based on tradition, guesswork, and elitist views.[12] Initially, cities allowed only certain occupations to be performed in homes, or they specified lists of occupations not allowed. As the century progressed, cities added layers of rules, permits, licenses, hearings, and other bureaucratic hurdles to home businesses.

Most cities retain elements of these regulatory regimes today. In a 2004 report on home businesses, the SBA found that "many zoning codes incorporate outright prohibitions, prescriptive requirements, or limits on various aspects of home-based businesses (e.g., number of employees, visitors, parking, exterior changes, or specific industries)."[13] Other common restrictions regard signage, renovations, outdoor activities, materials storage, deliveries, noise, odors, animals, square footage, types of occupations, number of visitors, truck parking, and retail sales on premises.[14]

Recent studies have found substantial variations among cities' regulation of home businesses, with many localities still imposing restrictions that appear excessively strict.[15] While some cities allow home businesses "by right," some require conditional-use permits for many types of businesses. Such permits may involve substantial paperwork, a public notice and comment period, and public hearings. After these processes, officials can still deny requests at their discretion. Such rules are sure to discourage home businesses in these cities (and, by extension, small business formation).

Second, there are industry-specific barriers to some types of home businesses. With cottage food, for example, state and local rules often specify which products can be sold, where they can be sold, and the sales volume allowed. Wyoming allows home businesses to sell just about any type of food that complies with federal laws within an annual sales limit of $250,000.[16] Rhode Island, on the other hand, only allows farmers to sell food made in their homes, and even these farmer sales are restricted in various ways.[17]

Other regulations prevent business owners from serving clients at their homes. In Nashville, for example, IJ represented Lij Shaw, a music producer who records musicians at his home studio, and Pat Raynor, a hair stylist who serves her clients in a single-chair salon in her house.[18] The two entrepreneurs wanted to work from home for cost and lifestyle reasons—Lij was raising his daughter, and Pat was short on money after her husband's death—but a Nashville zoning ordinance prohibited home businesses from serving clients on their property. Shaw and Raynor have a limited number of customers, and there was no evidence that their activities affected their neighbors, yet the city ordered them to end their home business activities. With IJ's help, the entrepreneurs fought back in court and in the press. In the midst of the pandemic, Nashville relented and in July 2020 temporarily relaxed its ban on home businesses that serve customers. However, that reprieve is scheduled to expire in 2023.

THE POLICY SOLUTIONS: LIBERALIZE ZONING AND OTHER STATE AND LOCAL REGULATIONS RESTRICTING HOME BUSINESSES

Several policy reforms would encourage the proliferation of home businesses to the benefit of many American workers and consumers. First, local zoning rules should be liberalized. Public policy should respect individual rights, and private property is a core right. People own their homes and should be able to use them as they see fit. As such, governments' default position should be allowing home-based businesses. On the other hand, one's right to use and enjoy their home is limited by the rights of others within neighborhoods, and local governments can consider negative externalities created by home businesses, such as traffic and noise. But the traditional planning goal in many cities to allow zero, or near zero, externalities from home businesses is clearly inapt, especially when the tolerance level for externalities from nonbusiness activities in residential areas is not zero.

Some common zoning restrictions on home businesses, moreover, have little to do with externalities at all—for example, limits on the business use of space within one's home. Furthermore, any negative externalities from home businesses need to be balanced against the positive benefits to neighborhoods. Most people think that entrepreneurs offering daycares, music lessons, tutoring, and handyman services in their neighborhoods are providing benefits, not creating a nuisance. Indeed, many neighborhoods have social media pages advertising services provided by locals. Municipal governments also should consider that restrictive zoning rules will push entrepreneurs' skills and income elsewhere and that home businesses often sprout into local brick-and-mortar businesses.

Policymakers in many states and cities have started to reconsider zoning rules because of today's changing society. IJ reports, for example, that since 2015, 30 states have either created new cottage food laws or significantly liberalized existing laws.[19] Home daycares are another area of substantial zoning reforms. In the past, many governments considered home daycares a "problem use" and barred them. With today's high demands for childcare by dual-working couples and pressure to increase daycare supply, at least 18 states have passed laws to preempt excessively tight local zoning restrictions on home daycares.[20]

Generally, local governments should reform their zoning laws to allow home-based businesses to operate by right, rather than requiring conditional-use permits. They should liberalize rules for parking and serving clients from homes. They should repeal rules limiting the amount of space allowed for business use within homes and other restrictions unrelated to externalities. General local ordinances related to parking, noise, and other nuisance issues should apply equally to homes used for businesses and all other homes.

Second, policymakers should loosen regulations surrounding certain indust- ries that benefit from home-based businesses. As the legalization of home brewing demonstrates, deregulation breeds entrepreneurship and economic development, and feared downsides usually don't materialize. When regulations are too restrictive, moreover, home businesses may go underground. Before Atlanta's deregulation of cottage food in 2012, for example, producers "were pro- hibited, under most circumstances, from selling any type of food that was not prepared in a commercial-grade kitchen used solely for commercial purposes." As a result, there were "a lot of home cooks selling baked goods under the table, without licensing or food safety training."[21]

Since the rules on home businesses vary widely across jurisdictions, places with restrictive rules should consider industry-specific reforms along the lines of less-regulated cities and states. With cottage food laws, for example, Rhode Island actually shuts down moms for selling home-baked cookies.[22] Yet we know that selling baked goods from home is a safe and beneficial activity because nearly all other states allow it. More broadly, state and local policymakers should study the experience of the five states—Montana, North Dakota, Oklahoma, Utah, and Wyoming—that have enacted "food freedom" laws allowing wide latitude to cottage food businesses.[23] Cities and states should also ensure that their daycare regulations permit home-based options.

Third, state governments should consider acting to preempt overly restrictive local rules and to provide a sort of "freedom baseline" for home businesses, as sev- eral states have done recently. Florida, for example, enacted legislation in 2021 requiring local governments to allow home business activities within rea- sonable limits.[24] Home businesses are subject to general zoning rules on parking, signage, storage of hazardous materials, and other typical items. But the Florida law blocks localities from implementing outright bans and punitive treatment of home businesses.

ACTION PLAN

Americans want to earn income from home—to test business ideas and to ben- efit their communities—and many others want to buy from them. A general rule of markets is that voluntary exchanges such as these are mutually beneficial and provide substantial gains for society as a whole. The American economy has shift- ed toward service industries and the internet; many Americans want jobs that are flexible; and many families need to juggle childcare and eldercare needs. Rather than creating barriers to home businesses, governments should work to facilitate them with rules that balance property rights with reasonable limits on externali- ties in residential neighborhoods.

State governments therefore should

- establish basic freedom guidelines for home businesses aimed at preventing unreasonable bans and restrictions at the local level;
- liberalize rules for cottage food businesses along the lines of Wyoming and other "food freedom" states; and
- preempt excessively tight local zoning restrictions on home daycare businesses.

Local governments should

- generally allow home-based businesses to operate by right rather than requiring conditional-use permits;
- recognize that home businesses form a crucial part of local economies and that some grow into brick-and-mortar businesses;
- adopt or revise zoning codes to treat activities related to home businesses, such as parking, equally as compared with similar nonbusiness activities; and
- repeal special, industry-specific restrictions on home businesses unrelated to actual neighborhood externalities.

NOTES

1. David Curry, "Etsy Revenue and Usage Statistics," Business of Apps, May 4, 2022.

2. "Frequently Asked Questions," U.S. Small Business Administration, Office of Advocacy, September 24, 2019.

3. "American Time Use Survey Summary," Economic News Release, U.S. Bureau of Labor Statistics, July 22, 2021.

4. Jennifer McDonald, "Entrepreneur from Home," Institute for Justice, January 2022.

5. Henry B. R. Beale, "Home-Based Business and Government Regulation," U.S. Small Business Administration, Office of Advocacy, February 2004.

6. For background, see Jennifer McDonald, "Flour Power," Institute for Justice, September 2018.

7. Julie Creswell, "The Home Cooks (and Start-Ups) Betting on Prepared Meals," *New York Times*, April 10, 2022.

8. Aaron Staples, Dustin Chambers, and Trey Malone, "How Many Regulations Does It Take to Get a Beer? The Economic Geography of Beer Regulations," Center for Growth and Opportunity at Utah State University Working Paper no. 2020.017, September 16, 2020.

9. "Stats and Data: National Beer Sales and Production Data," Brewers Association.

10. The name stems from the 1926 U.S. Supreme Court case *Village of Euclid v. Ambler Realty Co.*, under which the Court established that cities could separate land uses in zoning codes under their general police powers.

11. Anika Singh Lemar, "The Role of States in Liberalizing Land Use Regulations," *North Carolina Law Review* 97, no. 2 (January 2019): 293–354.

12. Olivia Gonzalez and Nolan Gray, "Zoning for Opportunity: A Survey of Home-Based-Business Regulations," Center for Growth and Opportunity at Utah State University Policy Paper no. 2020.006, March 2020; and Nolan Gray and Olivia Gonzalez, "Home-Based Businesses Are Coming. As COVID-19 Accelerates Remote Working, Are Cities Prepared?," *City Journal,* March 31, 2020.

13. Beale, "Home-Based Business and Government Regulation."

14. Patricia Salkin, "Modernizing Zoning for Home Occupations," *Zoning Practice* 9 (September 2006); and Robin Wheeler, "Zoning for Home-Based Businesses in New York," *New York Zoning Law and Practice Report* 10, no. 3 (November/December 2009).

15. M. Nolan Gray and Olivia Gonzalez, "Making Room for Home-Based Businesses: A Survey of 12 Zoning Ordinances," February 2017; and Jennifer McDonald, "Entrepreneur from Home," Institute for Justice, January 2022.

16. "Selling Homemade Food in Wyoming," Institute for Justice.

17. "Selling Homemade Food in Rhode Island," Institute for Justice.

18. McDonald, "Entrepreneur from Home."

19. "Recent State Reforms for Homemade Food Businesses," Institute for Justice.

20. Lemar, "The Role of States in Liberalizing Land Use Regulations."

21. Deborah Geering, "New Rules Boost Home-Based Food Businesses," *Atlanta*, October 24, 2012.

22. Anita Baffoni, "'There Has to Be a Way': Portsmouth Entrepreneur Urges State to Allow the Sale of Homemade Food," WPRI.com, March 11, 2021.

23. "Recent State Reforms for Homemade Food Businesses," Institute for Justice.

24. "CS/HB 403—Home-based Businesses," Florida Senate, 2021.

CRIMINAL JUSTICE

BY ILANA BLUMSACK AND SCOTT LINCICOME

THE ISSUE: CRIMINAL JUSTICE POLICY NEEDLESSLY DISCOURAGES MILLIONS OF AMERICANS FROM TAKING OR SWITCHING JOBS, THUS DEPRESSING THEIR LIVING STANDARDS AND THE BROADER ECONOMY

More than 30 percent of American adults have been arrested for a crime, and nearly 8 percent of adults—over 19 million Americans as of 2010—have a felony record (see Figures 1 and 2).[1] Employment opportunities are difficult for this population, often due to government policies instead of workers' ability or willingness to work.

Work is an important step for the reentry and reintegration of those with a criminal history into broader society. It substantially reduces recidivism, particularly in the months after release when reoffending is most likely to occur, and it increases workers' incomes and economic mobility—outcomes that also benefit the United States as a whole.[2]

Yet employment prospects for those with a criminal record (whether a conviction or merely an arrest) are dim. Bushway et al. (2022) estimated that 64 percent of unemployed men in their 30s have been arrested and that 46 percent have been convicted of a crime. Often, the record itself—not the underlying crime—is a significant reason for their unemployment.[3] Meanwhile, Larsen et al. (2022) found a strong connection between an individual's felony conviction and unemployment or labor force non-participation (especially for women), and that the country's increasing felony-history share since the 1980s translated to about 1.7 million Americans not working because of their record.[4] Other studies show a similar connection between a criminal record and non-employment.[5]

Criminal records also impair mobility: according to a 2010 Pew Charitable Trusts report, for example, formerly incarcerated individuals were twice as likely as those from similar economic backgrounds who had never been incarcerated to remain at the bottom of the income ladder, even 20 years after being released from prison.[7] These employment barriers exist not only for those convicted of crimes but for *any* individual with a criminal history, including those who were ultimately acquitted.[7]

Surely, not every individual with a criminal record deserves to be free of it and quickly reintegrated into the workforce, but millions of Americans who pose little risk to others are nevertheless shackled by their records. This includes people who were never actually convicted of a crime, those coerced into accepting dubious plea bargains by ambitious prosecutors, those convicted of drug possession, sports gambling, or other activities that have since been legalized, or those with decades-old convictions for nonviolent offenses.[8] For these people, there is simply no good reason why a criminal record should burden their employment prospects and

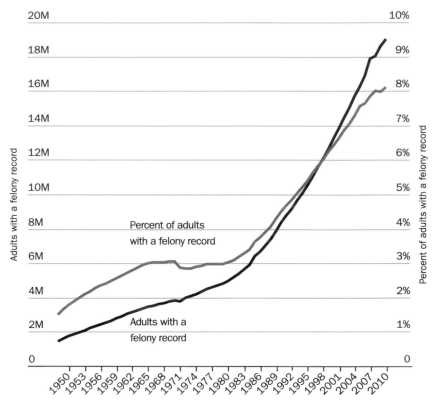

FIGURE 1 Between 1948 and 2010, the number and share of American adults with a felony record increased dramatically

Percent of adults with a felony record

Adults with a felony record

Source: Sarah K. S. Shannon et al., "The Growth, Scope, and Spatial Distribution of People with Felony Records in the United States, 1948–2010," *Demography* 54, no. 5 (2017): 1795–818.

social lives, yet state and federal criminal justice policy currently ensures that they are so burdened.

Licensing rules exacerbate the employment challenges of those with criminal records. As discussed in the Occupational Licensing chapter, these requirements place heavy financial and other burdens on qualified workers—burdens that are especially heavy for those with a criminal history. Many states also restrict the ability of people with criminal records to become licensed professionals in certain industries. For example, according to the Institute for Justice, 30 states allow licensing boards to deny an individual a license due to an arrest that ended with an acquittal, and 13 states allow the denial of a license without regard for rehabilitation or later conduct. These restrictions are generally limited to charges related to the occupation being pursued, but five states even permit licensing boards to deny an application based on any felony conviction, even if it is unrelated to the license at hand (see Figure 3).[9]

FIGURE 2 Between 1948 and 2010, the number and share of American men with a felony record increased dramatically

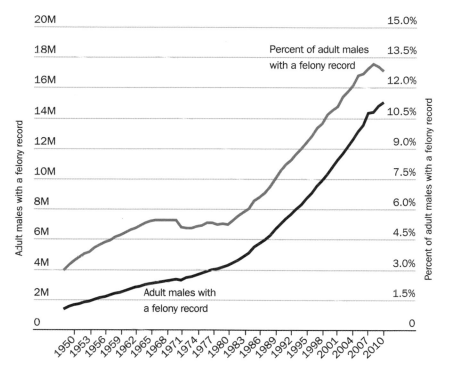

Source: Sarah K. S. Shannon et al., "The Growth, Scope, and Spatial Distribution of People with Felony Records in the United States, 1948–2010," *Demography* 54, no. 5 (2017): 1795–818.

These licensing restrictions increase unemployment and recidivism for individuals with a criminal history. According to a 2016 study from Arizona State University, states with many licensing restrictions on individuals with a criminal record saw a nearly 10 percent increase in recidivism rates, while states with fewer licensing restrictions experienced a 4.2 percent decrease in recidivism during that same period. As unemployment and underemployment are highly correlated with reoffending, reducing licensing barriers to those with criminal histories would very likely increase their employment and decrease criminal activity.[10]

A criminal record can also be a barrier to self-employment. For example, applicants to the Small Business Administration's (SBA) largest loan programs, the 7(a) and 504 programs, must disclose all criminal records and histories, including any expunged records. Loans are unavailable for those currently incarcerated, on parole or probation, or convicted within the past half year. The programs also require all applicants *ever* convicted of a felony to undergo an FBI fingerprint check and an SBA individualized character assessment prior to approval. It is unknown

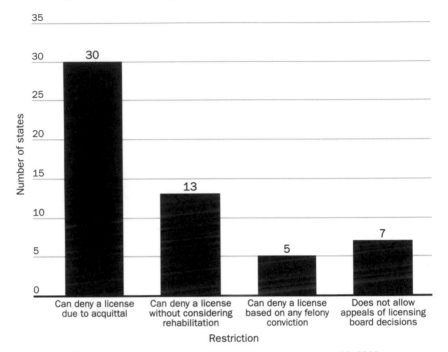

FIGURE 3 In 2022, dozens of states allowed a criminal history to serve as grounds for denying an occupational license

Source: Nick Sibilla, "Barred from Working," Institute for Justice, updated June 22, 2022.

how often the SBA denies an application based on the assessment or how often a potential lender stops the application process if these extra steps are necessary for approval.[11] Cato scholars have generally been critical of the SBA as a wasteful and unnecessary government intervention in the market.[12] As long as the agency exists, however, the harms arising from this discrimination should be considered.

Finally, many states deny driver's licenses to individuals with minor arrest records or unpaid court debts, thus harming their employment prospects.[13] As of 2017, for example, 11 million Americans had a suspended driver's license due to unpaid court debt; in New Jersey, 91 percent of license suspensions from 2004 to 2018 were for nondriving issues.[14] Federal law, meanwhile, reduces federal transportation funding to states that do not suspend driver's licenses of individuals convicted of drug offenses.[15]

A suspended driver's license impedes workers' ability to find employment because they need transportation or because many jobs (e.g., truck/bus drivers, certified nurse assistants, eye care workers, and even deli clerks) require a valid driver's license.[16] A 2007 New Jersey Department of Transportation survey of the state's residents found that 42 percent of respondents lost their jobs following a license suspension, with low-income and younger drivers being the most affected.[17] Newly unemployed workers may be unable to repay court debts (meaning a longer license suspension); others may choose to drive illegally and potentially face harsher fines or jail time.[18]

THE POLICY SOLUTIONS: ENACT EXPUNGEMENT, LICENSING REFORM, AND BROADER CRIMINAL JUSTICE REFORMS

Several policy reforms would improve the employment prospects of many American workers caught up in the criminal justice system, with little to no harm to its overall efficacy or to individuals without criminal records.

First, governments—particularly at the state level—should expand expungement of criminal records, which effectively seals an individual's record from public view and lets him or her legally answer that he or she does not have a criminal record in, for example, a job interview. (Expunged records are, however, still available to law enforcement.) Because expungement effectively nullifies a criminal record for most aspects of public life, it can improve employment outcomes for recipients. Starr and Prescott (2020) reviewed expungement recipients in Michigan and found that meaningful employment (jobs earning more than $100 per week) increased by 23 percent relative to beneficiaries' employment prior to expungement and that wage gains increased by a similar amount. These increases were sustained even years after individuals were granted expungement. Moreover, only 3.4 percent of expungement recipients were arrested within two years of being granted expungement—a lower rate, in fact, than the overall arrest rate in Michigan for the general population.[19]

Most states have expungement laws for certain offenses (often misdemeanors or nonviolent felonies) and have procedures in place for obtaining an expungement. However, the process is usually not easy: an eligible individual must wait several years after finishing the initial sentence, must not have any criminal history after finishing the sentence, and must proactively apply to be granted expungement. Also, many potential recipients are simply unaware of the possibility of expungement, and even if they are aware, they may struggle with the paperwork and other application requirements.[20]

Given these issues, the number of expungement beneficiaries is very low despite the procedure's many benefits. For example, because individuals had to petition the state of Michigan to receive expungement, Starr and Prescott found that, at most, 8.8 percent of eligible recipients in their sample of more than 9,000 cases had actually done so five years after gaining eligibility, even though applications were granted 75 percent of the time. Assuming similar percentages applied to the state's entire eligible population, it would mean that hundreds of thousands of Michiganders lost out on expungement for procedural reasons alone.

To improve these results and help millions of American workers in the process, governments should enact automatic expungement laws for qualified individuals.[21] After a waiting period in which the individual cannot reoffend, records for misdemeanors and certain felonies would be automatically expunged without the necessity of an application.[22] Several states have already implemented these changes, with Pennsylvania leading the way in 2018 and passing a "Clean Slate" law that automatically expunges nonconvictions (the individual was either acquitted or charges were dropped), and minor, nonviolent convictions after 10 years of good behavior.[23]

In terms of specific reforms, states should enact automatic expungement for misdemeanors and nonviolent felonies after a period of good behavior, as well as immediate expungement for any record in which the result was a nonconviction; expand automatic expungement to those with juvenile records who do not commit future crimes, as Michigan did in 2021; and automatically and immediately expunge the records of all individuals with a history of offenses that are no longer crimes in the state at issue (e.g., expunging possession and distribution charges after a state legalizes marijuana).[24] Several states automatically expunge certain records of marijuana offenses after decriminalization or legalization, but automatic expungement should be expanded to all current and future decriminalized offenses.[25] It also should apply to all eligible recipients, even if the arrests or convictions occurred many decades ago.[26]

Congress should enact similar automatic expungement laws for those with a federal criminal history.

State and federal legislation could still require a waiting period of a few years before criminal convictions are automatically expunged, while applying immediately to individuals not convicted of a crime. Recidivism is most common in the months following release.[27] By contrast, those who avoid additional convictions for several years after release are extremely unlikely to reoffend and thus pose very little risk to prospective employers, landlords, and others.[28] Automatically expunging criminal convictions after a relatively short waiting period is therefore a low-risk, high-reward policy.

If expungement is made more widely available to qualified individuals, it is preferable to "ban the box" policies (BTBs), which prohibit prospective employers from asking about job applicants' criminal history to increase employment among those with a criminal history. This policy, which is now law in numerous cities and counties and in at least 12 states, as well as for most federal agencies and contractors, was intended to reduce discrimination against individuals with a criminal past and increase employment of those with criminal histories.[29]

However, recent research, such as Doleac and Hansen (2020), has cast doubt on those hopes, finding that implementing BTBs actually reduced young, low-skilled male black employment by over 5 percent and that this effect persisted even years after the policy was implemented in a specific locale. Moreover, a recent field experiment of low-skilled job applications found that BTBs significantly reduced the likelihood that black applicants would receive a job interview when compared with identical white applicants.[30] Rather than improve employment outcomes, BTBs unintentionally reduce low-skilled black employment, as employers substitute race and educational attainment as proxies for criminal history.[31]

Policymakers should therefore repeal BTBs and instead embrace expungement. In such a case, the criminal histories of certain individuals, such as recent offenders or those with a history of serious felonies, would still be available, and employers would have less cause to statistically discriminate against certain groups. At the same time, individuals with expunged records would not be known to employers to have a criminal history, thus increasing their chances of finding gainful employment.[32]

Second, states should undertake several reforms to ease occupational licensing burdens on those with criminal records. Along with the general reforms recommended in the Occupational Licensing chapter, states should exclude all non-convictions from a licensing board's consideration, even if the charges are related to the license in question. Acquittals are essentially a sign of innocence, and it is thus absurd for licensing gatekeepers to consider them "criminal" conduct. Also, criminal records unrelated to the license in question or involving since-legalized activities should be excluded from the licensing board's consideration, and vague concepts such as "moral turpitude" should be dropped or very narrowly defined. Nor should states allow consideration of out-of-state criminal records in licensing decisions if the offenses in question are not crimes in the state where a license is being requested. Colorado governor Jared Polis, for example, recently signed an executive order barring state licensing boards from considering applicants' out-of-state marijuana-related convictions, as marijuana is now legal in Colorado.[33]

As with expungement, moreover, states should set a waiting period after which licensing boards may not consider convictions in their decisions if the individual has avoided further convictions.[34] And states should allow individuals to appeal their licensing decisions and receive rapid decisions on such appeals.

Third, to the extent the SBA remains in operation, despite Cato scholars' opposition to the agency, the federal government should cease discriminating against currently law-abiding applicants based on prior criminal history. Thus, as long as the SBA's loan programs are in operation, the agency should eliminate discretionary and subjective requirements, such as the character assessment, and allow all applicants not currently incarcerated, under indictment, or on probation or parole the same standardized application and approval process as that provided to other applicants.

Fourth, states should repeal laws suspending driver's licenses for unpaid court fines or debts. By the end of 2021, 18 states had done so; of the remaining 32 states, 18 mandate license suspension for unpaid fines or debts, while 14 leave the decision to a judge's discretion.[35] If full repeal of such laws is not possible, states should require that courts consider the driver's ability to pay in determining whether to suspend the license. Congress should also repeal current federal law encouraging states to suspend driver's licenses for drug convictions, as has been proposed in the Driving for Opportunity Act of 2021.[36]

Finally, broader problems in the U.S. justice system contribute to the employment challenges facing those with criminal histories. Overcriminalization—criminalizing even mundane actions, such as taking a neighbor's children to the bus stop or serving bar patrons pickle-infused vodka, or issuing harsh sentences for minor offenses, such as sentencing someone to life in prison for selling $20 worth of marijuana—greatly increases both the number of Americans with a criminal record and the number of Americans living behind bars.[37] Indeed, Agan et al. (2021) have shown that nonprosecution of nonviolent misdemeanors substantially reduces offenders' subsequent criminal activity and that avoiding a criminal record likely drives these results.[38] Yet mere possession of marijuana remains a crime in 19 states and under federal law.[39]

Meanwhile, coercive plea bargaining pressures innocent people to confess to crimes they did not commit, not only increasing the number of convictions but often subjecting individuals to significant time behind bars (and thus remaining out of the labor market).[40] Among minors, pretrial juvenile detention reduces the likelihood of graduating from high school and increases the chances that those minors will commit crimes as an adult.[41] These and other criminal justice policies should be reformed regardless of their effect on the labor market, but such reforms would undoubtedly also improve the employment and advancement prospects of millions of American workers.

ACTION PLAN

Many Americans are needlessly burdened by criminal records, which diminish their employment prospects, wages, and mobility. Several federal, state, and local reforms should be undertaken to increase these individuals' employment and living standards and to improve the U.S. economy in the process.

Specifically, Congress and state governments should

- enact automatic expungement laws for individuals arrested but not convicted of a federal, state, or local crime; individuals with convictions for a federal, state, or local offense that has since been legalized or decriminalized; and those convicted of federal, state, or local misdemeanors who have avoided additional convictions for two years, or those convicted of nonviolent felonies and who have avoided additional convictions for five years after serving their sentence.

Congress should also
- repeal the Fair Chance to Compete for Jobs Act of 2019, which expanded BTBs to most federal agencies and federal contractors;
- require that the SBA eliminate all subjective character assessments and ensure that all applicants not currently under indictment, incarcerated, or on parole or probation undergo the same application and assessment process; and
- repeal 23 U.S.C. § 159, which punishes states (via reduced transportation funding) for declining to suspend driver's licenses for drug offenses.

State governments should also
- repeal all BTBs;
- bar occupational licensing boards from considering license applicants' nonconvictions, convictions for offenses unrelated to the license sought, convictions more than two years old for misdemeanors and five years old for felonies where applicants have avoided additional convictions, and out-of-state convictions for offenses that are decriminalized or legal in the state of licensure, as well as vague concepts such as "moral turpitude";
- allow all occupational license applicants the opportunity to appeal licensing board decisions made on the basis of the applicants' criminal history; and
- repeal laws allowing or requiring the suspension of driver's licenses over unpaid fees, fines, or court debts.

Local governments should
- repeal their BTBs.

NOTES

1. Chidi Umez and Rebecca Pirius, "Improving Access to Licensed Occupations for Individuals with Criminal Records," National Council for State Legislatures, July 17, 2018; and Sarah K. S. Shannon et al., "The Growth, Scope, and Spatial Distribution of People with Felony Records in the United States, 1948–2010," *Demography* 54, no. 5 (2017): 1795–818.

2. Joe Labriola, "Post-prison Employment Quality and Future Criminal Justice Contact," *RSF: The Russell Sage Foundation Journal of the Social Sciences* 6, no. 1 (2020): 154–72.

3. Shawn Bushway et al., "Barred from Employment: More than Half of Unemployed Men in Their 30s Had a Criminal History of Arrest," *Science Advances* 8, no. 7 (February 18, 2022).

4. Ryan Larson et al., "Felon History and Change in U.S. Employment Rates," *Social Science Research* 103 (March 2022): Article 102649.

5. Scott Lincicome, "Not Ready for Prime Time," *The Dispatch*, November 4, 2021.

6. Pew Charitable Trusts, *Collateral Costs: Incarceration's Effect on Economic Mobility* (Washington: Pew Charitable Trusts, 2010).

7. Nick Sibilla, *Barred from Working: A Nationwide Survey of Licensing Barriers for Ex-Offenders* (Arlington, VA: Institute for Justice, August 2020).

8. Clark Neily, "Coercive Plea Bargaining: An American Export the World Can Do Without," *Decipher Grey*, April 23, 2021.

9. Nick Sibilla, "Barred from Working," Institute for Justice (website), updated June 22, 2022.

10. Stephen Slivinski, *Turning Shackles into Bootstraps: Why Occupational Licensing Reform Is the Missing Piece of Criminal Justice Reform* (Tempe, AZ: Center for the Study of Economic Liberty at Arizona State University, November 7, 2016).

11. David Schlussel and Margaret Love, "Federal Policies Block Loans to Small Business Owners with a Record," Collateral Consequences Resource Center, August 2, 2021.

12. Tad DeHaven and Veronique de Rugy, "Terminating the Small Business Administration," *Downsizing the Federal Government* (blog), Cato Institute, August 1, 2011.

13. "Existing Laws for Failure to Pay," Free to Drive.

14. Mario Salas and Angela Ciolfi, *Driven by Dollars: A State-by-State Analysis of Driver's License Suspension Laws for Failure to Pay Court Debt* (Charlottesville, VA: Legal Aid Justice Center, Fall 2017); and Nina R. Joyce et al., "Individual and Geographic Variation in Driver's License Suspensions: Evidence of Disparities by Race, Ethnicity and Income," *Journal of Transport and Health* 19 (December 2020): Article 100933.

15. "23 U.S. Code § 159—Revocation or Suspension of Drivers' Licenses of Individuals Convicted of Drug Offenses," Legal Information Institute, Cornell Law School.

16. Salas and Ciolfi, *Driven by Dollars;* and Alana Semuels, "No Driver's License, No Job," *The Atlantic*, June 15, 2016.

17. Jon A. Carnegie, *Driver's License Suspensions, Impacts and Fairness Study* (New Brunswick, NJ: New Jersey Department of Transportation, August 2007). See also William E. Crozier and Brandon L. Garrett, "Driven to Failure: An Empirical Analysis of Driver's License Suspension in North Carolina," *Duke Law Journal* 69 (2020): 1585–641.

18. Salas and Ciolfi, *Driven by Dollars*.

19. J. J. Prescott and Sonja Starr, "Expungement of Criminal Convictions: An Empirical Study," *Harvard Law Review* 133, no. 8 (2020): 2460–555.

20. Prescott and Starr, "Expungement of Criminal Convictions."

21. See Kristian Hernandez, "More States Consider Automatic Criminal Record Expungement," Pew Charitable Trusts, May 25, 2021; and see Gus Burns, "Up to 1 Million Michigan Residents May Be

Eligible for 'Clean Slate' Criminal Expungements," mlive.com, April 13, 2021.

22. Prescott and Starr, "Expungement of Criminal Convictions."

23. "Clean Slate, Expungement and Limited Access," Unified Judicial System of Pennsylvania.

24. "Clean Slate," Michigan Courts.

25. Restoration of Rights Project, "50-State Comparison: Marijuana Legalization, Decriminalization, Expungement, and Clemency," Collateral Consequences Resource Center, January 2022.

26. "California Lawmakers Eye Aiding Those with Criminal Records," Associated Press, March 3, 2021.

27. Slivinski, *Turning Shackles into Bootstraps.*

28. Prescott and Starr, "Expungement of Criminal Convictions."

29. Jennifer Doleac and Benjamin Hansen, "The Unintended Consequences of 'Ban the Box': Statistical Discrimination and Employment Outcomes When Criminal Histories Are Hidden," *Journal of Labor Economics* 38, no. 2 (2020): 321–74; and "Ban the Box: Federal Government Adopts Fair Hiring Practice," *National Law Review,* January 25, 2022.

30. Doleac and Hansen, "The Unintended Consequences of 'Ban the Box.'"

31. Peter Van Doren, "Ban the Box and Statistical Discrimination," *Cato at Liberty* (blog), Cato Institute, June 4, 2019.

32. Prescott and Starr, "Expungement of Criminal Convictions."

33. Alex Burness, "Colorado Regulators Won't Sanction Job-Seekers with Out-of-State Marijuana Convictions, Polis Orders," *Denver Post,* July 14, 2022.

34. Sibilla, *Barred from Working.*

35. "Existing Laws for Failure to Pay," Free to Drive.

36. Driving for Opportunity Act of 2021, H.R. 2453, 117th Cong. (2021).

37. James R. Copland and Rafael A. Mangual, *Overcriminalizing America: An Overview and Model Legislation for the States* (New York: Manhattan Institute, August 2018); and John Simerman and Jeff Adelson, "A Life Sentence for $20 of Weed? Louisiana Stands Out for Its Unequal Use of Repeat Offender Laws," *New Orleans Advocate,* December 20, 2021.

38. Amanda Y. Agan, Jennifer Doleac, and Anna Harvey, "Misdemeanor Prosecution," National Bureau of Economic Research Working Paper no. 28600, March 2021.

39. Claire Hansen, Horus Alas, and Elliott Davis Jr., "Where Is Marijuana Legal? A Guide to Marijuana Legalization," *US News and World Report,* May 27, 2022.

40. Neily, "Coercive Plea Bargaining."

41. E. Jason Baron, Brian Jacob, and Joseph P. Ryan, "Pretrial Juvenile Detention," National Bureau of Economic Research Working Paper no. 29861, March 2022.

ENABLING MOBILITY AND INDEPENDENCE

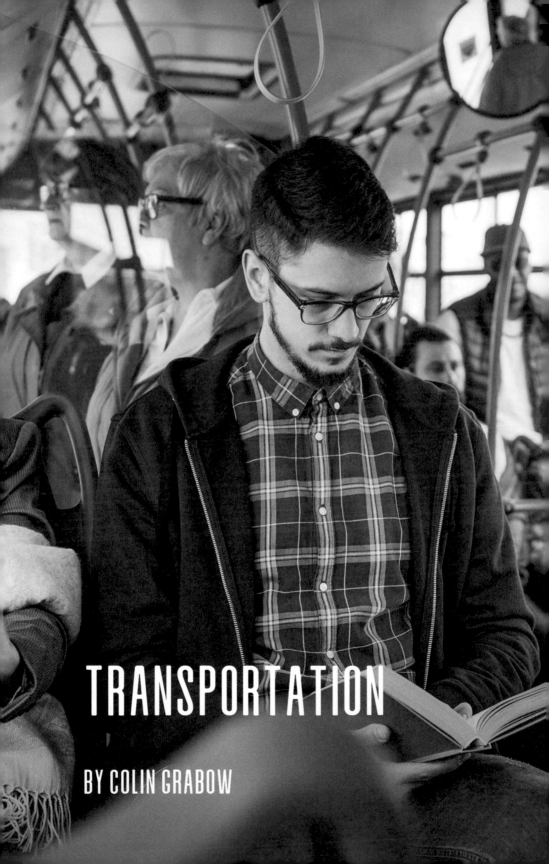

TRANSPORTATION

BY COLIN GRABOW

THE ISSUE: U.S. POLICY CONTRIBUTES TO AN INEFFICIENT AND COSTLY TRANSPORTATION SYSTEM THAT REDUCES WORKERS' TIME AND INCOMES

Travel within the United States is unnecessarily frustrating and expensive, with many parts of the country suffering from gridlocked streets and highways, unreliable and unpleasant mass transit, and rail and airline transport that often compare unfavorably with their overseas counterparts. American workers are all too familiar with domestic transport's subpar state. Between 2006 and 2019, commutes in the United States increased from 25 minutes to 27.6 minutes, while commutes in the European Union stayed at 25 minutes.[1] Wasted time is a wasted resource. Transport analytics firm INRIX calculated the total cost of auto congestion at $87 billion in 2018, or an amount equal to $1,348 per driver.[2] The cost of transportation is felt in more direct ways, too, ranging from higher prices for automobiles and gasoline to ballooning price tags for infrastructure projects that must be paid for with either increased taxes or user fees—costs that American workers usually can't avoid.

Unfortunately, U.S. policy inflates these costs in numerous ways, forcing American workers to pay more and get less for their transportation dollars.

A prime example is federal policies that increase the domestic price of automobiles—by far the primary transport mode for workers. As shown in Figure 1, nearly 85 percent of all commutes take place in cars, trucks, or vans, but acquiring a vehicle is expensive: the average price of a new automobile is now more than $47,000 ($20,000 for even a small car), and used car prices now average more than $27,000.[3]

While these prices reflect supply-demand dynamics and the cost of increasingly advanced features, they are also boosted by misguided government policies. For starters, there are tariffs: imported cars face a default 2.5 percent tax rate, while light trucks face a whopping 25 percent rate, thus increasing the price of these vehicles and diminishing consumer choice.[4] These harms are particularly pronounced for trucks, where the 25 percent tariff effectively bars many smaller, cheaper imports from the American market.[5] Many auto parts are also subject to tariffs, typically of 2.5 percent, while those from China face an extra 25 percent tariff pursuant to the "Section 301" case begun by the Trump administration. The United States also imposes antidumping duties on tire imports from South Korea, Taiwan, and Thailand and Section 301 tariffs on Chinese tire imports.[6] All of these duties further burden American drivers.[7]

Free trade agreements (FTAs) reduce or eliminate some of these added costs, but they often suffer from lengthy schedules for tariff elimination (for example, the U.S.-South Korea FTA's multidecade phaseout of the 25 percent truck tariff) or restrictive rules of origin containing various content, and even wage, mandates that reduce production efficiency and raise prices.[8] The latter rules, in fact, were found by the U.S. International Trade Commission to likely raise U.S. vehicle

FIGURE 1 Automobiles remain workers' primary means of getting to work

Percentages of all forms of transportation (2019)

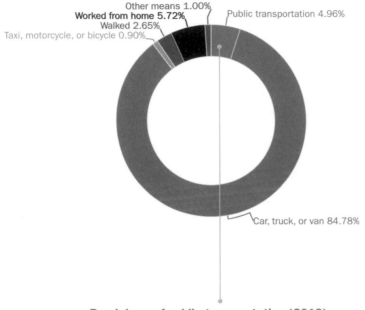

Other means 1.00%
Worked from home 5.72%
Walked 2.65%
Taxi, motorcycle, or bicycle 0.90%
Public transportation 4.96%
Car, truck, or van 84.78%

Breakdown of public transportation (2019)

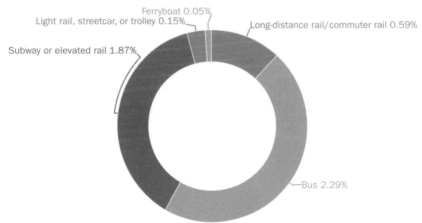

Ferryboat 0.05%
Light rail, streetcar, or trolley 0.15%
Subway or elevated rail 1.87%
Long-distance rail/commuter rail 0.59%
Bus 2.29%

Source: Michael Burrows, Charlynn Burd, and Brian McKenzie, "Commuting by Public Transportation in the United States: 2019," American Community Survey Reports, U.S. Census Bureau, April 2021.

prices or decrease consumption, while the Congressional Budget Office found that the rules would actually increase U.S. tariff (tax) revenue by billions of dollars.[9] Revisions to the North American Free Trade Agreement implemented in the United States-Mexico-Canada Free Trade Agreement, meanwhile, were found by an International Monetary Fund working paper to result in higher vehicle prices and to harm the automotive industries of all three countries.[10]

Automobile prices are further inflated by Corporate Average Fuel Economy (CAFE) standards. Enacted by Congress in 1975, CAFE standards require manufacturers to achieve a sales-weighted fuel economy average for their car and light-truck fleets. For autos that will be produced in model year 2026, an industry-wide fleet average of 49 miles per gallon will be required.[11] While these measures are meant to reduce fuel consumption—thus saving Americans money (according to CAFE proponents)—they are widely considered to impose a net cost on consumers because they increase automobile prices (a result of the high fixed-cost investments that automakers must undertake to comply with the rules). The regulations' environmental benefits are also dubious.[12]

CAFE standards' implicit tax in 2012 was estimated to be around $180 per vehicle ($225 in 2022 dollars) for those in the poorest income quintile; that amount would likely be higher today because the standards have become much more stringent over the last decade. Other studies find even more damaging effects in the longer term, with a per vehicle cost of $225 to $450 in 2018 prices for every one-mile-per-gallon increase in vehicle fuel economy.[13]

Government policies also interfere in the efficient distribution and sale of automobiles. Most notably, state laws restrict direct-to-consumer sales by automobile manufacturers; require auto dealers to be licensed; restrict when franchise relationships can be terminated, canceled, or transferred; restrict new dealerships in existing market areas; and require that manufacturers buy back vehicles or other accessories when a dealership franchise is terminated. Such measures are clear restraints on competition that result in higher vehicle prices and few, if any, consumer benefits. Estimates of these costs range anywhere from 2.2 percent to 8 percent of a car's value—adding hundreds, if not thousands, of dollars to a vehicle's sticker price.[14]

Policies also inflate the cost of driving and maintaining an automobile after its purchase. For example, Section 27 of the Merchant Marine Act of 1920, better known as the Jones Act, restricts domestic shipping to vessels that are U.S.-flagged and -built, as well as mostly U.S.-crewed and -owned. Owing to substantially higher crewing and construction costs, Jones Act–compliant tankers that move oil and refined products typically charge rates significantly higher than those of non-Jones Act vessels, ultimately manifesting themselves in increased gas prices.[15] Other laws, such as the Renewable Fuel Standard that mandates the blending of expensive biofuels into gasoline, tack on additional costs, while state and federal gas taxes further increase pain at the pump.[16]

In addition, there are increasing reports of shortages of qualified mechanics, undoubtedly aggravated by immigration restrictions and state occupational licensing laws (see the Occupational Licensing chapter).[17] These labor restrictions likely result in higher repair and maintenance costs for American drivers.

Next, government policies increase the cost and reduce the quality and supply of infrastructure in the United States, thus lengthening commutes and reducing economic activity. Congested transportation networks mainly reflect insufficient infrastructure or excess demand. Legislators have unsurprisingly focused their policy efforts on the former cause, as new infrastructure projects invariably bring opportunities for ribbon-cuttings and the touting of job numbers associated with these undertakings.

Unfortunately, numerous policies prevent the efficient provision of infrastructure. Protectionist Buy America requirements, which mandate the use of American materials (including iron and steel) in federally funded infrastructure projects, add both time and cost to infrastructure projects, as the price of materials is increased, competition is restricted, and finite resources are devoted to compliance instead of output. These laws might also impose indirect costs by inviting retaliatory measures from U.S. trading partners that restrict market access to American exports.

Tariffs on infrastructure-related items and materials further increase infrastructure costs. The United States still imposes 25 percent tariffs on steel and 10 percent tariffs on aluminum from most countries (see Table 1), with the notable exceptions of Japanese steel and European Union/UK steel and aluminum, which are now subject to less costly but still burdensome tariff rate quotas. A March 2022 analysis from the American Action Forum found that these tariffs imposed nearly $51 billion in additional costs—not including higher domestic prices resulting from tariff protection—in 2021 alone.[18] American steel prices remain well above those in Europe or global markets.[19]

Infrastructure projects are also hampered by laws such as the Davis–Bacon Act and the National Environmental Policy Act (NEPA). Passed in 1931, the Davis–Bacon Act requires that public works funded by the federal government pay at least the prevailing wage rates on nonfederal construction projects in the same locality as determined by the Department of Labor. However, as both think tank analysts and the Government Accountability Office (GAO) have pointed out, such determinations can be significantly higher than actual local prevailing wages, resulting in artificially high labor expenses and a 9.9 percent increase in infrastructure project costs, according to one estimate.[20]

The National Environmental Policy Act, which was passed in 1970, meanwhile, requires federal agencies to review the environmental impact of major projects that are funded by the federal government or require a federal permit, and the law lets opposition groups bring lawsuits challenging environmental reviews. Increased litigation, and the threat of even more litigation, has caused NEPA reviews to steadily become more onerous. As a report prepared for the Treasury

TABLE 1 Tariffs on infrastructure-related items and materials increase infrastructure costs

Tariffs	Value of affected U.S. imports (2021)	Tariff rate, percent	Additional tariff cost burden
Section 232, steel	7.2 billion	25.0	1.8 billion
Section 232, aluminum	6.1 billion	10.0	612.8 million
Section 232, derivative steel articles	418.9 million	25.0	104.7 million
Section 232, derivative aluminum articles	239.7 million	10.0	24.0 million
Section 301, List 1	24.7 billion	25.0	6.2 billion
Section 301, List 2	10.4 billion	25.0	2.6 billion
Section 301, List 3	126.4 billion	25.0	31.6 billion
Section 301, List 4A	105.1 billion	7.5	7.9 billion
Section 301, List 4B	206.3 billion	Suspended	0
Total	**280.6 billion**	**7.5–25.0**	**50.8 billion**

Source: Tom Lee and Jacqueline Varas, "The Total Cost of U.S. Tariffs," American Action Forum, March 24, 2022.

Department pointed out in 2017, the average time to complete a NEPA study increased from 2.2 years in the 1970s, to 4.4 years in the 1980s, to 5.1 years in the 1995 to 2001 period, to 6.6 years in 2011.[21] Such delays bring added costs and can even thwart important infrastructure projects.[22] State NEPA equivalents, such as the California Environmental Quality Act, which requires additional environmental impact analyses and further encourages litigation, can cause similar harms.[23]

The federal government's role in funding infrastructure is itself a contributor to higher transportation costs. By funding state and local infrastructure projects with no obvious federal nexus (in contrast, for example, to the interstate highway system), the federal government effectively functions as a costly and unnecessary middleman with no apparent value added to the process.

These policies help to explain why a 2021 Eno Center for Transportation study of transit projects in the United States, Canada, and Western Europe found U.S. projects to cost nearly 50 percent more on a per mile basis than their international counterparts (see Figure 2 for examples of American and international subway construction costs).[24]

Insufficient or degraded infrastructure, however, is only one element in the congestion puzzle. Further aggravating matters are policies that increase the demand for driving. One such example is a failure to apply pricing to the usage of roads and highways, leading to their overconsumption—and thus congestion—during periods of high demand.

FIGURE 2 U.S. underground subway projects typically cost more than their international counterparts

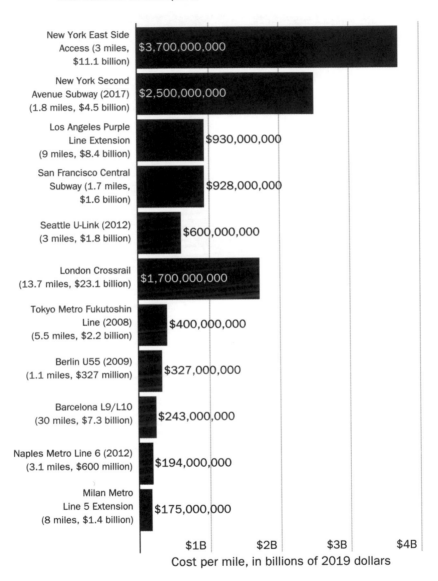

New York East Side Access (3 miles, $11.1 billion)	$3,700,000,000
New York Second Avenue Subway (2017) (1.8 miles, $4.5 billion)	$2,500,000,000
Los Angeles Purple Line Extension (9 miles, $8.4 billion)	$930,000,000
San Francisco Central Subway (1.7 miles, $1.6 billion)	$928,000,000
Seattle U-Link (2012) (3 miles, $1.8 billion)	$600,000,000
London Crossrail (13.7 miles, $23.1 billion)	$1,700,000,000
Tokyo Metro Fukutoshin Line (2008) (5.5 miles, $2.2 billion)	$400,000,000
Berlin U55 (2009) (1.1 miles, $327 million)	$327,000,000
Barcelona L9/L10 (30 miles, $7.3 billion)	$243,000,000
Naples Metro Line 6 (2012) (3.1 miles, $600 million)	$194,000,000
Milan Metro Line 5 Extension (8 miles, $1.4 billion)	$175,000,000

Cost per mile, in billions of 2019 dollars

Source: Ben Bradford, "Why Are Subways in the U.S. So Expensive?," Marketplace, April 11, 2019.
Notes: Costs were converted into U.S. dollars using the exchange rate for April 11, 2019.
Parentheses show year of completion, length of project in miles, and estimated total cost of project.

Also spurring demand for roads and highways are high housing prices that force commuters to flee to ever more far-flung suburbs as part of the "drive until you qualify" phenomenon. As discussed in the Housing Affordability chapter, a major driver of housing prices is zoning and other land-use regulations that restrict housing density and thus supply, which pushes workers farther from city centers and lengthens their commutes. The Entrepreneurship and Home Businesses chapter adds that zoning policies can prohibit even modest commercial enterprises, such as small retail stores, from operating in residential areas, increasing distance between consumers and businesses and thus placing needless demands on infrastructure and mass transit while boosting congestion. Finally, the aforementioned Jones Act discourages the use of coastal shipping owing to its high costs, and thus the law shifts cargo to land-based transportation modes such as trucking, which adds to congestion and increases road mainte nance costs and air pollution.

Government policies also needlessly increase the cost and decrease the quality and availability of mass transit and air travel in the United States. In 2019, approximately 7.8 million Americans commuted via bus, subway, elevated rail, long-distance train, commuter rail, light rail, streetcar, trolley, and ferryboat. While comprising just 5 percent of all workers overall, those reliant on public transportation comprise significantly higher percentages in some of the country's major cities, including New York (55.6 percent); Chicago (28.4 percent); San Francisco (36.3 percent); Seattle (25.1 percent); Philadelphia (25.5 percent); Washington (34.2 percent); and Boston (32 percent).[25]

As with automobiles and infrastructure, public transport is hampered by protectionist policies that increase the cost and difficulty of providing quality service. Buses and rolling stock, for example, are both subject to Buy America requirements. Transit buses acquired with federal public transportation funding are required to have at least 70 percent of their cost manufactured domestically, with final assembly taking place in the United States.[26] Rolling stock—including train control, communication, traction power equipment, and rolling stock prototypes—are subject to the same requirements.[27] The inefficiency and added cost of such protectionism contributes to higher prices—perhaps even dramatically so. Li et al. (2014), for example, found buses in Tokyo and Seoul to be half the price of American buses, and those produced in China were cheaper still; the paper's authors speculated that Buy America restrictions were a major driver of the cost differential.[28]

Ferries, meanwhile, are also made costlier by the Jones Act and the Passenger Vessel Services Act of 1886, which mandate domestically produced vessels for transporting of cargo (including cars) and passengers on U.S. waterways. State policy can add further costs. Washington State Ferries, which operates the largest ferry system in the United States, is required by state law to purchase new ferries constructed in state and at shipyards with state-sponsored apprenticeship programs. Given such restrictions, no more than two bids have been obtained for new ferries constructed during the last 35 years.[29]

Beyond increasing the cost of capital equipment through protectionist measures, government operation of transit services and a lack of market pressures can lead to waste and inefficiencies. This is no trivial matter: one pair of analysts calculated that more than 80 percent of the waste from suboptimal urban transit fares and frequencies can be attributed to political influences.[30] Notably, Jerch et al. (2016) found that the full privatization of public bus service alone could result in cost savings of $5.7 billion (2011 dollars), largely owing to a resulting reduction in public union power.[31] Once realized, such savings could be passed on to consumers/taxpayers or used to improve service offerings.

Amtrak offers a glaring example of the shortcomings of public transportation management. Suffering from inflated labor costs—the passenger rail operator's more than 20,000 employees racked up over $200 million in overtime in 2011— Amtrak also managed to lose money on 40 of 44 routes, according to a 2012 Cato Institute analysis.[32] It even lost $834 million over a 10-year period from food and beverage services.[33]

Public management also helps explain the low regard in which many of the country's airports are held and their typically poor showings in international comparisons.[34] Air travel miseries are compounded by an air traffic control regime that has fallen behind that of Canada and other countries on a variety of metrics.[35] Choice and competition among airlines, meanwhile, are restrained by cabotage laws that prevent foreign carriers from operating domestic routes. These inefficiencies and reduced competition inevitably result in higher prices and less flexibility for domestic airline travel. For example, airfares in the United States are substantially more expensive than similar flights in less-regulated Europe.[36] Although most workers are compensated by employers for the cost of business travel, they must still endure higher fares for personal travel, while increased worker travel costs for employers mean less money for employee compensation.

THE POLICY SOLUTIONS: REMOVE TARIFFS AND RED TAPE TO IMPROVE INFRASTRUCTURE AND GET AMERICA MOVING

Numerous policy options exist to improve the state of domestic transportation and make travel cheaper, faster, safer, and a more pleasant experience. To lessen the burden of auto ownership, federal policymakers should remove tariffs on autos and auto parts and repeal costly mandates such as the Renewable Fuel Standard and CAFE standards. Immigration rules and state occupational licensing requirements should be relaxed to ensure an adequate supply of mechanics and related personnel to service and maintain Americans' cars. At the state level, dealer franchise laws that boost car prices by reducing competition in auto sales should be eliminated. (Several states have already changed their laws to enable direct sales from manufacturers, such as Tesla.[37])

Once Americans acquire their automobiles, they should have first-class infrastructure on which to drive them. Toward that end, both federal and state Buy America requirements for materials used to build infrastructure and the Davis–Bacon Act should be repealed to reduce the cost of new construction and maintenance. Federal and state lawmakers should also examine the NEPA and state-level equivalents with an eye toward, if not repealing them, then at least streamlining their requirements, limiting frivolous or self-interested litigation, and ensuring that compliance with the law is not a multiyear ordeal.

Traffic congestion, meanwhile, can be ameliorated via congestion pricing in cities and dynamic tolling on highways that can replace the use of gas taxes and be efficiently administered by private entities instead of by the government. By implementing such surcharges during periods of high demand, such as rush hour, drivers can be encouraged to travel at alternative times or to use other forms of transportation. Such an approach has already been used in Stockholm, Sweden, where an approximately $3 fee paid for travel in the city center reduced traffic by 25 percent.[38] In the Washington, DC, area, meanwhile, the introduction of dynamic tolling on Interstate 66 has led to reduced travel times.[39]

More fundamentally, state and local governments should rethink and review zoning laws and the entire built environment—including the transportation network—with an eye toward maximum transportation flexibility and freedom. In addition to allowing mixed use buildings that give Americans the option of living in closer proximity to their workplaces, stores, and amenities, governments should allow their constituents to choose among modes by which to travel, including walking and bikes. Where demand for these modes exists, new alternatives could emerge and eliminate the need for a car, thus reducing congestion, the expense of auto ownership, and infrastructure maintenance.

On the federal level, repeal or a significant relaxation of the Jones Act has the potential to achieve multiple aims by reducing the cost of gas, alleviating traffic congestion by shifting more transport from trucks to coastal shipping, and reducing wear and tear on highways and bridges. Similarly, repeal or reform of this law and the Passenger Vessel Services Act could reduce the cost of travel for Americans that rely on ferries.

More commonly used forms of public transit can also be improved. Buy America requirements imposed on the purchase of transportation goods such as transit buses and light rail—thus raising costs and decreasing quality—should be removed. Privatization of publicly owned transit should also be embraced as a means of spurring greater efficiencies and removing politics from the provision of transportation services. On the heavy rail side, Amtrak is a leading candidate for outright privatization. As a privately managed entity in principle, the company could more easily shed staff and rein in labor costs while shuttering unprofitable lines. Those tasks are made far more difficult, however, by being a government entity in practice, subject to political pressures.

Beyond exiting its role in Amtrak, the federal government should seek ways to extricate itself from the provision of transportation and infrastructure by leaving such duties, wherever possible, to the marketplace or state and local governments. Congress should reexamine the federal government's purview of transportation and infrastructure provision and look for ways to devolve these responsibilities. In most instances, these are fundamentally local issues that should be provided at that level without the added inefficiency of an unnecessary layer of government involvement. Several privately administered toll roads have operated successfully in the United States for decades, and some infrastructure can even be provided without the government. The Dulles Greenway toll road in Northern Virginia, for example, was privately financed and built from 1993 to 1995 and today is owned by Macquarie Atlas Roads and operated by a U.S. subsidiary of Italian-based Autostrade per l'Italia S.p.A.[40] Privately financed infrastructure can also be found abroad. Switzerland, for example, is home to the construction of a $30–35 billion, 500-kilometer (approximately 310 miles) tunnel system that will transport freight 24/7 via driverless electric vehicles. The ambitious project is being fully funded by private investors, both foreign and domestic.[41]

Regarding airline travel, Congress should improve efficiency and quality by transferring air traffic control duties to privately managed entities, as is done in numerous countries. A 2005 Government Accountability Office study, for example, concluded that commercialized air traffic control systems in Australia, Canada, Germany, New Zealand, and the United Kingdom had cut costs, boosted investment in new technologies, and either maintained or increased safety after being reformed.[42] The federal government can also promote more efficient and competitive commercial airline operations through the repeal of prohibitions on foreign-owned airlines operating domestic routes. Notably, air cabotage liberalization within the European Union has yielded numerous benefits: along with the aforementioned price savings, a 2015 discussion paper found that liberalization increased the number of routes and flight frequencies; encouraged the entry of low-cost airline carriers, producing a more balanced distribution of airlines across EU airports; and improved overall accessibility.[43] A possible starting point could be opening the domestic airline market to countries with which the United States already has existing free trade agreements.

Local governments also can bolster the country's air transportation network through the privatization of government-owned airports. A 2016 Cato Institute report found that privatization and increased competition would boost the performance of U.S. aviation infrastructure, including reducing costs and encouraging more efficient pricing structures for airport and air traffic control usage.[44] A 2021

Reason Foundation analysis, meanwhile, noted that the majority of the 39 largest investor-owned airport companies accounted for one or more major airports selected by Skytrax passengers as among the world's 100 best.[45]

ACTION PLAN

Efficient transportation is vital to economic and human flourishing and essential for most American workers. We should be able to travel within the United States, be it to a local office or across the country, as easily as possible. Legislators at every level of government should move the conversation beyond simply spending more of American workers' hard-earned tax dollars on roads and bridges and look for ways to remove government barriers to a higher quality, lower cost, more robust, and more convenient transportation vision.

In particular, Congress should
- remove all tariffs on imports of automobiles and auto parts;
- reform U.S. antidumping laws to consider the costs for American consumers and other businesses, such as automakers and auto mechanics;
- repeal CAFE standards or dramatically lower them;
- repeal the Jones Act—alternatively, the law's impact can be mitigated by exempting energy shipments from the law or repealing its U.S.-built requirement, which dramatically raises the cost of purchasing new vessels, including tankers;
- repeal the Passenger Vessel Services Act;
- repeal Buy America requirements mandating the use of American materials and products in the construction of infrastructure projects as well as U.S. assembly and domestic content requirements for capital equipment;
- repeal the Davis–Bacon Act and related prevailing-wage requirements.
- if repeal of NEPA is impossible, reform the law to expedite all environmental reviews (e.g., subjecting them to a one-year deadline) and to limit litigation (e.g., providing a finite list of both actionable issues and parties allowed to bring a suit, a short statute of limitations for challenging a project, and a deadline for completing any such challenge). Only parties with a direct interest in a specific project should be able to challenge it. Lawsuits must also demonstrate not just that there has been environmental harm, but that such harm significantly exceeds a project's anticipated benefits. It is imperative that reform be wholesale and comprehensive rather than piecemeal efforts (such as solely truncating review timelines), as such reforms could perversely generate more litigation and delay;[46]
- repeal air cabotage laws restricting the ability of foreign airlines to offer domestic service, provided they comply with U.S. safety and labor requirements;

- privatize the U.S. air traffic control services; and
- privatize Amtrak.

State and local governments should

- repeal laws preventing direct auto manufacturer sales, dealer licenses, and other measures that limit competition in auto sales;
- revise occupational licensing laws to expand the available supply of auto mechanics;
- adopt congestion pricing to better account for externalities generated by increased traffic and to promote efficient vehicle flows during times of peak demand;
- substantially reduce or eliminate gas taxes and more efficiently meet revenue needs via dynamic tolling and private administration of major highways;
- reform state-level NEPA equivalents to expedite environmental reviews and limit litigation;
- eliminate zoning laws that severely restrict housing density and home businesses and prevent the development of mixed-use projects that could let workers live closer to their places of employment, other businesses, and amenities;
- accommodate alternative means of transportation, such as walking and bicycling, to alleviate pressure on roads and highways; and
- privatize airports and mass transit systems.

NOTES

1. "Census Bureau Estimates Show Average One-Way Travel Time to Work Rises to All-Time High," U.S. Census Bureau, March 18, 2021; and "Majority Commuted Less than 30 Minutes in 2019," Eurostat, October 21, 2020.

2. "INRIX: Congestion Costs Each American 97 hours, $1,348 A Year," INRIX, February 11, 2019.

3. Michael Burrows, Charlynn Burd, and Brian McKenzie, *Commuting by Public Transportation in the United States: 2019* (Washington: U.S. Census Bureau, April 2021); Sebastian Blanco, "New Car Price Keeps Climbing, with Average Now at Almost $47,100," *Car and Driver,* January 12, 2022; Kelley Blue Book, "Best Cars of 2022 and 2023: Best Compact Cars"; and Sean Tucker, "Average Used Car Price Drops," Kelley Blue Book, February 22, 2022.

4. *Harmonized Tariff Schedule of the United States* (Washington: U.S. International Trade Commission, October 30, 2020), pp. 87-1–87-33.

5. See Scott Lincicome, "America's Truck Shortage Reveals the Folly of Pandemic Protectionism," *Cato at Liberty* (blog), Cato Institute, October 21, 2020; and Daniel Griswold, "Why Are Pickups So Expensive? Blame the Chicken Tax," *Dallas Morning News,* March 13, 2022.

6. "Passenger Vehicle and Light Truck Tires from Korea, Taiwan, and Thailand, and Subsidized Passenger Vehicle and Light Truck Tires from Vietnam, Injure U.S. Industry, Says USITC," United States International Trade Commission, News Release no. 21-081, June 23, 2021. See "Notice of Action and Request for Public Comment concerning Proposed Determination of Action Pursuant to Section 301: China's Acts, Policies, and Practices Related to Technology Transfer, Intellectual Property, and Innovation," 83 Fed. Reg. 33608 (July 17, 2018); and also see "Notice of Modification of Section 301 Action: China's Acts, Policies, and Practices Related to Technology Transfer, Intellectual Property, and Innovation," 83 Fed. Reg. 47974 (September 24, 2018).

7. The tariffs on Chinese tire imports alone, for example, were estimated to produce an annual cost increase on tires of $816.7 million in 2009. See Gary Clyde Hufbauer and Sean Lowry, "US Tire Tariffs: Saving Few Jobs at High Cost," Peterson Institute for International Economics Policy Brief no. PB12-9, April 2012.

8. "Fact Sheet on U.S. Korea Free Trade Agreement Outcomes," Office of the United States Trade Representative Archives; and Brian Picone, Francisco de Rosenzweig, Gregory Spak, and David E. Bond, "United States Trade Alert: Mexico Requests Consultations With United States Concerning Automotive Rules of Origin Under US-Mexico-Canada Agreement," White & Case, August 24, 2021.

9. Liana Wong and M. Angeles Villarreal, "USMCA: Motor Vehicle Rules of Origin," Congressional Research Service, IF12082, April 21, 2022.

10. Mary E. Burfisher, Frederic Lambert, and Troy D. Matheson, "NAFTA to USMCA: What Is Gained?," IMF Working Paper no. 2019/073, March 26, 2019.

11. "USDOT Announces New Vehicle Fuel Economy Standards for Model Year 2024–2026," National Highway Traffic Safety Administration, press release, April 1, 2022.

12. See, e.g., Jinjoo Lee, "Americans Should Pay More for Gas, Not Less," *Wall Street Journal,* January 21, 2022.

13. Ryan Bourne, "Government and the Cost of Living: Income-Based vs. Cost-Based Approaches to Alleviating Poverty," Cato Institute Policy Analysis no. 847, September 4, 2018, pp. 12–14.

14. Bourne, "Government and the Cost of Living," p. 14.

15. U.S. Maritime Administration, *Comparison of U.S. and Foreign-Flag Operating Costs* (Washington: U.S. Department of Transportation, 2011); John Frittelli, "Shipping Under the Jones Act: Legislative and Regulatory Background," Congressional Research Service, R45725, November 21, 2019; and Gregory Meyer, "Why the US East Coast Imports Oil Despite Shale Boom," *Financial Times,* October 11, 2017.

16. Christopher M. Matthews, "As American Gasoline Prices Soar, Some Blame Ethanol," *Wall Street*

Journal, November 24, 2021.

17. Ed Garsten, "Repair Tech Shortage Costing Motorists Time and Money, CCC Study Shows," Forbes, March 15, 2022; and "Auto Mechanic Shortage, Delays Seen Growing," *Automotive News,* April 10, 2022.

18. Tom Lee and Jacqueline Varas, "The Total Cost of U.S. Tariffs," American Action Forum, May 10, 2022.

19. "Price History: Tables and Charts," SteelBenchmarker Report no. 391, July 25, 2022.

20. James Sherk, "Why the Davis–Bacon Act Should Be Repealed," Heritage Foundation, January 12, 2012; and *Statement Before the Subcommittee on Labor Standards of the House Committee on Education and Labor,* 96th Cong., 1st sess. (June 14, 1979) (statement of Elmer B. Staats, Comptroller of the United States).

21. Toni Horst et al., *40 Proposed U.S. Transportation and Water Infrastructure Projects of Major Economic Significance* (Washington: AECOM, Fall 2016).

22. Jerusalem Demsas, "Why Does It Cost So Much to Build Things in America?," *Vox,* June 28, 2021.

23. Brian Balkus, "Why America Can't Build," *Palladium Magazine,* June 9, 2022.

24. Romic Aevaz et al., *Saving Time and Making Cents: A Blueprint for Building Transit Better* (Washington: Eno Center for Transportation, July 2017).

25. Burrows, Burd, and McKenzie, "Commuting by Public Transportation."

26. Bill Canis and William J. Mallett, "Buy America and the Electric Bus Market," Congressional Research Service, IF10941, August 6, 2018.

27. "Buy America," Federal Transit Administration, U.S. Department of Transportation.

28. Shanjun Li, Matthew E. Kahn, and Jerry Nickelsburg, "Public Transit Bus Procurement: The Role of Energy Prices, Regulation and Federal Subsidies," National Bureau of Economic Research Working Paper no. 19964, March 2014.

29. Madeline Barch and Neil Bania, *Washington State Ferry Vessel Procurement* (Olympia, WA: Washington State Institute for Public Policy, December 2016).

30. Clifford Winston, "Have Car Won't Travel; The Sober—and Sobering—Case for Privatizing Urban Transportation," Brookings Institution, April 1, 1999.

31. Rhiannon Jerch, Matthew E. Kahn, and Shanjun Li, "Efficient Local Government Service Provision: The Role of Privatization and Public Sector Unions," National Bureau of Economic Research Working Paper no. 22088, March 2016.

32. Amtrak, *National Fact Sheet FY 2016* (Washington: Amtrak, July 2017); Amtrak, Office of Inspector General, "Management of Overtime: Best Practice Controls Can Help in Developing Needed Policies and Procedures," OIG-A-2013-009, March 26, 2013; and Randal O'Toole, "Stopping the Runaway Train: The Case for Privatizing Amtrak," Cato Institute Policy Analysis no. 712, November 13, 2012.

33. Ron Nixon, "Amtrak Losing Millions Each Year on Food Sales," *New York Times,* August 2, 2012.

34. Vanessa Barford, "Why Do So Many People Hate US Airports?," BBC, November 30, 2015.

35. Chris Edwards, "Air Traffic Control," in Cato *Handbook for Policymakers,* 9th ed. (Washington: Cato Institute, 2022).

36. Scott Lincicome, "How U.S. Air Travel Can Get (a Little of) Its Groove Back," *The Dispatch,* June 29, 2022.

37. Kristy Hartman and Laura Shields, "State Laws on Direct-Sales," National Council of State Legislatures, August 2021.

38. Justine Jablonska, "How Stockholm Broke Its Gridlock with Congestion Pricing," IBM, October 17, 2019.

39. Amir Nohekhan, Sara Zahedian, and Kaveh Farokhi Sadabadi, "Investigating the Impacts of I-66 Inner Beltway Dynamic Tolling System," *Transportation Engineering* 4 (June 2021): Article 100059.

40. See "Project Profile: Dulles Greenway," Federal Highway Administration Center for Innovative Finance Support; and Robert W. Poole, Jr., *Should Governments Lease Their Toll Roads?* (Los Angeles: Reason Foundation, August 2020).

41. "Switzerland's Underground Freight Project Gets Start Date," *Le News,* June 24, 2022.

42. "Air Traffic Control: Preliminary Observations on Commercialized Air Navigation Service Providers," U.S. Government Accountability Office, GAO-05-542T, April 2005.

43. Guillaume Burghouwt, Pablo Mendes de Leon, and Jaap De Wit, "EU Air Transport Liberalisation: Process, Impacts and Future Considerations," International Transport Forum Discussion Paper no. 2015-04, January 2015.

44. Robert W. Poole Jr. and Chris Edwards, "Privatizing U.S. Airports," Cato Institute Tax and Budget Bulletin no. 76, November 21, 2016.

45. Robert W. Poole Jr., *Annual Privatization Report 2021: Aviation* (Los Angeles: Reason Foundation, July 2021).

46. As of September 2022, Congress was considering NEPA reform, but specifics were limited and reforms were speculated to be less than comprehensive. Passage was also far from guaranteed. It is therefore uncertain at the time of this book's publication whether 2022 permitting reform efforts would result in meaningful improvements.

REMOTE WORK

BY ILANA BLUMSACK AND SCOTT LINCICOME

THE ISSUE: REMOTE WORK IS INCREASING (AND BENEFICIAL), BUT U.S. LAW HAS FAILED TO KEEP UP

In 2019, only an estimated 6 percent of American workers primarily worked remotely.[1] By February 2022, due in part to the COVID-19 pandemic, that figure had risen to 30 percent (see Figure 1). Even with some workers subsequently returning to the office, approximately 30 percent of all paid workdays were being done from home as of July 2022, up from about 5 percent in 2017–2018. According to a 2022 McKinsey and Company report, this translates to tens of millions of additional American workers now working from home all or most of the time.[2] Yet public policy has not adapted to this new reality, to the detriment of millions of American workers.

FIGURE 1 Remote work has increased dramatically since 2019

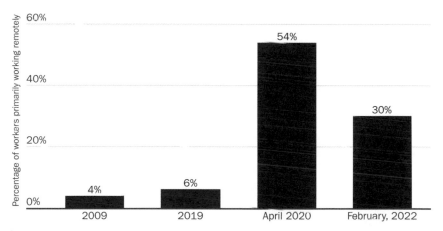

Sources: Patrick Coate, "Remote Work before, during, and after the Pandemic," National Council on Compensation Insurance, January 25, 2021; Lydia Saad and Ben Wigert, "Remote Work Persisting and Trending Permanent," Gallup, October 13, 2021; and Taylor Orth, "Many More Americans Prefer Working from Home than Currently Do," YouGov, February 11, 2022.

Multiple surveys conducted during the COVID-19 pandemic show remote work is popular among employees. A February 2022 Pew Research Center report found that of those working remotely, 76 percent prefer the arrangement, even as concerns over COVID-19 wane and more offices reopen to in-person work.[3] Barrero, Bloom, and Davis (2022) reported that 54 percent of unemployed respondents preferred to find a job that offered remote work.[4] The arrangement has proven particularly popular among parents, who can more easily juggle work and family obligations.[5] In fact, Barrero et al. (2022) found that many workers appear willing to trade wage increases for remote work because they so value the amenity.[6]

This wage tradeoff also benefits employers. Barrero et al. (2022) also found roughly 40 percent of businesses, including more than half of large companies, have expanded remote work arrangements in the last 12 months or plan to do so within the next year.[7] Barrero et al. (2021) reported that 40 percent of employed respondents were more productive in remote work, while only 15 percent reported decreased productivity.[8] Bloom et al. (2022) found that hybrid remote work increased employee retention by 35 percent and boosted overall worker productivity by 30 minutes per week.[9] Other recent studies of remote work have found similar employer benefits.[10]

Employers also have access to a larger pool of workers, including formerly marginalized ones. Businesses report, for example, an increase in hiring Americans with disabilities to fill remote positions, and the proliferation of remote work has made it easier for employers to hire workers located in different states or to abandon the expense of a physical headquarters altogether.[11]

The rise of remote work has empowered American workers to live where they want to live, instead of simply where their employer is located. A March 2022 Upwork survey reports, for example, that 11.7 percent of all respondents either had moved or were planning on moving due to remote work, a figure that would correspond to nearly 24 million people in the general American population.[12] This boost to American labor mobility and economic dynamism has profound benefits for not only the workers involved, but also the communities and regions to which they are moving and the economy overall.[13]

Although further changes to employees' and employers' use of remote work are inevitable as the United States continues to find its post-pandemic footing, it is increasingly clear that remote work will remain popular among, and utilized by, a large portion of the American workforce. Indeed, McKinsey estimated in Spring 2022 that 58 percent of job holders—the equivalent of 92 million people across a wide range of professions—could work remotely, and that more than half (55 million) of those workers could do so full time.[14] Even if these figures were, despite current attitudes, to decline significantly in the months ahead, it would represent a major shift in the workforce and the nation more broadly.

Unfortunately, policy has not kept pace with these trends and instead continues to impede remote work, especially at the state level.

First, states differ in their income tax treatment of remote employees across state lines. Most states determine an employee's tax treatment by his physical presence, so employees in most states are taxed by their state of residence (assuming they conduct their work there). However, a few states, such as Delaware, Nebraska, New York, and Pennsylvania, follow the "convenience of the employer" standard, thus basing an employee's income taxation on their employer's location.[15]

These differing rules can subject remote workers to double taxation. For example, an employee living and working in Maryland for a New York–based employer could be subject to both Maryland and New York state income taxes because New York is a convenience of the employer state, while Maryland is not.

Moreover, the convenience of the employer rule has already caused interstate taxation problems. In 2020, Massachusetts temporarily adopted these rules for now-remote workers who had physically worked in the state prior to the pandemic. This prompted New Hampshire to sue Massachusetts on the grounds that Massachusetts' regulation unfairly taxed New Hampshire workers, but the U.S. Supreme Court declined to hear the case.[16] The temporary Massachusetts measure expired in September 2021 without any Supreme Court clarification of how such interstate conflicts should be resolved.[17]

States also differ in withholding and filing income tax requirements on nonresidents or part-year residents. As the rise of remote work allows employees greater flexibility to work where they please, some employees may spend time working remotely in different locations across state lines. Employees may therefore be subject to state income tax withholding in multiple states, even if their periods of residence in those places were brief. In fact, most states require income tax withholding after just *one day of work* in that state (see Figure 2). And while states usually issue a tax credit for taxes paid to other states, an employee's overall tax burden might increase if one state has a higher income tax rate.[18] A hypothetical Oregon resident who temporarily works remotely from California, for example, would be subject to California's higher taxes on the California liability amount over and above the Oregon liability amount.[19] That worker would also need to be aware of a credit's availability and would expend time (and perhaps money) trying to earn it.

FIGURE 2 Most states require income tax withholding after just one day in the state

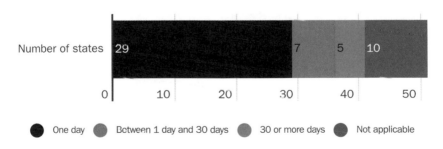

Source: Jared Walczak, "Eight Tax Reforms for Mobility and Modernization," Tax Foundation, January 5, 2022.
Note: Not applicable to Alaska, Florida, Nevada, New Hampshire, South Dakota, Tennessee, Texas, Washington, Wyoming, and Washington, DC.

Second, state tax policies have made remote work difficult for employers. Physical presence laws had previously intended for physical structures, such as office space or warehouses, to create a tax nexus, thereby subjecting the company to state corporate and sales taxes.[20] However, even one employee's continued presence working remotely may be enough to trigger tax nexus, even if the employer does not have any physical space or other connection to the state.[21] Similar concerns can arise for the majority of U.S. companies organized as "pass-through" entities not subject to corporate taxes (e.g., partnerships or S corporations), because remote workers' physical presence in a state can affect nonresident business owners' personal income tax liability.[22] These tax requirements can therefore discourage companies from hiring remote workers or offering the option to current employees, as the organizations will need to consider the tax implications of having workers in multiple or high-tax states in which the companies themselves are not located.[23]

Consider a corporation based in Virginia. An employee at the company can perform work remotely and decides to move to New Jersey in order to be close to grandchildren. That business would now be subject to New Jersey state corporate taxes, despite not having any sales or any physical connections in the state. Prior to the pandemic and the increased viability of remote work, physical presence laws were understood to account for company and employee utilization of local services, such as fire and police.[24] Yet this Virginia business would not be utilizing any New Jersey services, and the remote employee would be subject to New Jersey individual taxes to account for the employee's utilization of them.

State physical presence laws are not the only nexus issues facing companies in the digital age. In 2018, the Supreme Court ruled in *Wayfair v. South Dakota* that states can subject online retailers to state sales tax, even if the company does not have a physical presence in that state.[25] Since then, every state with a statewide sales tax has created economic thresholds over which remote sellers must collect and remit state sales taxes (economic nexus).[26] As Trevor Burrus and Matthew Larosiere argued at the time, the *Wayfair* decision represents an affront to limiting state power, as states can now tax retailers even though the companies lack any connection to the state beyond a few customers.[27] A similar issue exists for remote employers now too.

Finally, federal tax rules discriminate against remote work arrangements. As detailed in August 2022 comments to the Internal Revenue Service (IRS), the American Institute of CPAs (certified public accountants) warned that the agency's failure to update its guidance on the tax treatment of fringe benefits, business expenses, home offices, and related remote work issues has created "unnecessary confusion and stress" for employers, potentially subjecting them and their workers to significant costs or penalties.[28] It is unclear, for example, whether employer-provided work equipment (e.g., a laptop) is a taxable form of compensation. This type of uncertainty can discourage companies from offering remote work options. The CPA group further explained that federal guidance fails to account for major changes in technology, work culture, and remote work's benefits for employees and employers (which, as noted above, are significant). Thus, current policy erroneously assumes that a worker's home is in the same locality as his employer's office, and that employers "gain nothing" from remote or hybrid work arrangements.[29] As a result, remote workers can face additional tax burdens for engaging in what are now routine business transactions (e.g., regular travel to their employer's office).

Beyond taxes, state occupational licensing restrictions also burden remote workers. As discussed in the Occupational Licensing chapter, these requirements place heavy financial and time-related burdens on qualified workers. Moreover, licensure is oftentimes not transferable across state lines, thus limiting worker mobility. This lack of portability is a barrier to remote work across state lines, as employees may have to become relicensed when moving to another state.[30]

THE POLICY SOLUTIONS: REFORM STATE AND FEDERAL TAX POLICY, AND STATE OCCUPATIONAL LICENSING RULES, TO BETTER ACCOMMODATE REMOTE WORK

Given these problems, states should move to eliminate convenience of the employer laws to avoid double taxing remote workers and allow them more freedom to work wherever they want. Eliminating convenience of the employer rules would also benefit employers, as it would simplify accounting and lower related administrative costs—potentially making them more amenable to offering a remote work option. Moreover, most employment laws and regulations for remote workers—that is, minimum wage or paid leave mandates—are already assessed based on the remote employee's physical location.[31]

States should also significantly increase the number of days of residence needed to trigger state income tax withholding or filing obligations. With the proliferation of remote working possibilities, single-day thresholds for withholding income tax are both impractical for employers and employees and a barrier to remote employment. States should increase the minimum thresholds to indicate a significant period of consecutive residence, and not subject short-term residences to state income taxes. For example, Illinois and West Virginia recently raised their thresholds for withholding to 30 days, and Louisiana raised its threshold to 25 days.[32]

Granted, some convenience of the employer states may be reluctant to change their tax laws. In fact, the New York Department of Taxation and Finance actually increased the aggressiveness of its' convenience of the employer rule during the

COVID-19 pandemic.[33] Moreover, it may be difficult for all states to standardize their income tax withholding and filing requirements. Therefore, congressional action may be necessary to eliminate double taxation, consistent with the Commerce Clause of the United States Constitution.[34] First, Congress could require a minimum threshold of physical and working presence in a state—30 to 90 days—before the employee would be subject to that state's income taxes. These changes would standardize income tax treatments for remote employees and eliminate all convenience of the employer rules. Remote workers should not be taxed by states where they neither worked nor lived for a meaningful period.

Second, Congress should update nexus laws to better reflect our 21st-century business environment and stop discouraging companies from utilizing remote workers. Specifically, Congress should clarify the conditions needed to create a tax nexus in a given state. Congress could require, for example, that companies—regardless of business structure (e.g., corporations or partnerships)—must maintain either a physical building or a significant number of employees (such as 20 or more) in a state before being subject to that state's taxes. As Burrus and Larosiere argued after the *Wayfair* decision, the creation of a tax nexus should be based on a company's actual physical presence in a state and its ability to utilize state and local services.[35]

Third, the IRS and the Treasury Department should immediately update guidance regarding the tax treatment of issues related to remote work (e.g., fringe benefits, deductions, and home offices) to reduce the uncertainty that employers and remote or hybrid workers now face. In particular, federal guidance should recognize that it is quite common today for employees to work entirely or primarily from a residence that may be a long distance from their employer's office, and that remote and hybrid work arrangements reflect not only changing technology and American work culture but also that employers derive substantial benefits (e.g., increased profitability, employee retention, and new applicants) therefrom. These changes would help to ensure that current federal law does not impose higher taxes on remote workers than those paid by their in-office counterparts who engage in analogous transactions (e.g., travel to a corporate office).

Fourth, states should make it easier to transfer occupational licenses across state lines. In 2019 Arizona became the first state to universally recognize out-of-state licenses, and 17 additional states have since enacted similar laws universally recognizing at least some out-of-state licenses. As noted in the Occupational Licensing chapter, states should pass universal recognition laws to boost the freedom and mobility of American workers, remote or otherwise.

ACTION PLAN

Rather than being a blip during the depths of the COVID-19 pandemic, remote work has emerged as a popular and viable path of employment for many American workers, benefiting both them and the economy. Both federal and state legislators should take note, and reform tax and licensing laws to make remote work accessible and viable going forward. While states have a role to play in these reforms, ultimately, federal legislation will likely be necessary due to the interstate nature of remote work.

Specifically, the Treasury Department and IRS should

- immediately update outdated federal guidance on issues related to remote work to ensure that these rules no longer discourage or discriminate against remote work and remote workers. Any revised guidance should, consistent with federal law, recognize that remote and hybrid work are common arrangements that employers have voluntarily adopted for their commercial benefit.

Congress should

- prohibit state convenience of the employer rules;
- establish a clear minimum working and physical presence threshold before employees are subject to state income tax withholding and filing requirements—the threshold should be one that only subjects workers who resided in a state for a significant period of time to state income taxes, such as a minimum of 30, 60, or 90 days of consecutive work and residence; and
- update tax nexus laws to account for remote employees. Congress should require that businesses have a substantial physical presence in a state before being subject to state taxes. The physical presence should be determined by the utilization of office, warehouse, or storage space, or by the physical presence of a significant number of employees, in the state.

In the absence of congressional action, state governments should

- repeal convenience of the employer laws and reject any new proposals;
- require at least 30 days of residence to trigger state income tax withholding or filing obligations; and
- require businesses to have a substantial physical presence (office, several employees, etc.) in a state before being subject to state corporate, sales, or other applicable taxes.

State governments also should

- pass universal recognition laws to allow new, remote-working residents with out-of-state licenses to continue working in their licensed profession.

NOTES

1. Patrick Coate, "Remote Work before, during, and after the Pandemic," National Council on Compensation Insurance, January 25, 2021.

2. See Taylor Orth, "Many More Americans Prefer Working from Home than Currently Do," YouGov, February 11, 2022; and see Andre Dua et al., "Americans Are Embracing Flexible Work—and They Want More of It," McKinsey and Company, June 2022.

3. Kim Parker, Juliana Menasce Horowitz, and Rachel Minkin, "COVID-19 Pandemic Continues to Reshape Work in America," Pew Research Center, February 16, 2022.

4. See Jose Maria Barrero, Nicholas Bloom, and Steven J. Davis, "SWAA March 2022 Updates," March 1, 2022; and Jose Maria Barrero, Nicholas Bloom, and Steven J. Davis, "Why Working from Home Will Stick," National Bureau of Economic Research Working Paper no. 28731, April 2021.

5. Andrea Alexander et al., "What Employees Are Saying about the Future of Remote Work," McKinsey and Company, April 1, 2021.

6. Jose Maria Barrero et al., "The Shift to Remote Work Lessens Wage-Growth Pressures," Becker Friedman Institute Working Paper no. 2022-80, July 2022.

7. Barrero et al., "The Shift to Remote Work Lessens Wage-Growth Pressures."

8. Rebecca Stropoli, "Are We Really More Productive Working from Home?," Chicago Booth Review, August 18, 2021.

9. Nicholas Bloom, Ruobing Han, and James Liang, "How Hybrid Working from Home Works Out," National Bureau of Economic Research Working Paper no. 30292, July 2022.

10. Bryan Robinson, "3 New Studies End Debate over Effectiveness of Hybrid and Remote Work," *Forbes*, February 4, 2022.

11. Barrero et al., "The Shift to Remote Work Lessens Wage-Growth Pressures."

12. Adam Ozimek, "The New Geography of Remote Work," Upwork, March 10, 2022.

13. Adam Ozimek, "How Remote Work Is Shifting Population Growth across the U.S.," Economic Innovation Group, April 13, 2022. See also John A. Mondragon and Johannes Wieland, "Housing Demand and Remote Work," National Bureau of Economic Research Working Paper no. 30041, May 2022.

14. Dua et al., "Americans Are Embracing Flexible Work."

15. Mark Klein, Joseph Endres, and Katherine Piazza, "Tax Implications of COVID-19 Telecommuting and Beyond," *CPA Journal*, July 2021.

16. Klein, Endres, and Piazza, "Tax Implications of COVID-19 Telecommuting and Beyond."

17. Karen Hube, "What's Worse than Paying Taxes? Getting Taxed Twice for the Same Income," *Barron's*, March 19, 2022.

18. Jared Walczak, "Eight Tax Reforms for Mobility and Modernization," Tax Foundation, January 5, 2022.

19. Jeanne Sahadi, "Working Remotely in a Different State than Your Employer? Here's What That Means for Your Taxes," *CNN Business*, March 1, 2022.

20. Robert Freedman, "Remote Workers Complicate CFO's State Sales Tax Compliance," CFO Dive, September 8, 2021.

21. Klein, Endres, and Piazza, "Tax Implications of COVID-19 Telecommuting and Beyond."

22. Drew VandenBruhl and Jennifer W. Karpchuk, "Remote Work Creates a Spectrum of State and Local Tax Issues," *Tax Advisor*, December 1, 2021.

23. See Freedman, "Remote Workers Complicate CFO's State Sales Tax Compliance." See also Richard Goldstein, "Remote Legal Staff—Understanding the State and Local Tax Consequences of Remote Work," Berdon LLP, June 16, 2022.

24. Trevor Burrus and Matthew Larosiere, "*South Dakota v. Wayfair*: A Taxing Decision," *Cato at Liberty* (blog), Cato Institute, June 21, 2018.

25. Burrus and Larosiere, "*South Dakota v. Wayfair:* A Taxing Decision."

26. Klein, Endres, and Piazza, "Tax Implications of COVID-19 Telecommuting and Beyond."

27. Burrus and Larosiere, "*South Dakota v. Wayfair:* A Taxing Decision."

28. "AICPA Releases Comments Requesting Guidance Related to Remote Work," American Institute of CPAs, August 25, 2022.

29. American Institute of CPAs to Lily Batchelder and Charles P. Rettig, "Request for Guidance in Key Areas Related to Employees Working Remotely," August 25, 2022.

30. Michael Tanner and Kelly Lester, "Occupational Licensing Reform Moves Forward," *Cato at Liberty* (blog), Cato Institute, August 3, 2020.

31. Isaac Mamaysky, "The Future of Work: Exploring the Post-Pandemic Workplace from an Employment Law and Human Resources Perspective," *UC Davis Business Law Journal* 21, no. 1 (2021): 281–82.

32. Walczak, "Eight Tax Reforms for Mobility and Modernization."

33. Klein, Endres, and Piazza, "Tax Implications of COVID-19 Telecommuting and Beyond."

34. "Constitutional Authorities under Which Congress Regulates State Taxation," Congressional Research Service, R43842, January 2, 2015.

35. Klein, Endres, and Piazza, "Tax Implications of COVID-19 Telecommuting and Beyond."

36. Tatiana Follett, Zach Herman, and Iris Hentze, "Universal Licensure Recognition," National Conference of State Legislatures, March 2, 2021.

EMPLOYEE BENEFITS

BY VANESSA BROWN CALDER

THE ISSUE: WORK-RELATED BENEFITS, HEAVILY INFLUENCED BY GOVERNMENT POLICY, CAN REDUCE AMERICAN WORKERS' CHOICES, MOBILITY, AND FINANCIAL INDEPENDENCE

The American workforce is more diverse than it ever has been, and its needs are similarly diverse: some workers save for major purchases like housing, cars, or education, while others are approaching retirement; some balance family and childcare responsibilities, while others are just starting out; some Americans work to work, while many others work to live.[1]

Unfortunately, U.S. policy does not account for this diversity, especially when it comes to employee benefits. As a result, complex federal, state, and local rules governing employee compensation can deny workers the ability to determine the mix of pay and benefits that best reflects their priorities. Even worse, these laws and regulations can result in less total compensation, less schedule flexibility, fewer employment opportunities, and decreased mobility—thus harming the very workers the policies are intended to help.

Our diverse workforce is compensated through a combination of wages, salaries, and benefits: on average, nearly 30 percent of private sector workers' total compensation comes from employee benefits, and the number is higher for state and local government workers, for whom benefits make up 38 percent of their average total compensation.[2] Workers at larger firms, unionized workers, and private industry workers in certain industries—such as financial services, information technology, transportation, warehousing, and manufacturing—tend to receive a greater portion of their compensation as benefits, although the distribution of benefits that workers receive may vary somewhat across occupations.[3]

As shown in Figure 1, benefits consist of insurance, paid leave, supplemental pay (including bonuses and overtime), and other sources. Also, a portion of employee compensation is withheld for legally mandated payroll taxes that fund government-supported benefits including Social Security, Medicare, and unemployment insurance (UI).

Of course, not all benefits are monetary, and employers also provide other benefits to workers outside of those included in government figures. As discussed in the Remote Work chapter, for example, work-from-home constitutes a relatively new and increasingly important nonmonetary benefit that many workers prioritize above higher wages. For parents balancing work with family responsibilities, this perk appears to be especially highly valued: more than half of parents with children under age 18 said that COVID-19 has made them *more* likely to prefer working from home, either most of the time or part of the time.[4]

Because of the diversity of both the American workforce—in terms of age, needs, and preferences—and the types of benefits that satisfy worker needs, it is no wonder that different workers prioritize different portions of their

FIGURE 1 Benefits are around 30 percent of average U.S. worker compensation

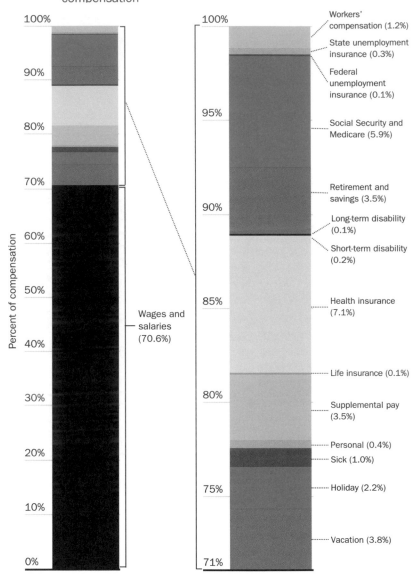

Source: "Table 1. Employer Costs for Employee Compensation by Ownership," Employer Costs for Employee Compensation, Bureau of Labor Statistics, December 2021.
Note: Chart shows private industry worker compensation.

compensation package differently. For example, a 2021 Morning Consult survey found that workers of all ages were about equally divided in saying that salary, benefits, or flexible work/remote work opportunities made for the most enticing job offers (see Figure 2). A separate 2021 poll by the American Psychological Association found that, when asked what perk they would like if they could only choose one, workers chose higher salaries/bonuses more frequently than benefits like retirement and insurance offerings (see Figure 3).

FIGURE 2 Competitive pay, benefits, and flexibility make for enticing job offers

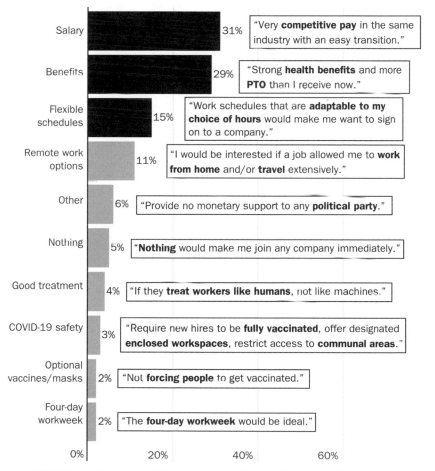

Employed adults were asked to describe, in their own words, something a company could do to make them want to **join immediately**

Category	%	Quote
Salary	31%	"Very **competitive pay** in the same industry with an easy transition."
Benefits	29%	"Strong **health benefits** and more **PTO** than I receive now."
Flexible schedules	15%	"Work schedules that are **adaptable to my choice of hours** would make me want to sign on to a company."
Remote work options	11%	"I would be interested if a job allowed me to **work from home** and/or **travel** extensively."
Other	6%	"Provide no monetary support to any **political party**."
Nothing	5%	"**Nothing** would make me join any company immediately."
Good treatment	4%	"If they **treat workers like humans**, not like machines."
COVID-19 safety	3%	"Require new hires to be **fully vaccinated**, offer designated **enclosed workspaces**, restrict access to **communal areas**."
Optional vaccines/masks	2%	"Not **forcing people** to get vaccinated."
Four-day workweek	2%	"The **four-day workweek** would be ideal."

Source: Alyssa Myers, "The Pandemic Has Forced People to Rethink What They Want from a Job, but Pay, Benefits Still Top the List," Morning Consult, August 2, 2021.

FIGURE 3 If employees could have only one extra perk, one-third want more money

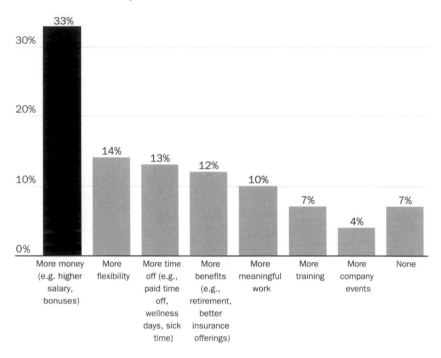

Source: "The American Workforce Faces Compounding Pressure: APA's 2021 Work and Well-Being Survey Results," American Psychological Association, 2021.

Given the wide variety of worker preferences regarding compensation, it is important that government policy allows employees to negotiate packages tailored to their specific wants and needs. If a worker prioritizes a higher salary or wages over other benefits, for example, that person should be able to request a compensation package heavily tilted toward wages instead of having policymakers dictate a different compensation mix through, for example, mandated or government-supported benefits and various taxes. In a well-functioning labor market with limited state interference, firms will compete for employees along these dimensions.

Unfortunately, various legal requirements, regulations, and government incentives deny workers control over their compensation. Even worse, these policies restrict employees and employers to fewer choices, and the policies can make it harder for workers to achieve major life goals, such as building wealth for retirement or changing jobs or locations. As a result, government benefits policies that were intended to help American workers can end up making many of them *worse off* in the long run.

As the Health Care chapter details, for example, the federal tax exclusion for employer-sponsored health insurance effectively ensures that more than 7 percent of workers' total compensation is provided through employer-sponsored health insurance. That is because workers face much higher taxes unless they turn a portion of their earnings over to their employer to use toward health care.

This encourages employers to make health care decisions (e.g., types of health insurance) on their employees' behalf—decisions that, especially in larger companies, likely fail to reflect workers' diverse health care preferences and needs.[5] In fact, employers usually offer their employees only one or two options for health coverage because any more would be costly and logistically complicated.[6]

The tax exclusion also harms workers in other, more subtle, ways. By reducing market competition for certain models of health care delivery and insurance and by encouraging unnecessary health care spending, the exclusion increases prices for medical care.

It also reduces workers' mobility. As explained in the Health Care chapter, the tax exclusion for employer-sponsored insurance creates implicit penalties and insecure health coverage for workers, fostering "job lock" (a situation where workers forgo better employment opportunities for fear of losing insurance coverage) and "entrepreneurship lock." Research therefore finds that the exclusion "reduces voluntary job turnover by 20% per year" and discourages workers from making the labor choices they desire.

Indeed, a majority of studies surveyed by AARP [formerly called the American Association of Retired Persons] in 2015 found that health insurance–related job lock reduced workers' propensity to change jobs, to start businesses, and to retire or work part-time.[7] Bae and Meckel (2022) found, moreover, that the Affordable Care Act's mandate that private insurance plans extend coverage to adult dependents under the age of 26 had the unintended consequence of increasing job lock among numerous parents who would have otherwise left their employers.[8] A reduction in workers' mobility also can increase employers' bargaining power and reduce lifetime earnings.

The tax exclusion (and the employer-sponsored health insurance that it encourages) also distorts workers' employment decisions in the event of a health crisis. For example, the Bradley et al. (2005) study of married women diagnosed with breast cancer found that the tax exclusion appeared to "create incentives to remain working and to work at a greater intensity when faced with a serious illness" just at the time women needed to invest more in their long-term health.[9] Bradley et al. (2012) found that men with employer-sponsored health insurance were more likely to remain working following an adverse health shock and more likely to lose their insurance under the same circumstances (e.g., because they can no longer work).[10]

Thus, current federal policy regarding health insurance is inconsistent with workers' best employment interests and also with their best health interests.

Other types of benefits subsidized by the federal government and tied to workers' employers, rather than to workers, raise similar concerns regarding worker choices, wasteful spending, and job lock. This includes various flexible spending accounts for qualified medical, dental, or dependent care expenses or pensions that employers control or manage for retirement savings.

Beyond these policies, other government-supported benefits also limit employee options, reduce benefit ownership, and potentially reduce workers' wealth. Federal programs like unemployment insurance, Social Security, and Medicare legally require employers to withhold a portion of employee compensation—compensation that could otherwise be paid as wages or benefits—to pay for future government-funded unemployment, retirement, and health entitlements. Sometimes, as in the case of Social Security, the withheld portion is a substantial share of compensation: Social Security mandates a 6.2 percent tax for the employer and 6.2 percent tax for the employee, or 12.4 percent total. Although half of the tax is directly paid by employers, the tax incidence (i.e., who actually ends up paying for it) falls almost entirely on employees.[11]

Together these payroll taxes constitute a significant burden on workers. Indeed, a 2019 report from the Joint Committee on Taxation found that a majority of American taxpayers, in most tax brackets, pay more in payroll taxes than in income taxes.[12] Unfortunately, not only are the tax burdens associated with government-funded benefits significant for workers, but they're also a bad deal. A 2012 Cato Institute analysis found, for example, that if workers who retired in 2011—just after the Great Recession—had been allowed to invest only the employee half of their Social Security payroll taxes over their working lifetime, they would have retired with more income than if they relied on just Social Security.[13] Such gains would surely be even better today, given the significant U.S. stock market gains since that paper was published.[14]

Just as importantly, major programs like Social Security and Medicare are long-term insolvent, which means that—unlike with private health care or retirement accounts—workers cannot be certain that their current tax contributions will be returned to them as future benefits. In fact, the Social Security Board of Trustees states that the program will run out of funds in 2034, which means immediate benefit cuts or tax increases will be necessary to reduce the funding shortfall.[15] Recent estimates suggest that workers beginning their work lives now will be *3 percent poorer* by the end of their work lives as a result of Social Security.[16]

Social Security also tips the scales against labor force participation, particularly for workers above its retirement age. For workers who would otherwise personally or financially benefit by working beyond Social Security's retirement age, the program puts a thumb on the scale against work. Liebman et al. (2009) found that workers respond to the cost of Social Security taxes by retiring earlier and reducing the hours they work.[17]

Medicare faces similar fiscal challenges, as the number of workers per Medicare beneficiary continues to decline. Medicare's Hospital Insurance trust fund is primarily funded by a 2.9 percent payroll tax on current workers, and the Congressional Budget Office projects that the fund will be exhausted by 2024.[18] Thus, Congress will soon need to increase taxes or premiums, curtail benefits, or implement some combination thereof. Such reforms might be worthwhile if Medicare were worth preserving, but the program has been found to perversely incentivize low-quality, high-cost health care.[19]

Federal UI may further discourage work and mobility. Under the current system, workers pay state and federal unemployment insurance payroll taxes and states determine eligibility, benefit formulas, and other details of benefit provision. Typically, UI benefits cover 50 percent of workers' pay for six months, but during economic recessions Congress generally boosts or extends unemployment benefits.

Expanded UI benefits frequently delay unemployed Americans' return to work and, in turn, the nation's economic recovery.[20] For example, the Federal Reserve Bank of New York estimated that extended unemployment benefits during the Great Recession increased the number of unemployed workers by approximately 4.5 million and 3.2 million in 2010 and 2011, respectively.[21] A 2021 Mercatus Center report surveyed the literature on the effect of UI benefit increases and found that expanded benefits increased the duration of recipients' unemployment in all 13 studies under review; meanwhile, three studies conducted during the pandemic found that states that terminated expanded benefits before the federal deadline increased employment and job acceptance rates compared to states that did not.[22] There is also some evidence that certain types of expanded benefits can discourage workers' geographic mobility in the United States and abroad.[23]

Finally, government policy also makes it more difficult for employers to provide workers scheduling and compensation flexibility. As discussed in the Private Sector Labor Regulation chapter, the federal Fair Labor Standards Act (FLSA) limits private sector workers' ability to be compensated for overtime with future time off that they might prefer. (Public sector workers, on the other hand, get to make this trade.) Local labor regulations, which govern everything from shift scheduling to work week and overtime rules, salary requirements, and worker lunch break schedules, make negotiating flexible work difficult or impossible.[24] These laws include associated legal and financial penalties for employers, which understandably deter employers from innovating existing business models in ways that increase employee flexibility. Research therefore shows that the FLSA and other overtime laws, while perhaps boosting some workers' pay, result in less-efficient working schedules for them and fewer jobs or hours for other workers. (See the Private Sector Labor Regulation chapter.)

Despite the problems associated with the current buffet of federally subsidized or mandated employee benefits, policymakers continue to advocate for additional benefit policies, such as paid family leave financed through additional payroll taxes. Enacting such programs would be a mistake, as they would reduce workers' choices and take-home pay.[25] For example, perhaps the best-known paid leave proposal—the FAMILY Act—would require increased payroll taxes and high administrative costs, yet benefit less than half of workers who need leave.[26] Moreover, although many employees desire paid family leave benefits, a 2018 Cato Institute survey indicates that Americans balk at government-supported paid leave once the cost associated with leave benefits is defined.[27] Federal paid family leave also has a variety of potential tradeoffs for employees, including harms to potential beneficiaries themselves.[28] For instance, the Das and Polachek (2014) study of California's subsidized leave program found that it increased unemployment and unemployment duration for women of childbearing age by 5 to 22 percent and 4 to 9 percent, respectively.[29]

THE POLICY SOLUTIONS: EXPAND WORKER CHOICE AND MOVE TO PORTABLE, PRIVATE BENEFITS

To empower all American workers and meet their diverse needs, policymakers must give them greater control over compensation, including employer and government-supported benefits.

First, Congress should replace the tax exclusion for employer-sponsored health insurance with an exclusion for contributions to private, portable health savings accounts (HSAs). As detailed in the Health Care chapter, Congress should convert the exclusion, and all other health-related targeted tax preferences, into an exclusion solely for HSA contributions; increase HSA contribution limits to a level at which most workers could deposit their employer's entire premium payment tax free (e.g., $9,000 for individuals and $18,000 for families) or to the level necessary to achieve revenue neutrality; add health insurance to the list of expenses that HSA holders can purchase with tax-free funds; and remove the insurance requirement so that taxpayers can pair an HSA with any type of coverage.[30] Enacting these reforms would raise employee wages, improve health care affordability, and give Americans control over their own health care decisions and priorities. Importantly, it would also reduce existing barriers to entrepreneurialism and workers' economic and geographic mobility.

Second, Congress should reform Social Security to give American workers more control over their retirement savings, including how the savings are invested and when workers can access them. As economist Rachel Greszler recently explained, Social Security was intended to prevent poverty, not to replace income. Thus, one reform possibility is to convert the program to a universal, flat, anti-poverty benefit, which would limit the number of recipients and thus eventually improve program solvency and reduce workers' payroll taxes. The lighter tax burden would, in turn, give workers more options and greater control over their remaining compensation, which they could save or invest as they see fit.[31]

Similarly, Congress should give the more than $800 billion that it currently spends on Medicare annually to enrollees directly as cash payments that they could more efficiently use in the private health care market. These Medicare checks would vary based on beneficiary health status and income, such that sicker and lower-income enrollees receive large-enough checks to secure standard insurance benefits while healthier and higher income enrollees receive smaller checks. In the long term, Congress should allow workers to invest their Medicare taxes in portable, inheritable personal savings accounts dedicated to their own retirement health needs.[32] As the Health Care chapter details, giving workers control over their health benefits would support innovation and efficiency in the health care marketplace.

At the very least, policymakers should increase the early retirement age and normal retirement ages for Social Security and Medicare to improve solvency and reduce the programs' existing work disincentives. Americans' life expectancy has increased by 17 years since Social Security was introduced, yet the full retirement age has barely changed. Many Americans are also working beyond the traditional retirement age of 65, through options like phased retirement, gig work, post-career consulting, and encore careers. Indexing the age of eligibility for benefits to life expectancy would not only help stabilize the Social Security and Medicare programs but also reflect these realities.[33]

Third, UI should be reformed to allow for greater worker control of benefits and to reduce existing work disincentives in the program. One way to increase workers' ownership of these benefits is to create personal unemployment insurance accounts, where workers contribute to an individual account via payroll taxes until they reach a certain level of benefits (for instance, 80 percent income replacement for six months).[34] Employees should be allowed to withdraw money from the account for any reason after they separate from an employer, and employees could contribute additional funds if they so desired.

Fourth, Congress and states should also rethink existing labor regulations that limit workers' flexibility and reduce their hours and employment opportunities. The FLSA, for example, makes it impossible for parents to take overtime compensation as future time off that they can spend with family. The proposed Working Families Flexibility Act would reform the FLSA to allow workers to take overtime pay as future time off if they so desire.

Fifth, rather than creating a new federal entitlement for paid family leave or any other new mandated benefits—policies that would likely be accompanied by a host of trade-offs and conditions—policymakers should ensure that parents and *all other workers* can achieve their personal objectives by creating tax-advantaged savings accounts. Currently, personal savings are disadvantaged compared to spending, with the exception of narrow government-specified savings goals.[35] Universal savings accounts would allow parents and Americans of all stripes to save for any reason and withdraw funds at any time without penalty, which would benefit workers at all income levels and of all ages. This reform could be paired with simplification of existing tax-advantaged savings accounts—for example, by setting a high annual contribution limit for universal savings accounts and sunsetting Roth IRAs, Coverdell Education Savings Accounts, and other savings accounts.[36]

Meanwhile, the provision of paid leave benefits should be left to employers, who are adopting these benefits rapidly: the share of first-time mothers who reported using paid leave and/or disability grew from 16 to 61 percent over the past 50 years and is continuing to grow.[37] Employers have the advantage of being able to provide a more diverse variety of benefits that are better tailored to their workforce than any program the government has to offer.

Finally, benefit-related reforms, as discussed in the Health Care, Childcare, Independent Work, Private-Sector Labor Regulation, and Remote Work chapters should also be pursued.

ACTION PLAN

Reforms to federal, state, and local policy will ensure that workers have the compensation, flexibility, and benefits that meet their diverse needs.

Congress should

- convert the tax exclusion for employment health insurance to an exclusion solely for HSA contributions and increase the associated HSA contribution limits;
- reform Social Security to a flat benefit and index Social Security's retirement age to life expectancy;
- transform Medicare into a cash payment program and allow current workers to invest their Medicare taxes in health savings accounts;
- replace unemployment insurance with personal unemployment insurance savings accounts;
- implement reforms to federal overtime regulations, such as those proposed in the Working Families' Flexibility Act, to allow employees to be compensated for overtime through future time off;
- consolidate the existing patchwork of tax-advantaged accounts into a single tax-advantaged universal savings account for personal and family savings; and
- forgo instituting federal paid family leave programs in favor of those offered by private companies, which are already rapidly adopting them.

State and local governments should

- relax local labor regulations that create rigid workplaces and barriers to flexible work, including shift scheduling, workweek and overtime rules, salary requirements, and lunch break laws.

NOTES

1. See, for instance, "Annual Data," Women's Bureau, U.S. Department of Labor.

2. See "Table 6. Employer Costs for Employee Compensation for Private Industry Workers by Establishment Size and Industry Group," Employer Costs for Employee Compensation, Bureau of Labor Statistics, December 2021.

3. The information industry includes workers engaged in software publishing, traditional and internet publishing, motion picture and sound recording, broadcasting, telecommunications, web search portals, data processing, and information services. Unionized workers receive 39.9 percent of their average compensation as benefits, while private industry workers at establishments with 500 workers or more receive 34.8 percent of their average compensation as benefits. Private industry workers in financial activities and information industries, as well as transportation, warehousing, and manufacturing, receive 33 percent or more of their average compensation as benefits. "Table 3. Employer Costs for Employee Compensation for State and Local Government Workers by Occupational and Industry Group," Employer Costs for Employee Compensation, Bureau of Labor Statistics, December 2021; "Table 4. Employer Costs for Employee Compensation for Private Industry Workers by Bargaining and Work Status," Employer Costs for Employee Compensation, Bureau of Labor Statistics, December 2021; and "Table 5. Employer Costs for Employee Compensation for Private Industry Workers by Establishment Size and Industry Group," Employer Costs for Employee Compensation, Bureau of Labor Statistics, December 2021.

4. Vanessa Brown Calder, "The Future of Working Parents," *Cato at Liberty* (blog), Cato Institute, April 25, 2022.

5. Michael F. Cannon, "End the Tax Exclusion for Employer-Sponsored Health Insurance," Cato Institute Policy Analysis no. 928, May 24, 2022.

6. Gary Claxton et al., *Employer Health Benefits: 2021 Annual Survey* (San Francisco: Kaiser Family Foundation, 2021), p. 65.

7. Dean Baker, "Job Lock and Employer-Provided Health Insurance: Evidence from the Literature," AARP, March 2015.

8. Hannah Bae and Katherine Meckel, "Dependent Coverage and Parental 'Job Lock': Evidence from the Affordable Care Act," National Bureau of Economic Research Working Paper no. 30200, July 2022. See also Maggie Shi, "Job Lock, Retirement, and Dependent Health Insurance: Evidence from the Affordable Care Act," Columbia University, May 2020.

9. Cathy J. Bradley et al., "Employment-Contingent Health Insurance, Illness, and Labor Supply of Women: Evidence from Married Women with Breast Cancer," Institute for the Study of Labor (IZA) Discussion Paper no. 1577, April 2005.

10. Cathy J. Bradley, David Neumark, and Meryl Motika, "The Effects of Health Shocks on Employment and Health Insurance: The Role of Employer-Provided Health Insurance," National Library of Medicine, National Center for Biotechnology Information, September 2012.

11. John Olson, "What Are Payroll Taxes and Who Pays Them?," Tax Foundation, July 25, 2016.

12. Robert Bellafiore, "New Report Shows the Burdens of Payroll and Income Taxes," Tax Foundation, March 26, 2019.

13. Michael D. Tanner, "Still a Better Deal: Private Investment vs. Social Security," Cato Institute Policy Analysis no. 692, February 13, 2012.

14. Ian Webster, "Stock Market Returns since 2012," Official Data Foundation.

15. Rachel Greszler, "Social Security's Unfunded Obligations Getting Worse," Heritage Foundation, June 10, 2022.

16. Charles Blahous, "Make Social Security Fairer to Workers," Morning Consult, October 22, 2021.

17. Jeffrey B. Liebman, Erzo F. P. Luttmer, and David G. Seif, "Labor Supply Responses to Marginal

Social Security Benefits: Evidence from Discontinuities," *Journal of Public Economics* 93, no. 11–12 (December 2009): 1208–23.

18. The Medicare payroll tax is divided between workers and employers, but the tax incidence mainly falls on workers. "The Outlook for Major Federal Trust Funds: 2020 to 2030," Congressional Budget Office, September 2020.

19. Michael F. Cannon, "Medicare" in *Cato Handbook for Policymakers,* 9th ed. (Washington: Cato Institute, 2022), pp. 425–32. See also Michael F. Cannon and Jacqueline Pohida, "Would 'Medicare for All' Mean Quality for All? How Public-Option Principles Could Reverse Medicare's Negative Impact on Quality," *Quinnipiac Health Law Journal* 25, no. 2 (Spring 2022): 181–258.

20. For negative employment effects, see Johannes F. Schmieder and Till von Wachter, "The Effects of Unemployment Insurance Benefits: New Evidence and Interpretation," National Bureau of Economic Research Working Paper no. 22564, August 2016.

21. Marcus Hagedorn et al., "Unemployment Benefits and Unemployment in the Great Recession: The Role of Equilibrium Effects," Federal Reserve Bank of New York, Staff Report no. 646, revised September 2019.

22. Michael D. Farren and Christopher M. Kaiser, "COVID-19 Expanded Unemployment Insurance Benefits May Have Discouraged a Faster Recovery," Mercatus Center Policy Brief, September 2021.

23. See, for instance, Ryan Nunn, Laura Kawano, and Ben Klemens, "Unemployment Insurance and Worker Mobility," Tax Policy Center, February 8, 2018 (finding that the Extended Benefits program, which ties weekly benefits to state unemployment rates instead of workers, "is associated with diminished worker mobility" across state lines); and Tania Fernandez-Navia, "Unemployment Insurance and Geographical Mobility: Evidence from a Quasi-natural Experiment," SSRN, April 29, 2021.

24. Warren Meyer, "How Labor Regulation Harms Unskilled Workers," *Regulation* 41, no. 2 (Summer 2018): 49–50.

25. FAMILY Act of 2021, H.R. 804, 117th Cong. (2021).

26. Rachel Greszler, "The Fiscal Effects of a Federal Paid Family Leave Program, Yet Another Unfunded Entitlement," Heritage Foundation Backgrounder no. 34733, March 4, 2020.

27. Emily Ekins, "Poll: 74% of Americans Support Federal Paid Leave Program When Costs Not Mentioned— 60% Oppose if They Got Smaller Pay Raises in the Future," Cato Institute, December 11, 2018.

28. Vanessa Brown Calder, "Parental Leave: Is There a Case for Government Action?," Cato Institute Policy Analysis no. 850, October 2, 2018, pp. 12–13.

29. Tirthatanmoy Das and Solomon W. Polachek, "Unanticipated Effects of California's Paid Family Leave Program," Institute for the Study of Labor Discussion Paper no. 8023, March 2014.

30. Michael F. Cannon, "End the Tax Exclusion for Employer-Sponsored Health Insurance," Cato Institute Policy Analysis no. 928, May 24, 2022.

31. *The Fierce Urgency of Now – Social Security 2100: A Sacred Trust: Hearing Before the Subcommittee on Social Security* 117th Cong. (2021) (testimony of Rachel Greszler, Research Fellow, Heritage Foundation).

32. Cannon, "Medicare," pp. 425–32.

33. John F. Early, "Unplugging the Third Rail: Choices for Affordable Medicare," Cato Institute Policy Analysis no. 871, June 6, 2019.

34. Veronique de Rugy, "A Better Form of Unemployment Protection," *Regulation* 44, no. 1 (Spring 2021): 6–8.

35. Ryan Bourne and Chris Edwards, "Tax Reform and Savings: Lessons from Canada and the United Kingdom," Cato Institute Tax and Budget Bulletin no. 77, May 1, 2017.

36. Account balances from existing savings vehicles could be rolled over into a universal savings account. Christina King, "Saving for Social Capital," U.S. Congress Joint Economic Committee: Ranking Member, Senator Mike Lee, May 26, 2020.

37. Vanessa Brown Calder, "Parental Leave: Is There a Case for Government Action?," Cato Institute Policy Analysis no. 850, October 2, 2018, pp. 2–5.

WELFARE REFORM

BY MICHAEL TANNER

THE ISSUE: THE U.S. WELFARE SYSTEM MAKES IT HARD TO MOVE FROM WELFARE TO WORK AND TO BECOME SELF-SUFFICIENT

The bulk of government efforts to fight poverty can be best described as throwing money at the problem. Contrary to public perception, the American welfare system is far from stingy. Although the exact number fluctuates yearly, the federal government funds more than 100 separate anti-poverty programs. Some 70 of these provide cash or in-kind benefits to individuals, while the remainder target specific groups.

Altogether, the federal government spent more than $1.1 trillion on welfare programs in 2021. State and local governments added about $744 billion in additional funding. Thus, government at all levels is spending roughly $1.8 trillion per year to fight poverty (not counting payments related to COVID-19). Stretching back to 1965, when President Lyndon Johnson first declared war on poverty, anti-poverty spending has totaled more than $25 trillion.[1]

Yet the results of all this spending have been disappointing. In terms of material deprivation, welfare payments have reduced poverty. In fact, a 2018 Cato Institute study suggests that if all benefits and other factors are fully accounted for, the true poverty rate may be under 3 percent.[2] Other studies are more cautious but still suggest that welfare programs reduce poverty rates by half or more. On the other hand, these studies also suggest that most of the improvement took place in the welfare programs' early years, and that the marginal gains of recent additional spending have been minimal.

More significantly, current welfare policy seems almost perversely designed to work against its overarching goal of enabling Americans to not just endure poverty more comfortably but to escape it altogether. This goal requires that the incentives within the welfare system encourage work, savings, and family formation. Overall, the system should make it as easy as possible for people to leave welfare for work, but several factors undermine that objective.

First, the magnitude of the current welfare system, with its multitude of overlapping programs—often with contradictory eligibility requirements, differing rules, mixed oversight, and divided management—is a bureaucratic nightmare.

For example, there are 34 housing programs run by seven different cabinet departments, including even the Department of Energy. There are 23 different programs providing food or food-purchasing assistance administered by three different cabinet departments. There are 13 different healthcare programs administered by three separate agencies within the Department of Health and Human Services as well as the Department of Veteran Affairs. Five cabinet departments oversee 15 cash or general-assistance programs. Altogether, 13 cabinet departments and four independent agencies administer at least one explicitly anti-poverty program.[3]

The complexity and lack of transparency make it difficult to measure whether programs are accomplishing their goals. Many existing programs have become fiefs for special interests, providing a bureaucratic roadblock to reform. And, while the overhead and administrative costs for most programs are modest (generally less than 5 percent), the costs do add up. Moreover, the sheer number of programs works to suck more people into the welfare system, increasing both cost and enrollment, without necessarily targeting those efforts to the people who are most in need.

Second, households in or near poverty that do receive assistance and participate in multiple programs can face marginal effective tax rates that are counterproductive, deterring work effort or putting a low ceiling on how much these families can increase their standard of living. In those cases, much of each additional dollar earned is clawed back through higher taxes or reduced benefits.

A 2013 Cato Institute study, for example, found that an unemployed single mother with two children who participated in seven common welfare programs—Temporary Assistance for Needy Families (TANF); food stamps (SNAP); Medicaid; housing assistance; Special Supplemental Nutrition Program for Women, Infants, and Children (WIC); energy assistance (LIHEAP); and free commodities—could take home an income higher than what she would have earned from a minimum-wage job in 35 states, even after accounting for the Earned Income Tax Credit (EITC) and Child Tax Credit (CTC), for which she would have been eligible, if employed. In fact, in Connecticut, Hawaii, Massachusetts, New Jersey, New York, Rhode Island, Vermont, and Washington, DC, welfare paid more than a $20 per hour job ($25.44 in 2022 dollars), and in five additional states it paid more than a $15 per hour job ($19.08 in 2022 dollars) job.[4] As a result, someone who left welfare for work could have found themselves worse off financially.

A 2012 Congressional Budget Office report looking at the example of Pennsylvania found that marginal tax rates, after accounting for the loss of benefits, could reach extremely high levels, discouraging labor-force entry and work hours. The report found that unemployed single taxpayers with one child would face an effective marginal tax rate of 47 percent for taking a job paying the minimum wage in 2012, and if their earnings disqualified them from Medicaid, they could have faced an astonishing marginal tax rate of 95 percent.[5]

Likewise, Maag et al. (2012), looking at a single parent with two children, found that in moving from no earnings to poverty-level earnings, this family faced a marginal tax rate that was as high as 25.5 percent in Hawaii.[6] A 2014 Illinois Policy Institute study found that a single mother with two children in that state who increased her hourly earnings from the minimum wage of $8.25 to $12 would increase her net take-home wage by less than $400 per year. Even worse, if she further increased her earnings to $18 an hour, her annual net income would *decrease* by more than $24,800 due to benefit reductions and tax increases.[7]

Although inflation and policy changes over the last decade have changed some of these studies' details, the general conclusions remain the same today. For example, the Federal Reserve Bank of Atlanta's Career Ladder Identifier and Financial Forecaster Policy Rules Database illustrates the public assistance program eligibility based on household incomes. The examples in Figures 1A and 1B depict the welfare benefits earned by a single parent with two children under five years of age. The most common welfare programs (TANF, SNAP, EITC, WIC, Medicaid, and Section 8 Housing Vouchers) were chosen to portray the benefit drop-off as household incomes increase.[8] The two counties in question, Los Angeles County, California, and Wake County, North Carolina, have very different eligibility rules for various programs leading to differing marginal tax rates in the two jurisdictions. Yet both show a sizable barrier to leaving welfare for work.

FIGURE 1A Across the country, income-related benefit "cliffs" can discourage welfare recipients from taking new jobs or working more hours

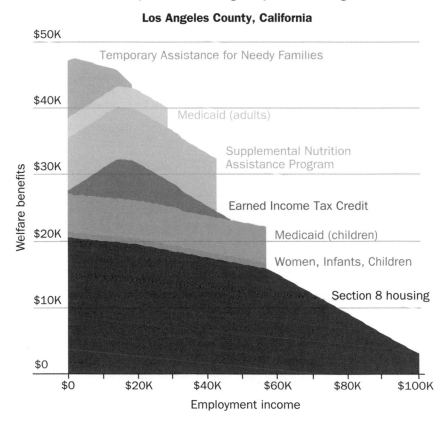

Source: Policy Rules Database Dashboard from the Federal Reserve Bank of Atlanta (2022).
Note: Data based on the most common welfare programs for a single parent with two children under the age of five.

FIGURE 1B Across the country, income-related benefit "cliffs" can discourage welfare recipients from taking new jobs or working more hours

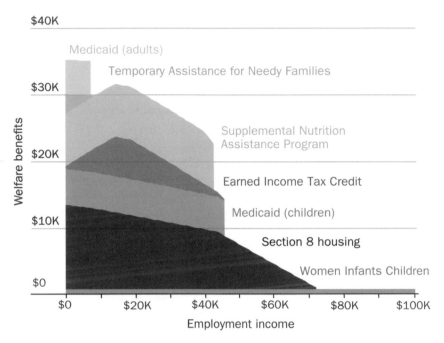

Wake County, North Carolina

Source: Policy Rules Database Dashboard from the Federal Reserve Bank of Atlanta (2022).
Note: Data based on the most common welfare programs for a single parent with two children under the age of five.

Third, many programs are designed in ways that further discourage economic and geographic mobility. Some also include a bias against marriage, which has been shown to be correlated with higher earnings and financial independence. A mother who marries the father of her children may lose a substantial portion of her benefits depending on her new spouse's income. Unmarried parents are better able to meet the income and asset eligibility tests for programs such as TANF and SNAP. For example, if a single mother with a net income of 125 percent of the federal poverty level marries someone with an income, it could push them over the threshold, and no one in the household would be eligible for SNAP. If they chose instead to cohabitate without marrying, the benefits would continue to flow. As detailed below, there is a similar mechanism in the EITC: benefits begin to phase out and are exhausted at lower income levels for married couples.[9]

Furthermore, the majority of welfare benefits today are provided not in cash but rather as in-kind benefits. This effectively infantilizes the poor: they are not expected to budget or choose among competing priorities the way that people who are not on welfare are expected to do, and they simply follow the government's choices, values, and priorities instead of their own. Indeed, direct cash assistance programs, including refundable tax credits, made up just 22 percent of federal assistance in 2020, down from roughly 29 percent two decades ago. In-kind programs—such as food stamps, housing assistance, and Medicaid— provide the poor with assistance, but only for specific purposes. In most cases, the payments are made directly to providers. The person being helped never even sees the money.

Virtually all programs go even further in limiting the use of benefits to government-approved purchases. For example, WIC can only be used to purchase certain foods determined by government regulation. SNAP's use is restricted to stores that stock a certain level of healthy food products, often eliminating the eligibility of small neighborhood stores. Even with cash programs like TANF, state lawmakers have enacted a host of restrictions around things like the locations where electronic benefit transfer cards may be used to access ATMs.

Thus, the current welfare system not only stigmatizes the poor, but also is one more factor pushing them into narrowly concentrated neighborhoods clustered around subsidized housing because the system relies on providers who are willing to accept government benefits (e.g., landlords willing to take Section 8 vouchers). Those neighborhoods often offer poor schools, few jobs, high crime rates, a lack of role models, and have been shown to inhibit residents' upward income mobility.[10]

One program that provides cash directly to the poor is the EITC, but it is rife with problems that discourage work and family formation. The EITC is specifically designed as a wage supplement and is tied directly to work to offset the high marginal tax rate that many poor people encounter when they leave welfare for work. The evidence suggests that the EITC increases work effort, and single mothers, in particular, have seen significant labor-force gains.

Studies also suggest that the EITC has been more successful than other welfare programs in reducing poverty. The Census Bureau claims that the poverty rate would be 2.5 percent higher in the absence of refundable tax credits.[11] As measured by the additional outlays needed to lift one million people out of poverty (using the supplemental poverty measure), refundable tax credits are clearly more cost-effective than other types of welfare programs.

As the EITC has grown, however, problems with the program have become more apparent. For example, the benefit level for childless workers is small and phases out quickly because the EITC focuses on families. The maximum credit available to a childless worker was only $1,502 in 2021, and all benefits phase out before the earned income hits $21,430 (the maximum credit for a single parent with one child was $3,618).[12] Childless workers under age 25 are not allowed to claim the EITC at all. As a result, they accounted for only 3 percent of EITC funding.

As noted above, moreover, the EITC can impose significant marriage penalties. According to the Tax Policy Center, "if a single parent receiving the EITC marries, the addition of the spouse's income may reduce or eliminate the credit."[13] Furthermore, the credit is mostly determined by the number of children in a family, thus making the maximum credit the same for a single parent as it is for a married couple. As a result, a married couple with two children would receive a maximum annual credit of $5,980—the same as for a single filer with two children. But the married couple would exhaust EITC benefits upon hitting $53,665 of total earned income, while the single parent would do so at only a few thousand dollars less ($47,915). Thus, the single parent can continue to receive benefits at higher income levels relative to the poverty level than married couples can—and the credit is more generous since the benefits are being distributed among the three people, rather than four.

Finally, as a refundable tax credit, the EITC is paid annually in the manner of a tax refund. While such a lump-sum payment can certainly help many low-income families, it still leaves them relying on wages throughout much of the year. In its current form, the EITC represents an income supplement, not a wage supplement, and does not address the year-round financial needs of low-income families who are often left living paycheck to paycheck, or worse, for the rest of the year.

THE POLICY SOLUTIONS: CONSOLIDATE AND DECENTRALIZE FEDERAL WELFARE PROGRAMS; MOVE TO CASH TRANSFERS; EMPHASIZE INDIVIDUAL CONTROL

Given the failure of more than 50 years of federal welfare policy to significantly reduce poverty or increase economic mobility, it should be apparent that the federal government does not know best. Nor have we demonstrated that we know enough about how to reduce poverty to impose a one-size-fits-all policy throughout the country. Five decades of failure should have taught us to be modest.

Wherever possible, Congress should shift both the funding and operational authority for welfare and other anti-poverty programs to the states. The "laboratories of democracy," as Justice Louis Brandeis described them, should be the primary focus of anti-poverty efforts, not an afterthought. That means more than simply giving states the authority to tinker with programs as they exist today. It means federal funding, even in block grant form, should not be accompanied by federal strings. Instead, states should be given control over broad categories of funding, with the ability to shift funds freely between programs at their discretion, but within a framework in which their efforts are rigorously evaluated and held accountable for achieving results. Some states may wish to emphasize job training or public service jobs. Others may feel that education provides the biggest bang for the buck. In some states, housing may be a priority; in others, the need for nutrition assistance may be greater. Some may wish to impose strict eligibility requirements, while others may choose to experiment with unconditional benefits, even a universal basic income.

Moreover, states that have successfully reduced poverty while also reducing the number of people on the welfare rolls should be allowed to shift funds to other priorities entirely. Success should be rewarded. States that fail to achieve results, after accounting for factors beyond their control, should have their funding reduced, with any shortfall made up from state funds. Failure should not be subsidized.

While shifting funds from the federal government to the states represents a good first step, the states should go even further by moving away from in-kind benefits and to direct cash payments. While it is reasonable for taxpayers to seek accountability for how their funds are used, this paternalism may be both unnecessary and self-defeating. For starters, arguments that the poor can't be trusted with cash are too often based on erroneous and racially biased stereotypes rather than on sound evidence. In fact, studies from states that drug-test welfare recipients suggest that the use of drugs is no higher among welfare recipients than among the general population.[14] And numerous studies have shown that even when welfare recipients are given totally unrestricted cash, they do not increase their expenditure on "temptation goods" like tobacco or alcohol.[15]

Furthermore, cash benefits can allow the poor to decide for themselves how much of their income should be allocated to rent, food, education, or transportation. They might also choose to save more or invest in learning new skills that will help them earn more in the future. A 2015 Financial Industry Regulatory Authority report found that 53 percent of American households with incomes less than $25,000 had no investment accounts, compared to just 1 percent of households making over $150,000 a year without investment accounts.[16] We can't expect people to behave responsibly if they are never given any responsibility.

Cash benefits also could encourage mobility, helping to break up geographic concentrations of poverty that can isolate the poor from the rest of society and reinforce the worst aspects of the poverty culture, especially if those benefits are received early in life. Armed with money instead of vouchers redeemable only at certain locations, the poor could escape bad neighborhoods the same way vouchers and tax credits allow children to escape bad schools. Doing so can produce tremendous results: Chetty et al. (2016), for example, found that families that moved into low-poverty areas before their children entered their teen years saw the children go on to earn 31 percent more later in life than did comparable children who remained in high-poverty areas. Beyond higher earnings, children from families that moved saw a wide range of other positive outcomes. They were more likely to attend college, less likely to be single parents, and more likely to live in better neighborhoods when they grew up and left home.[17]

Any cash payment system should be designed to help low-income Americans solve their immediate problems without becoming ensconced in the welfare system. Thus, Congress could encourage states to expand existing cash-diversion programs, which provide lump-sum cash payments in lieu of traditional welfare benefits.[18] Currently in use in 32 states and DC, these programs are designed to assist families facing an immediate financial crisis or short-term need. The family is given a single cash payment in the hope that if the immediate problem is resolved, there will be no need for going on welfare. In exchange for receiving the lump-sum payment, welfare applicants in most states—but not all—give up their eligibility for TANF for a period ranging from a couple of months to a year.[19] Several studies indicate that for individuals who had not previously been on welfare, diversion programs significantly reduced their likelihood of ending up there. Studies also suggest that diversion participants are subsequently more likely to work than become traditional recipients of welfare.[20]

Finally, Congress should reform the EITC to turn it into a pure wage supplement. Benefits should be available to childless adults and should not rise with the number of children in a family. Payments should arrive monthly rather than in an annual lump sum. Any additional cost due to expansion should be paid for by reductions in other welfare programs.

ACTION PLAN

Provision of public welfare to at least some people may be justified, according to certain ethical viewpoints, but is insufficient and counterproductive to effectively deliver human flourishing. We should not judge the success of our efforts to end poverty by how much charity the state redistributes to the poor, but by how few people need such charity in the first place.

Truly improving the lives of the poor is not a question of spending slightly more or less money, tinkering with the number of hours mandated under work requirements, or rooting out fraud, waste, and abuse. We need a new debate, one that moves beyond our current approach to fighting poverty to focus on what works rather than noble sentiments or good intentions—a system built on work, individual empowerment, and Americans' philanthropic impulse.

Congress should therefore
- consolidate all current welfare and anti-poverty programs;
- shift remaining welfare programs to the states with as few strings as possible;
- encourage states to transition from in-kind benefits to cash grants;
- encourage states to make greater use of welfare diversion (lump-sum cash) programs; and
- transform the EITC into a pure wage supplement linked to work rather than family size/composition.

State governments should

- transition from in-kind benefits to cash grants;
- review benefit levels; phaseout ranges and asset and income tests to reduce "welfare cliffs" and disincentives to work, savings, and family formation;
- avoid arbitrary and punitive restrictions on the use of benefits;
- expand the use of diversion programs and lump-sum payments in lieu of traditional benefits; and
- make greater use of federal waivers to experiment with different ways to deliver benefits, combine programs, and change program incentives.

NOTES

1. Author's calculations based on the following sources: "Fiscal Year 2022 Budget Summary," U.S. Department of Education, May 2021; "FY 2021 Performance Budget Justification," Appalachian Regional Commission, February 2020; "Assets for Independence Demonstration Program," Federal Grants Wire; "Appropriations Committee Releases Fiscal Year 2022 Labor, Health and Human Services, Education, and Related Agencies Funding Bill," Committee on Appropriations, U.S. House of Representatives, July 11, 2021; "Justification of Estimates for Appropriations Committees," Administration for Children and Families, U.S. Department of Health and Human Services, 2022; "Children's Health Insurance Program," Congressional Budget Office; "Commodity Supplemental Food Program: Tentative Caseload Assignments for the 2022 Caseload Cycle," Food and Nutrition Service, U.S. Department of Agriculture; "Community Development Block Grants Section 108 Loan Guarantees," Federal Grants Wire; "Mayor Bowser Applauds HUD for $38.8 Million Investment in Affordable Housing," Washington, DC, Department of Housing and Community Development; Joseph V. Jaroscak, "Community Development Block Grants: Funding and Allocation Processes," Congressional Research Service, R46733, March 24, 2021; Patrick A. Landers et al., "Federal Spending on Benefits and Services for People with Low Income: FY2008–FY2020," Congressional Research Service, R46986, December 8, 2021; "Drug-Free Communities Support Program Grants," U.S. Department of Health and Human Services; "FY 2021 Food and Administrative Funding for Emergency Food Assistance Program," U.S. Department of Agriculture; Katie Jones and Maggie McCarty, "USDA Rural Housing Programs: An Overview," Congressional Research Service, R47044, March 8, 2022; "State Administrative Expenses for Child Nutrition," Federal Grants Wire; "Food Distribution Program on Indian Reservations," U.S. Department of Agriculture, January 2020; "Graduate Assistance in Areas of National Need," U.S. Department of Education, January 22, 2021; "FY 2022 Operating Plan," Health Resources and Services Administration, U.S. Department of Health and Human Services, May 2022; "High School Graduation Initiative Also Known as School Dropout Prevention Program," U.S. Department of Education, August 5, 2014; "Indian Child Welfare Act Title II Grants," Federal Grants Wire; "Native American Programs: Summary of Resources," U.S. Department of Housing and Urban Development, 2022; "Fiscal Year 2023: The Interior Budget in Brief," Bureau of Indian Affairs, U.S. Department of the Interior, 2022; "Job Opportunities for Low-Income Individuals," Federal Grants Wire; Gary Guenther, "Internal Revenue Service Appropriations, FY2022," Congressional Research Service, IF11979, March 25, 2022; "Migrant Education—High School Equivalency Program," U.S. Department of Education, November 30, 2015; "Migrant Education Program: Funding Status," Office of Elementary and Secondary Education, U.S. Department of Education; "Budget of the United States Government: Fiscal Year 2023," Office of Management and Budget, White House; "Projects for Assistance in Transition from Homelessness," Federal Grants Wire; "Promoting Safe and Stable Families: Title IV-B, Subpart 2,

of the Social Security Act," U.S. Department of Health and Human Services, June 10, 2021; "Public Housing Fund: Summary of Resources," U.S. Department of Housing and Urban Development, 2022; Kara Clifford Billings, "School Meals and Other Child Nutrition Programs: Background and Funding," Congressional Research Service, R46234, May 23, 2022; "Special Programs for the Aging, Title III, Part D, Disease Prevention and Health Promotion Services," Federal Grants Wire; "Special Programs for the Aging, Title III, Part B, Grants for Supportive Services and Senior Centers," Federal Grants Wire; "Special Programs for the Aging, Title III, Part C, Nutrition Services," Federal Grants Wire; "State Administrative Matching Grants for the Supplemental Nutrition Assistance Program," Federal Grants Wire; "The President's Fiscal Year 2022 Budget Request," Child Welfare League of America, June 4, 2021; "Summer Food Service Program," Economic Research Service, U.S. Department of Agriculture, August 3, 2022; "Temporary Assistance for Needy Families," Congressional Budget Office, May 2022; "Title V Delinquency Prevention Program," SAM.gov; "Transitional Living Program Fact Sheet," Family and Youth Services Bureau, U.S. Department of Health and Human Services; "Undergraduate Scholarship Program for Individuals from Disadvantaged Backgrounds," Federal Grants Wire; "Contribution Factor and Quarterly Filings —Universal Service Fund (USF) Management Support," Federal Communications Commission; "The President's Budget Request for Refugee and Asylum Services: Fiscal Year (FY) 2020," National Immigration Forum, April 3, 2019; Joe Belden and Michael Feinberg, "Leaky Roof? A USDA Home Repair Program Is an Option," *Daily Yonder,* June 15, 2022; "Guaranteed Rural Housing Loans (Section 502)," U.S. Department of Housing and Urban Development, January 2004; Anna Maria Garcia, "Weatherization Program Notice BIL 22-1," U.S. Department of Energy, March 30, 2022; "Weatherization Assistance Program," Office of Energy Efficiency and Renewable Energy, U.S. Department of Energy; "FY 2022 Congressional Budget Justification: Training and Employment Services," Employment and Training Administration, U.S. Department of Labor, 2022; "WIOA Pilots, Demonstrations, and Research Projects," Federal Grants Wire; "WIC Farmers' Market Nutrition Program," National Sustainable Agriculture Coalition, May 2019; "WIC Program Grant Levels by Fiscal Year," Food and Nutrition Service, U.S. Department of Agriculture, July 19, 2022; "Memorandum: The Child Care and Development Fund (CCDF) in FY2021 Reconciliation Proposals," Congressional Research Service, February 17, 2021; "Federal Grant Funding," National Association of Community Health Centers; "Public and Indian Housing, Family Self-Sufficiency," U.S. Department of Housing and Urban Development, 2020; Brynne Keith-Jennings, "Introduction to Puerto Rico's Nutrition Assistance Program," Center on Budget and Policy Priorities, November 3, 2020; "Supportive Housing for Persons with Disabilities (Section 811)," Office of Housing, U.S. Department of Housing and Urban Development; Maggie McCarty, Libby Perl, and Katie Jones, "Overview of Federal Housing Assistance Programs and Policy," Congressional Research Service, RL34591, March 27, 2019; "Appropriations Committee Releases Fiscal Year 2022 Transportation, and Housing and Urban Development, and Related Agencies Funding Bill," Committee on Appropriations, U.S. House of Representatives, July 11, 2021; "FCC Announces Updated Lifeline Minimum Service Standards and Indexed Budget Amounts," Benton Institute for Broadband and Society, July 30, 2021; "Low-Income Housing Tax Credit (LIHTC)," Office of Policy Development and Research, U.S. Department of Housing and Urban Development; "Ryan White HIV/AIDS Program Funding," Health Resources and Services Administration, U.S. Department of Health and Human Services; "National School Lunch Program," Economic Research Service, U.S. Department of Agriculture, Economic Research Service, January 13, 2022; "Section 8 Housing Assistance Payments Program," Federal Grants Wire; "Senior Farmers Market Nutrition Program," National Sustainable Agriculture Coalition, July 2019; "Child Nutrition Discretionary Grants Limited Availability," Federal Grants Wire; "FY 2022 Congressional Budget Justification: State Unemployment Insurance and Employment Service Operations," Employment and Training Administration, U.S. Department of Labor, 2021; "Unemployment Insurance," Federal Grants Wire; Adrienne L. Fernandes-Alcantara, "Federal Youth Employment and Job Training Programs," Congressional Research Service, IF11640, August 31, 2020; and Libby Perl, "Veterans and Homelessness," Congressional Research Service, IF10167, February 15, 2022.

2. John F. Early, "Reassessing the Facts about Inequality, Poverty, and Redistribution," Cato Institute Policy Analysis no. 839, April 24, 2018.

3. Author's calculations based on the sources in note 1.

4. Michael Tanner and Charles Hughes, "The Work versus Welfare Trade-Off: 2013," Cato Institute White Paper, August 19, 2013, p. 3.

5. "Illustrative Examples of Effective Marginal Tax Rates Faced by Married and Single Taxpayers: Supplemental Material for Effective Marginal Tax Rates for Low- and Moderate-Income Workers," Congressional Budget Office, November 2012, p. 13.

6. Elain Maag et al., "How Marginal Tax Rates Affect Families at Various Levels of Poverty," *National Tax Journal* 65, no. 4 (December 2012): 759–82.

7. Erik Randolph, "Modeling Potential Income and Welfare-Assistance Benefits in Illinois: Single Parent with Two Children Households and Two Parents with Two Children Household Scenarios in Cook County, City of Chicago, Lake County and St. Clair County," Illinois Policy Institute, Special Report, December 2014, p. 45.

8. Author's calculations based on "Benefits Cliffs Across the U.S.," Policy Rules Database Dashboard, Federal Reserve Bank of Atlanta.

9. Elaine Maag and Adam Carasso, "Taxation and the Family: What Is the Earned Income Tax Credit?," in *The Tax Policy Briefing Book* (Washington: Tax Policy Center, 2020).

10. Raj Chetty and Nathaniel Hendren, "The Impacts of Neighborhoods on Intergenerational Mobility I: Childhood Exposure Effects," National Bureau of Economic Research Working Paper no. 23001, May 2017; and Vincient Whatley, "The Importance of Neighborhoods and Intergenerational Economic Inequality in the United States," Washington Center for Equitable Growth, November 19, 2021.

11. "Income, Poverty and Health Insurance Coverage in the United States: 2019," press release, U.S. Census Bureau, September 15, 2020.

12. "Earned Income and Earned Income Tax Credit (EITC) Tables," Internal Revenue Service, January 21, 2022.

13. C. Eugene Steuerle, "Biden's Expanded EITC Adds Significant Marriage Penalties," *Tax Vox* (blog), Tax Policy Center, August 3, 2021.

14. Harold Pollack and Lisa R. Metsch, "Welfare Reform and Substance Abuse," *Milbank Quarterly* 83, no. 1 (2005): 65–100; and "Drug Testing Welfare Recipients: Recent Proposals and Continued Controversies," Office of the Assistant Secretary for Planning and Evaluation, U.S. Department of Health and Human Services, October 2011.

15. David K. Evans and Anna Popova, "Cash Transfers and Temptation Goods: A Review of Global Evidence," World Bank Policy Research Working Paper no. 6886, May 2014; and Paul Y. Yoo et al., "Unconditional Cash Transfers and Maternal Substance Use: Findings from a Randomized Control Trial of Low-Income Mothers with Infants in the U.S.," *BMC Public Health* 22 (2022).

16. Gary Mottola, "A Snapshot of Investor Households in America," FINRA Investor Education Foundation, September 2015.

17. Raj Chetty, Nathaniel Hendren, and Lawrence F. Katz, "The Effects of Exposure to Better Neighborhoods on Children: New Evidence from the Moving to Opportunity Experiment," *American Economic Review* 106, no. 4 (2016): 855–902.

18. Although more states have authorized lump-sum payments than any other type of diversion program, the Department of Health and Human Services reports that these programs are rarely used in practice. Montana, Utah, and Virginia appear to have the most extensive experience with the concept. "Table I.A.1: Formal Diversion Payments," TANF Policy Tables, Welfare Rules Database, Urban Institute.

19. "Table I.A.1: Formal Diversion Payments."

20. Carmen Solomon-Fears, "Welfare Reform: Diversion as an Alternative to TANF Benefits," Congressional Research Service, RL30230, June 16, 2006.

IMPROVING LIVING STANDARDS

CHILDCARE

BY RYAN BOURNE

THE ISSUE: STATE AND FEDERAL POLICIES MAKE CHILDCARE MORE EXPENSIVE, THUS WEAKENING PARENTAL CHOICE, WORK INCENTIVES, AND LABOR FLUIDITY

Childcare in the United States is expensive, particularly in some of the country's wealthiest places. High prices hit poorer American workers in the pocketbook and reduce financial payoffs to changing jobs, working more hours, or moving to higher-cost states or cities for better work opportunities.

Child Care Aware of America data show that, for 2020, full-time center-based care for an infant cost an average of $24,400 per year in Washington, DC, and $22,600 in Massachusetts.[1] Family care—that is, childcare in the home of the childcare worker—in these states is cheaper, but it still came in at $18,400 and $14,000, respectively. Given that these figures are averages, they mask much higher prices for childcare in certain counties.

In some states, childcare is significantly cheaper. In Mississippi and Arkansas, for example, full-time center-based infant care costs, on average, only $5,800 and $6,400 annually. But, relative to incomes (which are also lower in these states), childcare in these states is still a very large expense for working families.

For example, average annual prices for center-based infant care for one child in Mississippi (the most affordable state) still reach 7.3 percent of a married couple's median income. This share rises to as high as 16.7 percent in California, despite the state's higher pay. For households that earn less than the median income, childcare costs can potentially take up huge chunks of the family budget. The United States vies with Switzerland and the United Kingdom for having the highest net out-of-pocket childcare costs for an illustrative two-earner family.[2]

For single-parent households on the margins of the workforce, the cost of formal childcare can be astounding. The price of full-time center-based care ranges from 26.3 percent of median income in South Dakota to a huge 79.4 percent in the District of Columbia (see Figure 1). Although these figures may not represent all single-parent households' lived experiences, given their actual childcare choices, the data nevertheless show how unaffordable formal childcare is for single parents. Importantly, it may be that many poorer families are forced into using informal services due to the high costs of formal care, contrary to their true preferences.

The cost of childcare has recently become even more salient because the pandemic has reduced the dwindling supply of childcare services and workers. Between December 2019 and March 2021, the number of home-based and center-based childcare providers decreased by 6,957 and 8,899, respectively.[3] Although much of this decline was driven by a collapse in demand as parents stayed home, it is widely reported that caregivers are leaving the profession permanently, leading to significant staffing difficulties at childcare businesses around the country.[4]

FIGURE 1 On average, childcare costs were 26 to 79 percent of single parent median income in 2020

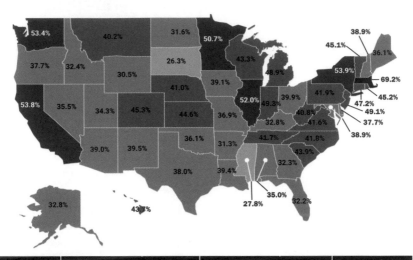

State	Percent of single-parent median income	State	Percent of single-parent median income	State	Percent of single-parent median income
District of Columbia	79.4%	Wisconsin	43.3%	Oregon	37.7%
Massachusetts	69.2%	Pennsylvania	41.9%	Missouri	36.9%
New York	53.9%	North Carolina	41.8%	Maine	36.1%
California	53.8%	Tennessee	41.7%	Oklahoma	36.1%
Washington	53.4%	Virginia	41.6%	Nevada	35.5%
Illinois	52.0%	Nebraska	41.0%	Alabama	35.0%
Minnesota	50.7%	West Virginia	40.8%	Utah	34.3%
Indiana	49.3%	Montana	40.2%	Alaska	32.8%
New Jersey	49.1%	Ohio	39.9%	Kentucky	32.8%
Michigan	48.9%	New Mexico	39.5%	Idaho	32.4%
Connecticut	47.2%	Louisiana	39.4%	Georgia	32.3%
Colorado	45.3%	Iowa	39.1%	Florida	32.2%
Rhode Island	45.2%	Arizona	39.0%	North Dakota	31.6%
Vermont	45.1%	Maryland	38.9%	Arkansas	31.3%
Kansas	44.6%	New Hampshire	38.9%	Wyoming	30.5%
South Carolina	43.9%	Texas	38.0%	Mississippi	27.8%
Hawaii	43.7%	Delaware	37.7%	South Dakota	26.3%

Source: Child Care Aware of America, *Demanding Change: Repairing Our Child Care System* (Arlington, VA: Child Care Aware of America, February 2022).

Theory and evidence suggest that, if driven by a lack of workers or centers, higher childcare prices can worsen labor market outcomes, particularly for workers with lower levels of attachment to the labor market. For example, research from overseas, such as Powell (2002), has found that higher childcare prices reduce the propensity for parents to work.[5] In the United States, meanwhile, mothers' odds of full-time employment have been found to be lower, and part-time employment higher, in states with expensive childcare.[6] Of course, parents should be free to decide how best to care for their children, but it is nevertheless noteworthy that mothers spend more time caring for their own children both in states where childcare is more expensive and as childcare costs increase, after controlling for other factors.

Statistical analysis has also found that moving to a state with less-affordable childcare lowers the retention rates of married mothers in the labor market.[7] But this is only the observed effect: many relocations simply do not occur because of the deterrent to moving that these sorts of childcare cost differentials create. In other words, some families cannot move (for work or lifestyle reasons) because childcare costs in their desired destination are too high.

Expensive childcare therefore leads to parents being unable to afford the types of childcare they would prefer or that would be better suited to their work needs. This can create a barrier to better job matching, human capital accumulation, and physical mobility that could deliver higher wages or better opportunities, along with a more vibrant and productive economy overall.

That childcare is expensive is not—contrary to what many critics say—a "market failure" in need of government intervention. For starters, that prices tend to be disproportionately higher in places with high incomes might simply suggest that as we get richer, we demand more high quality childcare. Childcare may also suffer from "Baumol's cost disease" because it remains a labor-intensive service that is difficult to automate.[8] That is, as wages throughout the economy rise with productivity growth, childcare providers must compete for workers with other, higher-paying options, so we would imagine that this type of service would get relatively more expensive over time.

Baumol effects and rising incomes are not, however, the only factors putting upward pressure on childcare prices. Many government policies, particularly at the state level, raise the cost of providing childcare, thus constraining supply into the sector—both reducing its availability and raising prices without a proportionate improvement in quality or safety. These state-level requirements include staff-child ratio requirements, occupational licensing requirements, and zoning restrictions.

Staff-child ratio requirements. These requirements raise the net cost of providing childcare by reducing workers' revenue potential. This reduction either lowers wages for childcare providers, thus discouraging them from entering the sector, or makes it more expensive and complicated for some centers to operate at a given capacity, leading to fewer centers or home-based settings. Either way, the supply of childcare is reduced, increasing market prices.

Empirical research confirms that stringent staff-to-child ratios substantially increase prices with little beneficial effect on observed childcare quality. Thomas and Gorry (2015), for example, used variation in state regulation requirements and prices to estimate that loosening the staff-child ratio by just one child across all age groups (regulations tend to vary by child age) would reduce center-based care prices by 9–20 percent.[9] This echoed earlier research showing that increasing the number of children that any care provider could look after by two would reduce prices by 12 percent.[10]

These trends unsurprisingly affect American workers, particularly those with lower incomes. Thomas and Gorry's work shows, for example, that the higher prices associated with a tighter regulation are associated with a small but measurable fall in the number of mothers working.[11] In a separate paper, Hotz and Xiao (2011) found that the effects of these regulations are particularly regressive.[12] Using an extensive dataset across three census periods, the authors found that tightening the staff-child ratio by one child reduces the number of childcare centers in the average market by 9–11 percent without increasing employment at other centers. Crucially, this supply reduction occurs wholly in lower-income areas, leading to significant substitution to home daycare. In other words, this regulation reduces the availability of childcare in lower-income neighborhoods, making it more difficult for poor families to juggle childcare and work responsibilities while increasing prices, which can then deter other households from moving to that area.

Just as importantly, there is no evidence of a net quality benefit from tighter childcare ratio regulation. Contrary to the theory that a higher staff-to-child ratio will lead to more interaction time and better child development, meta-analyses have found "small, if any, associations with concurrent and subsequent child outcomes."[13] Advocates of government-imposed staff-child ratios also ignore the fact that if higher prices induced by regulation drive poorer households toward informal care settings or even out of work, the effects on those affected children's development are wholly unobserved.

Occupational licensing requirements. Educational qualifications and training requirements for caregivers have similarly large effects on childcare prices, albeit with more mixed effects on quality. The economic harms—reduced availability, higher prices, discriminatory effects, etc.—of occupational licensing in childcare services mirror those discussed generally in the Occupational Licensing chapter. Most obviously, tighter educational or training requirements further restrict the pool of potential childcare providers, thus increasing prices. Thomas and Gorry found that requiring lead providers to have even a high school diploma can increase prices by 25–46 percent. Hotz and Xiao likewise found that increasing the average required years of education of center directors by one year reduces the number of childcare centers in the average market by 3.2–3.6 percent.

That childcare experience and educational requirements vary widely by state calls into question the validity and necessity of the most restrictive childcare licensing regimes (as further discussed in the Occupational Licensing chapter). In California, for example, personnel in childcare centers must have at least 12 postsecondary semester credits in early childhood education and development and six months of experience working in a licensed center with children of the relevant age. Center directors must have four years of relevant experience in a center or, alternatively, a degree in child development with two years' experience.[14] In Washington, DC, recent restrictions are even more stringent: center directors must have a bachelor's degree in early childhood education, ordinary childcare providers in centers are required to have an associate's degree in early childhood education, and assistant teachers and home childcare providers need at least a Child Development Associate (CDA) credential by December 2023.[15]

The overall harms of these restrictive licensing systems disproportionately manifest themselves in low-income markets because related quality improvements (proxied by accreditation for the center) overwhelmingly occur in just high-income areas. These types of childcare regulations thus enshrine into law the policy preferences of wealthier childcare consumers but eliminate access and raise prices to formal childcare for poorer consumers, with little improvement in quality.

Zoning restrictions. As discussed in the Entrepreneurship and Home Businesses chapter, many state and local governments have considered home daycares a "problem use" and have therefore used zoning restrictions to ban them. Such restrictions reduce the availability of childcare in the affected neighborhoods and further increase the price of childcare services.

Childcare regulation is overwhelmingly a state responsibility, but the federal government plays a role in two important ways: restrictive federal immigration policies and federal childcare subsidies.

Restrictive federal immigration policies. The supply of potential childcare workers, au pairs, and babysitters is further reduced through lengthy foreign labor certification processes, low visa caps, and limited visa availability for nannies living outside the home of care. Despite these restrictions, more than 20 percent of childcare workers (around 318,400) in 2019 were foreign-born (more than half of those were noncitizens), with substantial benefits for American parents. Cortes (2008) found, for example, that for every 10 percent increase in low-skilled immigrants among the labor force, prices for "immigrant-intensive services," including childcare, fell by 2 percent.[16] Furtado (2015), meanwhile, showed "immigrant inflows are associated with reductions in the cost of childcare and other household services," allowing high-skilled native mothers to work more or have more children.[17] And East and Velasquez (2022) have found that new immigration restrictions tend to reduce these same individuals' labor supply.[18]

Federal childcare subsidies. Meanwhile, federal subsidies entrench onerous state childcare regulations. The Childcare Development Block Grant authorizes and governs the federal childcare subsidy program known as the Child Care and

Development Fund (CCDF), which provides financial assistance to low-income families. The Child Care and Development Block Grant (CCDBG) Act of 2014 requires that providers receiving grant funds meet group size limits, age-specific child-to-provider ratios, and staff qualification requirements, as determined by the state—regulations that, as noted above, reduce supply and increase prices.[19]

THE POLICY SOLUTIONS: LOOSEN STATE REGULATION OF CHILDCARE STAFFING AND LICENSING AND OF HOME-BASED BUSINESSES; EXPAND IMMIGRATION; AND REFORM FEDERAL CHILDCARE SUBSIDIES

Even though rising childcare prices are not a conventional market failure, policymakers and much of the public see it as a problem requiring government action. However, the most common proposals to counteract high out-of-pocket costs largely entail shifting them from parents to taxpayers through state and federal subsidies. The COVID-19 relief bill of March 2021, for example, included $39 billion in childcare subsidies, and President Biden has demanded a major new subsidy program for childcare as part of his Build Back Better legislation.

Subsidies, however, can *worsen*, rather than improve, the affordability problem while also constraining options for certain groups. Around the world, subsidy eligibility requirements associated with childcare subsidies tend to crowd out the use of home-based care. While parents often say they prefer these arrangements, estimates show that 75 percent of children in America receiving subsidies through the Childcare Development Fund are cared for in a childcare center.[20] Furthermore, under the recent Democratic plan, families would either be granted a voucher to use at certain providers or be able to request a government-subsidized slot. This will push up demand, raising prices for those who do not enjoy subsidized care. Or if the subsidy levels are set too low to cover provider costs, then providers might be driven out of business. Subsidies also inevitably come with regulatory strings that raise the costs of provision or lessen the availability of care in certain geographic locations by making it unprofitable.[21]

Rather than throwing taxpayer dollars at demand-side subsidies, legislators should reform policies that contribute to childcare being so expensive in the first place. The best solution to high childcare costs would be for state governments to repeal legislation that entrenches regressive childcare regulations. In a more open and diverse market, providers would still have to work to provide the types of care that households want. Indeed, one can imagine childcare facilities working to deliver voluntary accreditation regimes to assure parents of staff-child ratios or the educational backgrounds of their childcare workers if that is what some parents desire. But this kind of quality assurance does not need to be provided by government, particularly in the internet age where reviews are easily accessible. Voluntary standards are common and successful in other important markets (e.g., food portion sizes), and there is no reason to think that such an approach would not work in childcare too.

State governments should desire a free market in childcare, which would deliver pluralism in the forms of care available to parents, based on their own needs and assessments of quality. There is no inherent reason why a wide range of options should be unavailable, given the large numbers of people with experience caring for children. This would free parents to choose whom to pay to care for their children according to their own preferences about the features of the service, whether that be through babysitters, au pairs, nannies, reciprocal after-school parent arrangements, home daycare, or formal centers.

If full repeal of these sorts of staffing regulations is impossible politically (as it likely is), states can still undertake several specific reforms to reduce childcare costs and help parents. First, given that the industry is so labor-intensive, achieving the biggest price savings requires encouraging states to loosen regulations on childcare staff. These rules are often justified as ensuring children's health and safety, or improving child development outcomes, but often seem to have more to do with protecting large institutional childcare providers or raising salaries for certain workers.

Restrictive staff-to-child ratios and educational occupational licensing requirements on caregivers are especially ripe for reform. The evidence that ratio regulation and staff educational requirements have such a regressive impact on the availability and cost of childcare suggests that these rules—if they cannot be repealed entirely—should be relaxed to expand supply and allow consumers to choose their level of care, subject to a more reasonable regulatory baseline.

Second, liberalizing zoning codes to allow more home daycares to operate in the relevant jurisdictions is another obvious reform to increase childcare supply. As discussed in the Entrepreneurship and Home Businesses chapter, policymakers in at least 18 states —concerned about the rising cost of childcare—have already passed laws to preempt excessively tight local zoning restrictions on home daycares.[22] States should also relax or rescind overly prescriptive rules about the structural layout of childcare properties. In California, for example, childcare facilities must have at least 25 square feet of indoor space and 75 square feet of outdoor space per child.

Third, the federal government should make it easier for migrants—particularly low-skilled migrants—to move here, thus increasing the supply of potential caregivers and further reducing childcare prices. As already mentioned, evidence suggests the arrival of low-skilled immigrants in the United States toward the end of the 20th century led to substantial cost reductions, while also increasing fertility rates of U.S. citizens (allowing more people to have the number of children they would like and could afford in a better policy environment).[23] This effect would be even more powerful for childcare costs in a world where the state regulatory barriers to new childcare supply had been relaxed.

Finally, Congress should abolish direct federal childcare subsidies entirely. Any subsidies to parents should instead take the form of simple strings-free cash transfers to those in need so that parents can decide how best to use those funds in line with their children's and family's specific needs. (See the Welfare Reform chapter for more.) Short of this change in approach, Congress should amend the CCDF and CCDBG programs by removing the link between funds and state childcare regulations to discourage these types of regulation and encourage the aforementioned reforms.

ACTION PLAN

Short of the full repeal of state childcare staffing regulations, state governments should strive to pare down the stringency of existing rules through legislative revisions or curbing the power of relevant agencies.

At a minimum, state governments should amend the relevant laws and regulations to

- relax mandated staff-to-child ratios for children of all ages;
- eliminate any outdoor space requirement regulations;
- carve out exemptions to, or preempt, zoning codes that restrict home-based childcare businesses; and
- repeal licensing provisions that require childcare providers or center directors to hold bachelor's degrees, associate's degrees, or Child Development Associate qualifications.

Meanwhile, Congress should

- eliminate, or at least liberalize, the current statutory restrictions on the visa categories most commonly used for immigrant childcare workers, such as the J-1 visa for au pairs and the EB-3 immigrant visa, while expanding other visa programs such as the H-2B visa for unskilled workers;[24]
- exempt childcare workers from the EB-3 immigrant visa cap and expand the H-2B visa to year-round work rather than limiting its use to seasonal jobs;
- encourage removal of the J-1 au pair program's age cap of 26 and English proficiency requirement, which may be unnecessary in certain childcare settings. Processing of these visas should also be accelerated; and
- amend the CCDF and CCDBG programs to eliminate the link between federal funds and state childcare regulations.

NOTES

1. Child Care Aware of America, *Appendices of Demanding Change: Repairing Our Child Care System* (Arlington, VA: Child Care Aware of America, February 2022).

2. "Net Childcare Costs for Parents Using Childcare Facilities," Organisation for Economic Co-operation and Development, 2021.

3. Child Care Aware of America, *Demanding Change: Repairing Our Child Care System* (Arlington, VA: Child Care Aware of America, February 2022).

4. Child Care Aware of America, *Demanding Change*.

5. Lisa M. Powell, "Joint Labor Supply and Childcare Choice Decisions of Married Mothers," *Journal of Human Resources* 37, no. 1 (Winter 2002): 106–28.

6. Leah Ruppanner, Stephanie Moller, and Sayer Liana, "Expensive Childcare and Short School Days = Lower Maternal Employment and More Time in Childcare? Evidence from the American Time Use Survey," *Socius: Sociological Research for a Dynamic World* 5, (2019): 1–14.

7. Christin Landivar, Liana Ruppanner, and William J. Scarborough, "Are States Created Equal? Moving to a State with More Expensive Childcare Reduces Mothers' Odds of Employment," *Demography* 58, no. 2 (2021): 451–70.

8. See, for example, Eric Helland and Alexander Tabarrok, *Why Are the Prices So Damn High? Health, Education, and the Baumol Effect* (Arlington, VA: Mercatus Center at George Mason University, 2019).

9. Diana W. Thomas and Devon Gorry, "Regulation and the Cost of Child Care," Mercatus Center Working Paper, August 2015.

10. Randal Heeb and Rebecca M. Kilburn, "The Effects of State Regulations on Childcare Prices and Choices," RAND Labor and Population Working Paper, January 2004.

11. Thomas and Gorry, "Regulation and the Cost of Child Care."

12. V. Joseph Hotz and Mo Xiao, "The Impact of Regulations on the Supply and Quality of Care in Child Care Markets," *American Economic Review* 101, no. 5 (August 2011): 1775–805.

13. Michal Perlman et al., "Child-Staff Ratios in Early Childhood Education and Care Settings and Child Outcomes: A Systematic Review and Meta-Analysis," *PLOS ONE*, January 19, 2017.

14. "Child Care Center Provider Requirements," State of California—Health and Human Services Agency, Department of Social Services.

15. See "Center Director New Educational Requirements," Office of the State Superintendent of Education, DC.gov; "Teacher New Educational Requirements," Office of the State Superintendent of Education, DC.gov; and "Assistant Teacher New Educational Requirements," Office of the State Superintendent of Education, DC.gov.

16. "Occupation Recode for 2018 and Later Based on 2018 OCC Codes (OCCP): PRS-Childcare Workers, by Citizenship Status," U.S. Census Bureau, ACS 1-Year Estimates Public Use Microdata Sample; and Patricia Cortes, "The Effect of Low-Skilled Immigration on U.S. Prices: Evidence from CPI Data," *Journal of Political Economy* 116, no. 3 (June 2008): 381–422.

17. Delia Furtado, "Immigrant Labor and Work-Family Decisions of Native-Born Women," *IZA World of Labor* (2015): 1–10.

18. Chloe N. East and Andrea Velasquez, "Unintended Consequences of Immigration Enforcement: Household Services and High-Educated Mothers' Work," *Journal of Human Resources,* forthcoming, 2022.

19. "Child Care and Development Block Grant Act (CCDBG) of 2014: Plain Language Summary of Statutory Changes," Office of Child Care, Administration for Children and Families, November 18, 2014.

20. "Characteristics of Families Served by the Child Care and Development Fund (CCDF) Based on Preliminary FY2019 Data," Office of Child Care, Administration for Children and Families.

21. Ryan Bourne, "The 'Build Back Better' Childcare Disaster," *Cato at Liberty* (blog), Cato Institute, October 22, 2021.

22. Anika Singh Lemar, "The Role of States in Liberalizing Land Use Regulations," *North Carolina Law Review* 97, no. 2 (January 2019): 293–354.

23. Delia Furtado, "Fertility Responses of High-Skilled Native Women to Immigrant Inflows," *Demography* 53, (2016): 27–53.

24. "Visa Options for Nannies and Childcare Workers," Khalique Law PLLC, March 22, 2022.

K-12 EDUCATION

BY NEAL MCCLUSKEY

THE ISSUE: COMPULSORY, "ONE-SIZE-FITS-SOME" K-12 PUBLIC EDUCATION DOES NOT MEET STUDENTS' AND PARENTS' DIVERSE NEEDS AND COSTS A GREAT DEAL FOR THE OUTCOMES WE GET

Elementary and secondary schooling is important to the workforce and economy, tasked with providing the next generation of American workers with foundational skills and knowledge. But the current system—dominated by an archaic, stagnant government schooling model—is ineffective for far too many students while costing taxpayers large sums of money. It also foments needless cultural strife. As a result, K–12 education in the United States has become more of an anchor than an engine for society and the economy.

The current system may seem set in stone: students start attending public schools at age five, to which they are assigned by their home addresses at the time. They then progress through elementary, middle, and high schools and graduate at the age of 18, hopefully prepared to enter the workforce or go to college. This is not, however, how education has always been delivered in the United States. Compulsory schooling, in fact, was not adopted in all states until the early 20th century, and regular widespread use of public schooling was also limited until around that same time (see Figures 1 and 2).[1]

Public schooling grew only in fits and starts, largely because families were already obtaining education in accordance with their needs. "Book learning," such as reading, writing, and arithmetic, was complemented by learning real-world skills such as farming (working with parents) or other trades (through apprenticeships). Meanwhile, the primary goal of mass public schooling for many of its early advocates was not preparing children for a successful work life but turning them into patriotic members of their states and country who shared basic Protestant beliefs and supported the American system of government.

As the country became increasingly industrialized, the attention of elites was directed toward getting more children into schools in order to remove them from the workforce (for their sake and to end competition with older laborers); to assimilate immigrants; and to create an "efficient" system that identified children's abilities and prepared them for the type of work, often industrial, for which experts deemed them suited.[2] Major parts of this reform included larger districts and schools, including high schools; ability tracking based on IQ tests; and overall "scientific" management.

Yet even as work in the United States has changed radically since the 1940s, the basic structure of K–12 education has remained essentially unchanged. The policy goal, on the other hand, has evolved from mainly workforce and character development to academic achievement, precipitated by shocks such as the Cold War

FIGURE 1 Near-ubiquitous public school enrollment is a relatively recent phenomenon in the United States

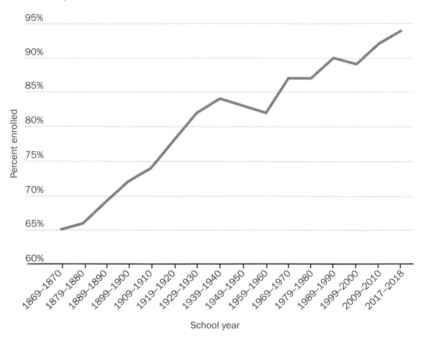

Source: U.S. Department of Education, National Center for Education Statistics, Digest of Education Statistics, 2020.

technology race and the 1983 federal report "A Nation at Risk," which decried falling academic performance and its impact on American global competitiveness.[3] A new focus on standards and accountability to improve academic achievement resulted in the 2002 No Child Left Behind Act (NCLB), which mandated nationwide math and reading proficiency by 2014, as determined by state standardized tests, and imposed penalties for public schools failing to make adequate yearly progress toward that goal. Further centralization occurred with the Common Core in 2010, a federally supported effort to have all students use the same curricular standards and to measure their progress with shared standardized tests. Amid a bipartisan backlash against this trend, Congress passed the 2015 Every Student Succeeds Act, which ended the goal of adequate yearly progress and federal Common Core coercion.

The demise of standards-based reform reflects diverse Americans seeing education as being about many things—character development, creativity, and more—not merely about standardized test scores. But public schooling is inherently one-size-must-fit-all, with all families in a district required to pay taxes for it, and policies increasingly made at the state and federal levels. The NCLB-based

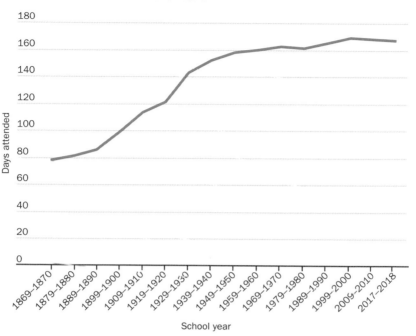

FIGURE 2 Widespread regular public school attendance did not become the norm until after World War II

Days attended (y-axis): 0, 20, 40, 60, 80, 100, 120, 140, 160, 180

School year (x-axis): 1869–1870, 1879–1880, 1889–1890, 1899–1900, 1909–1910, 1919–1920, 1929–1930, 1939–1940, 1949–1950, 1959–1960, 1969–1970, 1979–1980, 1989–1990, 1999–2000, 2009–2010, 2017–2018

Source: U.S. Department of Education, National Center for Education Statistics, Digest of Education Statistics, 2020.

system put almost all children on a test-centric curriculum with a heavy emphasis on college enrollment, an endpoint that looked like the best outcome to policy-makers but that is not well suited to students who are poor test-takers, are interested in hard-to-test creative pursuits, or want technical skills training.

Indeed, college often does not produce what employers are seeking: employees with hard, up-to-date skills, not just theoretical knowledge. To make up for that, many employers take college grads and put them through expensive on-the-job training in what they will actually do.[4]

High schools' inattention to non-college career paths is particularly concerning given the high cost of college and the hundreds of thousands of high school students who annually enter the workforce immediately upon graduating.[5] As discussed in the Introduction, American workers today are far more likely to work in services and jobs that require creativity and "soft skills" than they are to be put in shifts on an assembly line, and many non-college jobs can be lucrative and rewarding. Today's public schools, however, leave students unprepared for many jobs because the main goal of K–12 schooling is test scores and college attendance, not career and technical education.

Even for families focused on college, public schooling is too often unresponsive. The pandemic starkly illustrated this problem, with many public schools remaining closed to in-person instruction even as the COVID-19 danger subsided and many parents needed to return to work, leaving them scrambling for childcare arrangements.[6] Recent studies, such as Goldhaber et al. (2021), have found that these remote-learning arrangements imposed substantial costs on students, both academically and emotionally, and forced many parents to work fewer hours or exit the workforce entirely.[7] Meanwhile, private schools, which must attract paying families to stay in business, were much more likely to have returned to in-person instruction.[8]

In addition to being hidebound, public K–12 education has become increasingly costly, without providing commensurate improvements in the academic achievement on which it has been focused. As Figure 3 shows, inflation-adjusted per student spending on K–12 education in the United States has grown markedly over the decades, from $6,427 in the 1970–1971 school year to $15,621 in 2018–2019, a more than 143 percent increase. Of course, this is the average; some jurisdictions spend appreciably more, including an average total annual expenditure per pupil of $26,799 in New York State and nearly $30,000 in the District of Columbia.[9]

FIGURE 3 Inflation-adjusted, per pupil spending on public schooling has increased more than 143 percent since 1970

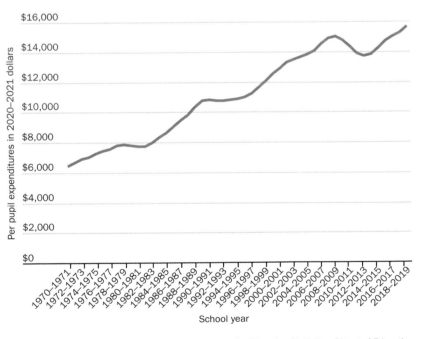

Source: U.S. Department of Education, National Center for Education Statistics, Digest of Education Statistics, 2021.

These expenditures totaled almost $800 billion in 2018–2019 and are paid by current and future American workers through various taxes, with state and local (especially property tax) sources constituting the vast majority of revenues.[10] Thus, "free" public education is anything but.

High and ever-increasing per student expenses might be acceptable if the public K–12 system were achieving commensurate gains in student performance, but test scores for the "final products" of our public schooling system--high school seniors—have been basically stagnant for decades. As shown in Figure 4, the share of U.S. students scoring in the top level on the long-term-trend National Assessment of Educational Progress (NAEP), a federal test given to a representative sample of students that is comparable across time, has hovered around 7 percent in math and 6 percent in reading since the 1970s.

The long-term NAEP has not been reported for 17-year-olds since 2012, but the "main" NAEP results for essentially the same group, although less comparable from beginning to end, reveal similar trends. As shown in Figure 5, the share of test-takers scoring "proficient" on this test declined between 1992 and 2019 for

FIGURE 4 Despite more spending, the share of 17-year-olds achieving top National Assessment of Educational Progress scores has stagnated since 1970

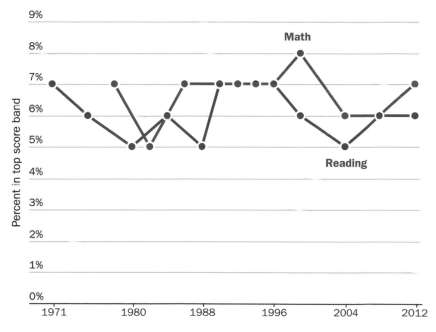

National Center for Education Statistics, National Assessment of Educational Progress, Long-term Trend: Summary of Major Findings, 2012.

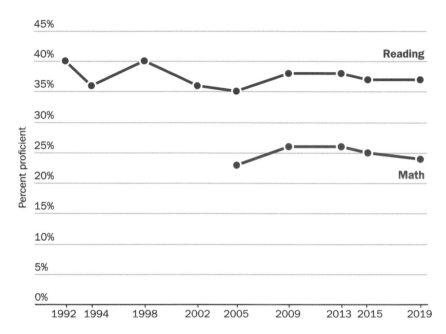

FIGURE 5 The percentage of 12th graders scoring proficient on the National Assessment of Educational Progress exam has stagnated in the 21st century

Source: National Center for Education Statistics, National Assessment of Educational Progress.

reading and stagnated in math between 2005 and 2019. Per pupil spending, meanwhile, rose from $10,713 in the 1992–1993 school year to $14,022 in 2005–2006 and then to $15,621 in 2018–2019.

Results have been better for younger students and many racial or other student subgroups over time, but the final broad results for high school seniors show that greatly increased taxes and spending have not produced lasting academic benefits for the K–12 system's "end product" (students graduating from high school and moving into the workforce or higher education). And this stagnation has occurred as overall wealth has increased markedly, with real per capita gross domestic product rising from $24,303 in 1970 to $58,619 in 2019—thus, worsening living conditions cannot explain poor K–12 progress.[11]

Even working families that prefer the system's focus on academic achievement and college admission have been forced to spend more every year to achieve essentially the same ultimate objective.

THE POLICY SOLUTIONS: LET FAMILIES CONTROL FUNDING AND GIVE EDUCATORS AUTONOMY TO CREATE DIVERSE DELIVERY METHODS AND CONTENT

American elementary and secondary education is essentially a government monopoly, with immediate control by elected school boards and heavy direction from state and the federal governments. It also is the victim of "capture" by people employed by the schools and their associations because most students cannot vote, and parents' time is mostly taken up by their jobs and raising their children. Thus, teacher unions and administrator groups have the most potent combination of personal stakes and ability to act on them. They no doubt care about school children, but they also have normal human incentives to maximize their pay/membership and to minimize their accountability to others. This employee capture and government schools' market power have rendered the system inefficient and unresponsive to the needs of the country's diverse children and families. K–12 education needs to be fundamentally changed, with funding following individual students so that families can choose among myriad educational models and objectives.

There are many ways to effectuate this change, starting with vouchers, which allow government funding to follow a child to a chosen school. Another option is tax-credit-connected education savings accounts (ESAs), in which people donate funds to groups that put the money into savings accounts on which families can draw for expenses such as private school tuition, tutoring, or therapies for children with disabilities. Under such ESAs, donors receive tax credits for their contributions, giving families maximum choice and giving funders the freedom to direct donations to approaches that work. And because no one is compelled to fund these choices or participate in the program, incentives to demand heavy regulation of the program are minimized.

Short of private school choice is charter schooling, in which private groups ask public entities for permission to run a public school that is free of many rules and regulations governing traditional public schools. Accountability comes from having to attract enough families to fund operations and meeting performance objectives laid out in the school's charter. Charter schooling is much more limited than private school choice because charter schools are public schools and hence are subject to standardized testing and punishments for underperformance. Charter schools are also often still subject to many public schooling regulations and cannot be religious. Charter schools can, though, specialize in areas like career and technical education, the arts, and more, making charter schooling preferable to traditional public schooling.

This new educational system would encourage diversity of educational options and competition among providers, thus increasing quality and innovation, tempering costs, inhibiting regulatory capture, and meeting the varied needs of *all* students. Research has repeatedly shown that more competition drives public schools to improve their academic performance, making choice the proverbial tide that lifts all boats.[12] Research also suggests that students randomly selected into voucher programs perform better on standardized tests than students who applied but did not receive a voucher, though not by much (and outcomes vary by program).[13] That said, these latter results may well be because private schools typically are not as focused on standardized tests, especially state tests, as are public schools. Thus, private school scores are less likely to reflect testing strategies or a long-term fixation on testing.

More choice would also produce significant cost savings: while the national average per pupil expenditure in public schools is nearly $16,000, average private school tuition is about $12,000.[14] Private schools often have revenue sources in addition to tuition, but were American families given $12,000, it would open access to numerous schools while significantly easing tax burdens that the current system places on today's families and future generations.

Freedom from state standards and testing mandates would maximize educational variety, allowing educators to provide offerings tailored to the needs of unique subsets of children. Autonomy over teacher hiring, school hours, school calendars, and more is also important. But perhaps the greatest advantage of expanded school choice is that schools would need to attract families to stay in business, thus making them more responsive to family needs. This dynamic played out during the pandemic, with private schools much more likely to be open in-person than public schools and more likely to satisfy parents.[15]

Expanded choice allows families to select arrangements that are best for them and their children; it is also the best path forward to efficiently and effectively train the future American workforce. As the Higher Education chapter details, for many people the returns on a four-year college education cannot justify the increasingly high cost of tuition and student debt. With cultural attitudes warming to careers that do not require a college degree (and many employers eager to offer them), moreover, there has been renewed interest in career and technical options for high-school-age students. For example, farming equipment manufacturer John Deere has created an apprenticeship program open to high school students.[16] Nazareth Prep in Pittsburgh coordinates apprenticeships for students in the Manchester Craftsmen's Guild, Energy Innovation Center, and Carnegie Science Center.[17]

Schools might also prepare students for other types of employment through essentially early internships. For example, Cristo Rey Catholic schools—a network of 38 schools enrolling about 12,300 students—partner with local companies for which students work part-time and the businesses provide the schools some funding, a win-win-win scenario. In 2011, IBM helped found the P-TECH school in New York City, where students prepare for "new collar" jobs that require postsecondary training but not a full degree.[18] Were educational choice more widespread, such options would no doubt be greater. Also, directly funding students allows families to freely choose these alternatives, mitigating concerns about racially or otherwise biased "tracking" (dividing students into classes based on their perceived abilities) and making it more likely that students want to learn in these environments rather than being shunted there.

ACTION PLAN

There is much that federal and state governments and school districts can do to decentralize elementary and secondary education so that it is much less constrained and more responsive to families and students.

Congress should

- change federal law to allow districts to choose among numerous tests so that they can have more flexibility in what they provide—the Every Student Succeeds Act is less prescriptive than NCLB but still mandates that all public schools use state standards and administer state tests; and
- consider significant cuts to federal K–12 spending because there is no constitutional authority for it, and use block grants to distribute what funds remain to states.

State governments should

- enact private school choice, preferably tax-credit-connected education savings accounts, in which donors to groups that bundle ESAs get income, property, or other tax credits for their donations;[19]
- consider coupling ESAs with personal-use credits for families that pay for private school;
- consider scholarship tax credits, in which donors to private school scholarship funds receive tax credits;
- consider ESAs that receive deposits directly from the state;
- consider vouchers, which involve direct state funding only for private school tuition, if other private school choice vehicles are unavailable; and
- pursue charter schooling only if private school choice is politically impossible. Regulations should be minimized and full state funding should follow students to the schools.

Local districts should

- allow some part of district funding to follow students to schools of choice, if permitted by state law. There is no active example of this, but Douglas County, Colorado, enacted a local voucher program in 2011 that was struck down by the Colorado Supreme Court in 2015 for allowing vouchers to be used at religious schools;[20] and
- consider cutting property taxes, enabling residents to save money and use it for their individual needs.

NOTES

1. Michael S. Katz, "A History of Compulsory Education Laws," *Fastback* 75, Phi Delta Kappa Educational Foundation, 1976.

2. Moses Stambler, "The Effect of Compulsory Education and Child Labor Laws on High School Attendance in New York City, 1898–1917," *History of Education Quarterly* 8, no. 2 (Summer 1968): 189–214; David B. Tyack, *The One Best System: A History of American Urban Education* (Cambridge, MA: Harvard University Press, 1974), 126-146.

3. National Commission on Excellence in Education, *A Nation at Risk: The Imperative for Educational Reform* (Washington: U.S. Department of Education, 1983).

4. Dana Wilkie, "Employers Say College Grads Lack Hard Skills, Too," Society for Human Resource Management, October 21, 2019.

5. "College Enrollment and Work Activity of Recent High School and College Graduates Summary," Bureau of Labor Statistics, April 16, 2022.

6. Abha Bhattarai, "'I'm Barely Clinging onto Work': Exhausted Parents Face Another Wave of School Shutdowns," *Washington Post,* January 8, 2022.

7. See Dan Goldhaber et al., *The Consequences of Remote and Hybrid Instruction during the Pandemic* (Cambridge, MA: Center for Education Policy Research, Harvard University, 2022); and Tim Henderson, "Stateline: Working Parents Face Continued Chaos Despite Reopened Schools," Pew Research Center, February 24, 2022.

8. Michael B. Henderson, Paul E. Peterson, and Martin R. West, "Pandemic Parent Survey Finds Perverse Pattern: Students Are More Likely to Be Attending School in Person Where COVID Is Spreading More Rapidly," *Education Next* 21, no. 2 (Spring 2021): 34–49.

9. "Table 236.75: Total and Current Expenditures per Pupil in Fall Enrollment in Public Elementary and secondary Schools, by Function and State or Jurisdiction: 2018–19," Digest of Education Statistics, 2021, U.S. Department of Education, National Center for Education Statistics.

10. "Table 236.20. Total Expenditures for Public Elementary and Secondary Education and Other Related programs, by Function and Subfunction: Selected Years, 1990--91 through 2018–19," Digest of Education Statistics, 2021, U.S. Department of Education, National Center for Education Statistics; and "Table 235.10. Revenues for Public Elementary and Secondary Schools, by Source of Funds: Selected Years, 1919–20 through 2018–19," Digest of Education Statistics, 2021, U.S. Department of Education, National Center for Education Statistics.

11. U.S. Bureau of Economic Analysis, "Real Fross Domestic Product per Capita [A939RX0Q048SBEA]," Federal Reserve Economic Data, Federal Reserve Bank of St. Louis, August 9, 2022.

12. "The 123s of School Choice: What the Research Says about Private School Choice Programs in America," EdChoice, April 1, 2022, pp. 25–30.

13. See EdChoice, "The 123s of School Choice," pp. 9–12.

14. "Average Private School Tuition Cost," Private School Review.

15. Corey A. DeAngelis and Neal McCluskey, "Decentralize K–12 Education," Cato Institute Pandemics and Policy series, September 15, 2020.

16. "John Deere Announces New Registered Apprenticeship Program," John Deere, July 17, 2019.

17. "Internship Program," Nazareth Prep.

18. "Learn about P-Tech's History," P-Tech.

19. Jason Bedrick, Jonathan Butcher, and Clint Bolick, "Taking Credit for Education: How to Fund Education Savings Accounts through Tax Credits," Cato Institute Policy Analysis no. 785, January 20, 2016.

20. Nic Garcia, "Douglas County Voucher Program Unconstitutional, Supreme Court Rules," *Chalkbeat: Colorado,* June 29, 2015.

HEALTH CARE

BY MICHAEL F. CANNON AND JEFFREY A. SINGER

THE ISSUE: FEDERAL AND STATE HEALTH CARE POLICIES INCREASE PRICES AND DECREASE SUPPLY AND INNOVATION

The health sector serves American workers poorly. Prices are sky-high. While the quality of care is often exceptional, in many areas quality is so low as to be dangerous to patients' health. The cause of these problems is a dense thicket of state and federal laws that deny workers the right to make their own decisions about their health care, including the right to control whether, to what extent, and where to spend their earnings on health care.

The tax code is the greatest obstacle to workers controlling their health care decisions. For nearly as long as there has been a federal income tax—and for longer than modern health insurance has existed—the federal tax code has effectively penalized workers unless they surrender a sizeable share of earnings to their employer; enroll in a health insurance plan the employer chooses, purchases, controls, and revokes upon separation; and pay any remaining portion of the insurance premium directly.

This system's implicit penalties are large. Suppose two jobs offer the same total compensation but one offers $22,221 in health benefits (the cost of the average employer-sponsored family plan in 2021), while the other instead offers $22,221 in cash wages. The federal tax code penalizes a worker who chooses the latter job: at a marginal tax rate of 33 percent, the tax code effectively creates a $7,333 per year penalty if the worker wants to take that $22,221 as cash in order to choose her own health plan. To avoid that implicit penalty, most (though not all) workers obtain health insurance through an employer.

Since employers finance health benefits by reducing cash wages and other compensation, this feature of the tax code denies workers control of a sizeable share of their income.[1] In the above hypothetical, the worker loses control over $22,221 of earnings, as well as her choice of health plan, to the employer. In 2022, workers, in the aggregate, lost control of nearly $1.3 trillion of their earnings—$944 billion that their employers paid toward employee health benefits, plus another $327 billion that workers paid directly. If workers declined their employers' health benefits and instead took that $1.3 trillion as cash wages, they would have had to pay a total of $352 billion in implicit penalties.

Employer-sponsored health insurance is therefore a compulsory system in which workers must participate on pain of higher taxes or criminal penalties if they fail to pay those higher taxes. Figure 1 shows that the $1.3 trillion that employers and workers spend on health benefits is the largest source of compulsory health spending in the United States. As Figures 2 and 3 show, the United States ranks ninth among advanced nations in terms of compulsory health spending as a share of overall health spending and first in terms of compulsory health spending as a share of gross domestic product (GDP), and the federal tax code is the principal reason why.

FIGURE 1 Employee health benefits are the largest source of compulsory health spending in the United States

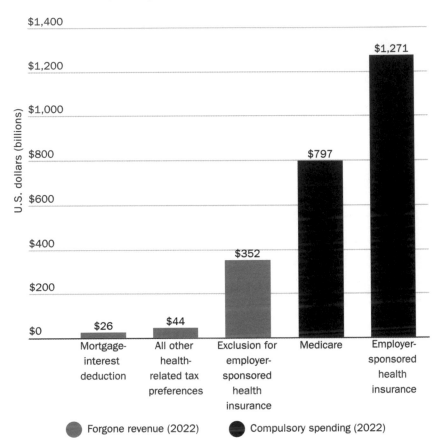

Sources: U.S. Office of Management and Budget, "Tax Expenditures," in *Analytical Perspectives: Budget of the U.S. Government, Fiscal Year 2022* (Washington: Government Publishing Office, 2021), pp. 111, 113; "The Budget and Economic Outlook: 2021 to 2031," Congressional Budget Office, February 2021, p. 5; Boards of Trustees, "2021 Annual Report of the Boards of Trustees of the Federal Hospital Insurance and Federal Supplementary Medical Insurance Trust Funds," Federal Hospital Insurance and Federal Supplementary Medical Insurance Trust Funds, August 31, 2021, p. 111; National Health Statistics Group, "Table 5-6—Private Health Insurance by Sponsor: Calendar Years 1987–2020," Office of the Actuary, Centers for Medicare & Medicaid Services, Department of Health and Human Services; National Health Statistics Group, "Table 16—National Health Expenditures (NHE), Amounts and Average Growth Annual Growth from Previous Year Shown, by Type or Sponsor, Selected Calendar Years 2011–2028," Office of the Actuary, Centers for Medicare & Medicaid Services, Department of Health and Human Services; and author's calculations.

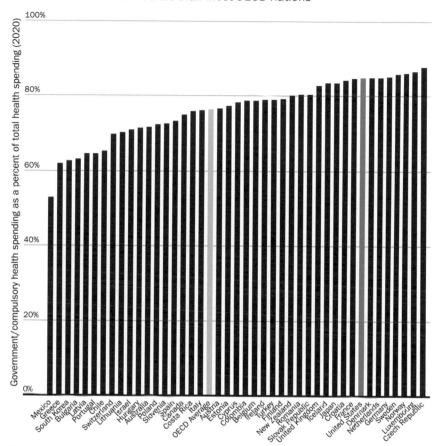

FIGURE 2 Compulsory spending comprises a larger share of health spending in the United States than most OECD nations

Source: "Health Spending: Government/Compulsory, % of Health Spending, 2020," Organisation for Economic Co-operation and Development, https://data.oecd.org/chart/6LrL.
Note: OECD = Organisation for Economic Co-operation and Development.

This feature of the federal tax code—the "tax exclusion" for employer-sponsored health insurance—has done enormous harm to workers. As Feldstein and Friedman (1977) wrote, "It can with justice be said that the tax [exclusion] has been responsible for much of the health care crisis."[2] The exclusion reduces access to quality, affordable health insurance and medical care in three ways.

First, it increases prices for health insurance and medical care. Since the tax code penalizes every dollar workers do not devote to health benefits, it encourages workers to demand excessive levels of health insurance coverage. Excessive coverage, in turn, leads to greater medical consumption and higher prices—because patients care less about both price and quantity when someone else is paying—

FIGURE 3 As a share of GDP, compulsory health spending is higher in the United States than any other OECD nation

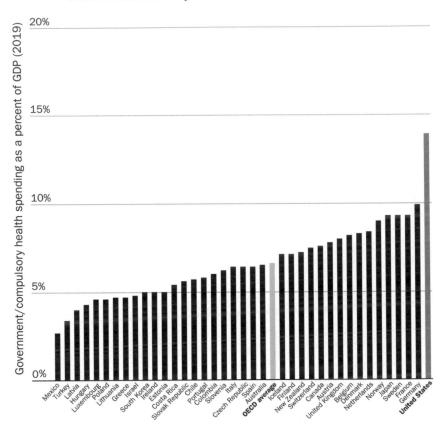

Source: "Health Spending: Government/Compulsory, % of GDP, 2020 or Latest Available," Organisation for Economic Co-operation and Development, https://data.oecd.org/chart/6CTC.
Note: OECD = Organisation for Economic Co-operation and Development; GDP = gross domestic product.

which, in turn, push health insurance premiums higher. Finkelstein (2007) estimated that the growth in health insurance in the latter part of the 20th century, of which the exclusion was a major driver, is responsible for half the growth in per capita health spending over that time.[3] Tilipman (2022) found that employers offer overly broad provider networks that leave the average worker $620 worse off per year.[4] By encouraging workers to consume excessive levels of health insurance and medical care, the exclusion creates a deadweight economic loss on the order of 1 percent of GDP (i.e., $230 billion in 2021).[5]

Second, the exclusion reduces choice, competition, and innovation in health care. Employers offer workers fewer health plan options than workers would have on the open market. Eighty percent of covered workers have only one or two health plan types from which to choose.[6] The exclusion also tilts the playing field in favor of particular ways of financing and delivering medical care (i.e., fee-for-service payment and fragmented delivery) at the expense of other payment arrangements (e.g., prepayment or capitation) and delivery systems (e.g., integrated health systems and coordinated care). The exclusion thus inhibits entry and competition by innovative health plans that reduce premiums and improve quality on dimensions where the health sector is weak.

Third, the exclusion has, for decades, stripped workers of their health insurance coverage after they get sick. The average worker changes jobs a dozen times by age 52.[7] Absent the exclusion, workers could purchase health insurance that remained with them between jobs—coverage that neither disappears nor charges higher premiums because an enrollee falls ill. As Professor Sherry Glied, an economic adviser to presidents Clinton and Obama, noted, "Before the passage of Medicare, many Americans over sixty-five were covered by health insurance policies that were guaranteed renewable for life" because more than 70 insurance companies offered such guaranteed-renewable health insurance.[8]

Instead, the exclusion penalizes workers unless they enroll in health insurance that automatically disappears when they change jobs, or when the employer drops coverage, or when enrollees lose a spouse to divorce or death, or when they age off a parent's plan, or when they retire, or when they become too sick to work. Workers in poor health are roughly twice as likely to end up with no insurance if they obtained coverage from a small employer versus purchasing it directly from an insurer.[9] Indeed, Congress created Medicare in 1965 in part because "many [workers] who had insurance coverage before retirement were unable to retain the coverage after retirement [...] because the policy was available to employed persons only."[10] Decade after decade, the tax code has penalized workers who choose secure health insurance and forced them into less-secure health insurance.

As the Employee Benefits chapter discusses further, these implicit penalties—and the insecure coverage on which they make workers dependent—lead to "job lock" and "entrepreneurship lock," where workers forgo better professional opportunities for fear of losing access to health insurance.[11] The exclusion reduces voluntary job turnover by 20 to 25 percent per year, which prevents workers "from making their preferred labor mobility choice, such as to change jobs, start a business, reduce work hours, or exit the labor force to stay home with children or retire."[12] Workers who have health insurance through their own employer are less likely to start or own their own businesses than workers who have health insurance through a spouse or Medicare.[13] Reducing worker mobility also increases employers' bargaining power and, given the linkage between job-to-job transitions and wage growth, may reduce workers' lifetime earnings.[14]

Yet, even after workers gain control of their health care dollars, numerous state and federal laws would still block them from using those dollars to obtain health care services that best suit their needs.

First, state clinician-licensing laws impede the widespread use of telehealth and erect barriers to the free flow of health care services across state lines. Patients are free to travel to another state to receive medical treatment from any doctor in that state. In most cases, however, patients cannot receive services from those same doctors at home via telemedicine. Most states allow clinicians to provide telehealth services to in-state patients only if the provider has a license from that state.[15] The ostensible purpose of clinician-licensing laws is to improve quality, but licensing actually inhibits quality by preventing patients from consulting with top specialists around the country.

The barriers that clinician-licensing laws create to interstate telehealth stem from the fact that states currently define the locus of the practice of medicine as the location of the patient. This arbitrary legal definition prevents patients from receiving services from a clinician who does not hold a license from the state where the patient is. Even if the clinician held licenses in all 49 other states, this rule would still strip the patient of the right to purchase services from that clinician.

Government licensing of clinicians leaves workers with fewer choices, higher prices, less convenient access to care, and fewer innovative services.

Second, clinician-licensing laws further decrease the available local supply of health care services and thus further increase prices. The effects of licensing restrictions became clear during the early days of the COVID-19 pandemic, when the governors of several of the hardest-hit states suspended licensing requirements to allow out-of-state practitioners to come to the aid of their states' residents.[16] These emergency actions tacitly recognized that clinician-licensing laws block access to care. As the Occupational Licensing chapter discusses, licensing restrictions discourage interstate mobility and employment in the relevant professions, while increasing the cost of related services.

Clinician-licensing laws also dictate what categories of clinicians may practice in the state and the specific services that each type of clinician may offer (i.e., the clinician's scope of practice). Questions about scope of practice typically descend into special-interest turf wars. When lobbyists for nurse practitioners and physician assistants seek to change laws so that their clients may practice independently of physicians or expand their scope of practice to meet their expertise— allowing them to compete with physicians to provide more services—lobbyists for physicians resist.[17]

State legislators are not competent to adjudicate such matters, so they side with whichever special-interest group has the most political clout. The American Medical Association boasts that it has blocked more than 100 attempts to expand midlevel clinicians' scopes of practice since 2019.[18] Patients, by contrast, have little say in the matter and end up paying higher prices because scope-of-practice restrictions prevent midlevel clinicians from providing services they are competent to perform at a lower price than physicians charge.

In response to the COVID-19 public health crisis, many states temporarily broadened many midlevel clinicians' scopes of practice. In rare cases, states have relaxed scope-of-practice restrictions for other reasons. To address the demand for health care professionals, for example, a growing number of states have abandoned the federal guideline that Certified Registered Nurse Anesthetists practice under the supervision of physicians.[19] In many states, certified registered nurse anesthetists can practice independently, providing broader access to anesthesia services, particularly in rural areas. In these cases, states are again implicitly admitting that clinician-licensing laws restrict access to care.

Third, state and federal laws also block physicians in foreign jurisdictions from providing medical care to willing U.S. patients. State licensing boards require international medical school graduates who have completed postgraduate specialty training and hold licenses to practice in other countries to repeat their entire postgraduate training in an accredited U.S. institution before receiving a state medical license. As a result, many foreign-trained doctors take positions in ancillary medical fields such as nursing, lab technician, or radiology technician instead of starting all over again. Government regulation deprives U.S. patients of the benefit of these physicians' human capital and the lower prices that would come with greater competition.

Finally, state "certificate of need" (CON) laws require providers to obtain government authorization before offering new services or opening or expanding health care facilities. These laws are not about ensuring new services or facilities meet minimum standards. Rather, they are about allowing the government to decide whether local health care markets need more competitors. Since incumbent providers heavily influence CON authorities, all too often the answer is "no." As of January 2022, 35 states and the District of Columbia had some form of CON law on the books, with the scope of restrictions varying widely.[20]

By restricting entry into health care markets, CON laws increase prices and negatively impact quality. A 2022 Palmetto Promise Institute review of dozens of academic studies found that CON laws correlate with higher per unit costs, higher expenditures, less access to care, and lower quality care.[21] They also render state health care systems sclerotic and unable to meet changes in demand, such as during public health emergencies. CON laws nevertheless persist because incumbent providers fiercely resist reform or repeal.

THE POLICY SOLUTIONS: EXPAND HEALTH SAVINGS ACCOUNTS; REMOVE BARRIERS TO INTERSTATE TELEHEALTH; ADOPT UNIVERSAL LICENSE RECOGNITION; EXPAND SCOPE OF PRACTICE LIMITATIONS; ALLOW FOREIGN DOCTORS TO PRACTICE HERE; AND REPEAL CERTIFICATE OF NEED LAWS

The most effective way to bring health insurance and health care within the reach of more workers is to drive down health care prices, and the most effective way to reduce health care prices is to make patients more cost-conscious. Figure 4, for example, summarizes a series of experiments that found cost-conscious patients forced providers to reduce prices by up to 32 percent over two years for services including hip and knee replacements, knee and shoulder arthroscopy, cataract removal, colonoscopy, CT and MRI scans, and laboratory tests.

The most important thing policymakers can do to make patients more cost-conscious is to return to workers the $1.3 trillion of earnings that the federal tax code puts under their employers' control. Returning those funds to workers would lead them to demand lower prices because they would reap the savings. It would also constitute an effective tax cut larger than the Reagan tax cuts of 1981, as Figure 5 shows.

Congress can deliver that $1.3 trillion tax cut by expanding tax-free health savings accounts (HSAs) and making the tax exclusion available only for HSA contributions. These accounts currently allow about 30 million workers to shield about $42 billion of their earnings per year from the exclusion's implicit penalties. This means HSAs currently reclaim for workers only about 4 percent of the $1 trillion of their earnings that the exclusion puts under their employers' control, as Figure 6 depicts.

Dramatically expanding HSAs would allow workers to take that $1 trillion as cash income that they control. The vast majority of workers could then deposit those funds in an HSA without any tax consequences. Returning control over that $1 trillion to the workers who earned it would put workers at the center of the health sector, create greater cost-consciousness, force providers and insurers to lower prices, and improve employment opportunities and independence by letting workers purchase secure health insurance that does not tie them to one employer. As the Independent Work chapter explains, freelancers, gig workers, and other independent workers should also be allowed to open and contribute tax-free funds to these expanded HSAs.

State and federal policymakers should also take steps to reduce or eliminate restrictions on the supply of health care services.

FIGURE 4 Cost-consciousness lowers prices

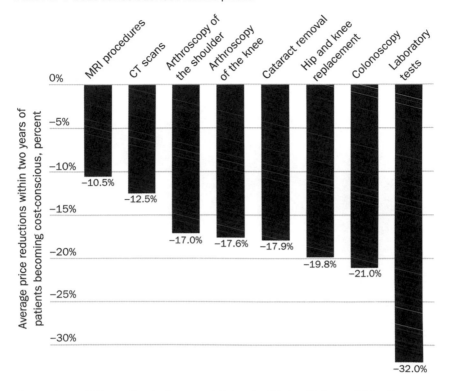

Source: James Robinson, Timothy Brown, and Christopher Whaley, "Reference Pricing Changes the 'Choice Architecture' of Health Care for Consumers," *Health Affairs* 36, no. 3 (March 2017), https://doi.org/10.1377/hlthaff.2016.1256.

First, states should eliminate obstacles to telehealth delivery across state lines. Doing so would increase access to care, enable patients to take advantage of expertise in areas of the country that may be otherwise beyond their reach, and increase competition among health care providers, thus lowering prices and improving quality of care. Early in the COVID-19 pandemic, many states temporarily removed barriers to the delivery of telehealth across state lines, but some of those measures have since lapsed.[22]

In 2021, however, Arizona learned from its pandemic experiences and became the first state to allow patients to receive telehealth services from clinicians in any state.[23] Out-of-state telehealth providers must obey Arizona's laws governing standards of care and scopes of practice. Arizona's professional licensing boards may review, discipline, and even ban out-of-state providers if they violate Arizona standards of care. They must show proof of malpractice insurance coverage. Patients may bring malpractice claims against out-of-state telehealth providers in Arizona courts. Other states and territories should follow Arizona's example.

FIGURE 5 Expanding health savings accounts would return a larger share of GDP to workers than past tax cuts

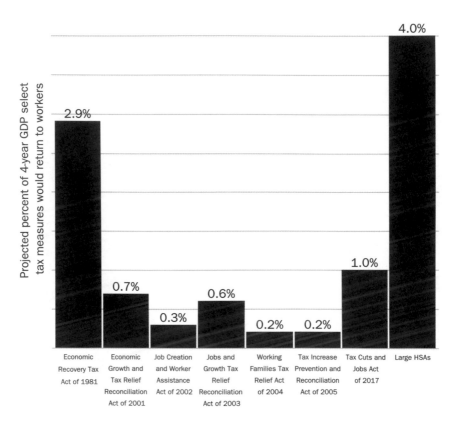

Sources: Jerry Tempalski, "Revenue Effects of Major Tax Bills, Updated Tables for all 2012 Bills," Office of Tax Analysis, Department of the Treasury, February 2013; National Health Statistics Group, "Table 5-6—Private Health Insurance by Sponsor: Calendar Years 1987–2020," Office of the Actuary, Centers for Medicare & Medicaid Services, Department of Health and Human Services; and National Health Statistics Group, "Table 16—National Health Expenditures (NHE), Amounts and Average Growth Annual Growth from Previous Year Shown, by Type or Sponsor, Selected Calendar Years 2011–2028," Office of the Actuary, Centers for Medicare & Medicaid Services, Department of Health and Human Services; Congressional Budget Office, "Re: Cost Estimate for the Conference Agreement on H.R. 1, a Bill to Provide for Reconciliation Pursuant to Titles II and V of the Concurrent Resolution on the Budget for Fiscal Year 2018," letter to Kevin Brady (chairman of the House Committee on Ways and Means), December 15, 2017; and Office of Management and Budget, "Historical Tables, Budget of the United States Government, Fiscal Year 2019," February 12, 2018, p. 27; and author's calculations.

Note: GDP = gross domestic product; HSA = health savings account.

FIGURE 6 Employer-sponsored health insurance premiums dwarf HSA contributions

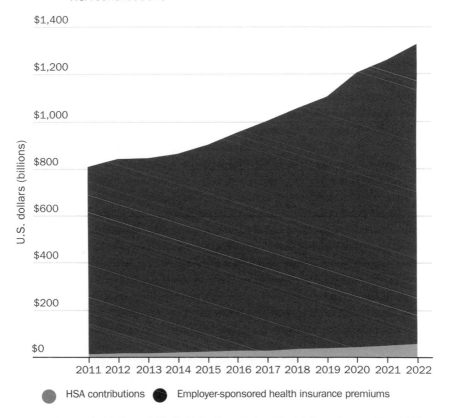

Sources: Centers for Medicare & Medicaid Services, National Health Expenditures tables, 2019, https://www.cms.gov/files/zip/nhe-projections-2019-2028-tables.zip-0; Devenir Research, "2021 Midyear HSA Market Statistics & Trends, Executive Summary," September 16, 2021; and author's calculations.
Notes: * = author's calculations 2022 estimated; HSA = health savings account.

Federal policymakers can also remove barriers to interstate telehealth services.[24] While states have constitutional authority to regulate the practice of medicine for residents within their borders, telehealth services that cross state lines are interstate commerce that Congress has the authority to liberalize under Article 1, Section 8 of the Constitution. Congress should use that authority to define the locus of the practice of medicine as the location of the *clinician*, not—as states currently do—the location of the patient. Doing so would free patients to consult with top specialists via telehealth in any part of the country.

Second, states should reform burdensome clinician-licensing restrictions. They should recognize out-of-state licenses for clinicians who establish a business presence within the state. In early 2019, Arizona became the first state to enact universal license recognition.[25] Since then, 16 states have enacted variations of Arizona's universal license-recognition law.[26] This reform makes it easier for health care practitioners to provide services to patients in various parts of the country. However, five states, including Arizona, require clinicians to establish a residence. Eleven other states, including New Jersey, Pennsylvania, and Missouri, don't. State lawmakers in all 50 states and the District of Columbia should enact universal license recognition without a residency requirement.

States should go even further by recognizing the out-of-state licenses of clinicians who provide short-term in-person care in another state. Examples include clinicians who provide care during temporary stints in medically underserved areas, clinicians who practice very close to the border of a neighboring state, and out-of-state clinicians who specialize in rare conditions or who help manage fragile patients too unstable for transfer. Truly universal license recognition would also make it easier for locum tenens (i.e., "fill in") providers and out-of-state specialists to provide itinerant temporary health services to remote and underserved communities by removing the barriers that unnecessary licensing applications and fees create.

States should also take immediate action to make medical care more accessible by relaxing scope-of-practice regulations. States that did so temporarily during the pandemic should make those measures permanent. States should allow pharmacists and pharmacy technicians broader scope to perform vaccinations, prescribe hormonal contraceptives, and prescribe HIV pre-exposure prophylaxis and post-exposure prophylaxis. They should expand pharmacists' scope of practice to include tuberculosis skin testing and interpretation; testing and administering of prescription medications for patients with influenza and other viral illnesses or common bacterial infections, such as strep throat; the ability to prescribe non-sedating or low-sedating antihistamines, corticosteroids, and decongestants; and the ability to extend routine noncontrolled chronic medication prescriptions for an additional 30–60 days.[27] Expanding pharmacists' scope of practice can save workers time and money by avoiding unnecessary visits to a doctor's office.

Scope-of-practice restrictions bar many other health care professionals from practicing to the full extent of their training.[28] States should permit optometrists who have the training to offer simple eye surgical procedures to patients; let appropriately trained doctorate-level psychologists prescribe psychotherapeutics; and let dental therapists (analogous to physician assistants) and dental hygienists practice independently and to the full extent of their training.[29]

Ultimately, state lawmakers should relinquish the tasks of defining clinician categories and scopes of practice, with which they have no expertise. States should instead certify competing private third-party organizations to perform these tasks. Such organizations could include medical malpractice liability insurers, specialty boards, and health systems.[30] Many private organizations already offer certification in specific skills, such as specialty certificates for physician assistants in cardiovascular and thoracic surgery or emergency medicine, and for registered nurses in AIDS and pediatric care. Competing private certification organizations would experiment with lower-cost ways of ensuring competence, which would broaden access to care and reduce the student-debt load of clinicians.

Third, states and the federal government can further increase the supply of health care services by increasing immigration and recognizing foreign medical licenses. Canadian provinces, Australia, and most European Union countries allow foreign doctors to practice under the supervision of a domestic physician for a designated period. When the supervisory period is complete and the foreign doctors pass those countries' licensing exams, the doctors receive a license. In many cases, these countries require foreign doctors to practice for a certain period in an underserved area.[31] Workers in the United States would benefit from similar licensing programs for foreign physicians. Governor Phil Murphy of New Jersey patterned a public health emergency measure on the provisional-license model.[32] Other states should do the same.

Finally, states should repeal CON laws. Doing so would reduce prices, improve health care quality, and increase access to care. During the pandemic, 20 states suspended their CON laws. Four other states issued emergency certificates of need, bypassing the usually months-long certificate application process. These steps were tacit admissions that CON laws create barriers to care and impede the health sector's ability to respond quickly to shifts in demand, such as public health emergencies.[33] State lawmakers should heed these lessons and repeal CON laws immediately and permanently.

ACTION PLAN

Workers should be free to control their earnings and to choose from an array of competing health insurers, providers, and clinicians the health insurance and medical care that meets their individual needs. Tax laws and numerous restrictions on the supply of health care are standing in the way.

To return $1.3 trillion to the workers who earned it, Congress should
- apply the tax exclusion solely to funds that individuals or employers deposit in the worker's HSA;
- increase HSA contribution limits dramatically to, say, $9,000 for individuals and $18,000 for families;
- remove the requirement that HSA holders enroll in high-deductible health insurance or any health insurance;
- allow HSA holders to purchase health insurance, of any type and from any source, tax free with HSA funds; and
- ensure that these reforms also apply to independent workers.

These changes would deliver to workers the largest effective tax cut of their lifetimes. It would reorient the health sector toward the needs of patients by making health care and insurance better, more affordable, and more secure.

To expand the supply of health care services in the United States, Congress should

- enact legislation defining the "locus of care" when providing telehealth services as where the practitioner is—not where the patient is.

And state governments should

- enact universal licensing recognition, recognizing occupational licenses from all 50 states, the District of Columbia, and U.S. territories;
- enact legislation allowing patients to receive telehealth services from health care practitioners from all 50 states, the District of Columbia, and U.S. territories;
- enact legislation recognizing the licenses of health care practitioners from any of the 50 states, the District of Columbia, and U.S. territories who
- wish to provide short-term in-person care to patients;
- enact legislation that broadens scope-of-practice regulations to allow clinicians to practice to the full extent of their training;
- enact legislation creating provisional licensing programs for trained and experienced foreign health care practitioners;
- certify competing, private, third-party organizations to define clinician categories, define educational requirements and scopes of practice for those categories, and certify individual clinicians' competence to practice;[34] and
- repeal CON laws.

NOTES

1. Michael F. Cannon, "End the Tax Exclusion for Employer-Sponsored Health Insurance: Return $1 Trillion to the Workers Who Earned It," Cato Institute Policy Analysis no. 928, May 24, 2022.

2. Martin S. Feldstein and Bernard Friedman, "Tax Subsidies, the Rational Demand for Insurance, and the Health Care Crisis," *Journal of Public Economics* 7, no. 2 (April 1977): 155–78.

3. Amy Finkelstein, "The Aggregate Effects of Health Insurance: Evidence from the Introduction of Medicare," *Quarterly Journal of Economics* 122, no. 1 (February 2007): 1–37.

4. Nicholas Tilipman, "Employer Incentives and Distortions in Health Insurance Design: Implications for Welfare and Costs," *American Economic Review* 112, no. 3 (March 22): 998–1037.

5. See Christopher J. Conover, "Health Care Regulation: A $169 Billion Hidden Tax," Cato Institute Policy Analysis no. 527, October 4, 2004, p. 28n81; "Table 1: National Health Expenditures and Selected Economic Indicators, Levels and Annual Percent Change: Calendar Years 2012–2028," Centers for Medicare & Medicaid Services; "Table 5–6—Private Health Insurance by Sponsor," Centers for Medicare & Medicaid Services; "Table 16— National Health Expenditures (NHE), Amounts and Average Growth Annual Growth from Previous Year Shown," Centers for Medicare & Medicaid Services; and authors' calculations. But see David Powell, "The Distortionary Effects of the Health Insurance Tax Exclusion," *American Journal of Health Economics* 5, no. 4 (Fall 2019): 428–64.

6. Gary Claxton et al., *Employer Health Benefits: 2021 Annual Survey* (San Francisco: Kaiser Family Foundation, 2021), p. 65.

7. "Number of Jobs, Labor Market Experience, and Earnings Growth: Results from a National Longitudinal Survey," Economic News Release, Bureau of Labor Statistics, August 31, 2021; and "Employee Benefits in the United States, March 2020," Bureau of Labor Statistics Bulletin no. 2793, September 2020.

8. Sherry Glied, *Revising the Tax Treatment of Employer-Provided Health Insurance* (Washington: AEI Press, 1994), p. 19n76.

9. Mark V. Pauly and Robert D. Lieberthal, "How Risky Is Individual Health Insurance?," *Health Affairs* 27, no. S1 (2008).

10. "Health Insurance Coverage: United States—July 1962–June 1963," National Center for Health Statistics series 10, no. 11, Department of Health, Education and Welfare, August 1964, p. 5.

11. For a review of the literature, see Jonathan Gruber and Brigitte C. Madrian, "Health Insurance, Labor Supply, and Job Mobility: A Critical Review of the Literature," National Bureau of Economic Research Working Paper no. 8817, February 2002.

12. Benjamin W. Chute and Phanindra V. Wunnava, "Is There a Link between Employer-Provided Health Insurance and Job Mobility? Evidence from Recent Micro Data," Institute of Labor Economics Discussion Paper no. 8989, April 2015; Brigitte C. Madrian, "Employment-Based Health Insurance and Job Mobility: Is There Evidence of Job-Lock?," *Quarterly Journal of Economics* 109, no. 1 (1994): 27–54; and Andrew Sherrill and John E. Dicken, "Health Care Coverage: Job Lock and the Potential Impact of the Patient Protection and Affordable Care Act," Government Accountability Office report no. GAO-12-166R, December 15, 2011.

13. Robert W. Fairlie, Kanika Kapur, and Susan Gates, "Is Employer-based Health Insurance a Barrier to Entrepreneurship?," *Journal of Health Economics* 30, no. 1 (January 2011): 146–62.

14. Fatih Karahan et al., "Do Job-to-Job Transitions Drive Wage Fluctuations over the Business Cycle?," *American Economic Review* 107, no. 5 (May 2017): 353–57.

15. Shirley Svorny, "Liberating Telemedicine: Options to Eliminate the State-Licensing Roadblock," Cato Institute Policy Analysis no. 826, November 15, 2017.

16. Jeffrey A. Singer, "States Lead the Way in Coronavirus Crisis with Emergency Removal of Occupational Licensing Obstacles—Why Not Make Them Permanent?," *Cato at Liberty* (blog), Cato Institute, March 18, 2020.

17. Singer, "States Lead the Way in Coronavirus Crisis"; and Alexis S. Gilroy et al., "States Relax Physician

Assistant Supervision and Delegation Laws," Jones Day, March 2020.

18. "AMA Successfully Fights Scope of Practice Expansions That Threaten Patient Safety," Scope of Practice, American Medical Association.

19. "Governor Ducey Takes Step to Free Up More Physicians to Address COVID-19," news release, Office of the Governor Doug Ducey, March 24, 2020.

20. Jack Pitsor and Anna Parham, "Repeal or Retool? States Assess Certificate of Need Laws," National Conference of State Legislatures, January 12, 2022.

21. Matthew D. Mitchell, "South Carolina's Certificate of Need Program: A Comprehensive Review of the Literature," Palmetto Promise Institute, March 2022.

22. "U.S. States and Territories Modifying Requirements for Telehealth in Response to COVID-19," Federation of State Medical Boards, June 15, 2022.

23. Arizona House Bill 2454, May 5, 2021.

24. Svorny, "Liberating Telemedicine."

25. Matthew D. Mitchell and Anne Philpot, "Arizona Makes the Right Move on Occupational Licensing," Mercatus Center, George Mason University, April 30, 2019.

26. "State Reforms for Universal License Recognition," Institute for Justice.

27. Jeffrey A. Singer and Courtney M. Joslin, "How States Can Promote Health Care Access and Affordability While Enhancing Patient Autonomy," R Street Policy Study no. 214, November 2020.

28. Jeffrey A. Singer, "Health Care Scope of Practice Laws Reveal Another Weakness in Response to COVID-19 Pandemic," *Cato at Liberty* (blog), Cato Institute, March 26, 2020.

29. "Optometrist Scope of Practice," National Conference of State Legislatures, March 31, 2021; "Idaho Becomes Fifth State to Allow Psychologists to Prescribe Medications," American Psychological Association, April 5, 2017; Naomi Lopez, "The Reform That Can Increase Dental Access and Affordability in Arizona," *0-Related Reforms* (blog), Goldwater Institute, April 10, 2017; and "Direct Access States," American Dental Hygienists' Association, January 2020.

30. Shirley Svorny and Michael F. Cannon, "Health Care Workforce Reform: COVID-19 Spotlights Need for Changes to Clinician Licensing," Cato Institute Policy Analysis no. 899, Cato Institute, August 4, 2020.

31. "International Medical Graduates: Obtaining a Licence to Practise in Canada," Royal College of Physicians and Surgeons of Canada. See also Paul J. Larkin Jr., "COVID-19 and the Provisional Licensing of Qualified Medical School Graduates as Physicians," *Washington and Lee Law Review Online* 76, no. 2 (April 6, 2020): 81–90; and Kevin Dayaratna, Paul J. Larkin Jr. and John O'Shea, "Reforming American Medical Licensure," *Harvard Journal of Law & Public Policy* 42, no.1 (January 2019): 253–78.

32. Michael Sol Warren and Keith Sargeant, "N.J. to Allow Foreign Doctors Help Treat Coronavirus. No Other State Has Done This," NJ.com, April 17, 2020; and Svorny and Cannon, "Health Care Workforce Reform."

33. *Hearing on S.B. 6: RIP for Public Employees/Teachers Before the Alaska Senate Labor and Commerce Committee, 32nd Legislature* (April 14, 2021) (testimony of Jeffrey A. Singer, Senior Fellow, Cato Institute).

34. Svorny and Cannon, "Health Care Workforce Reform."

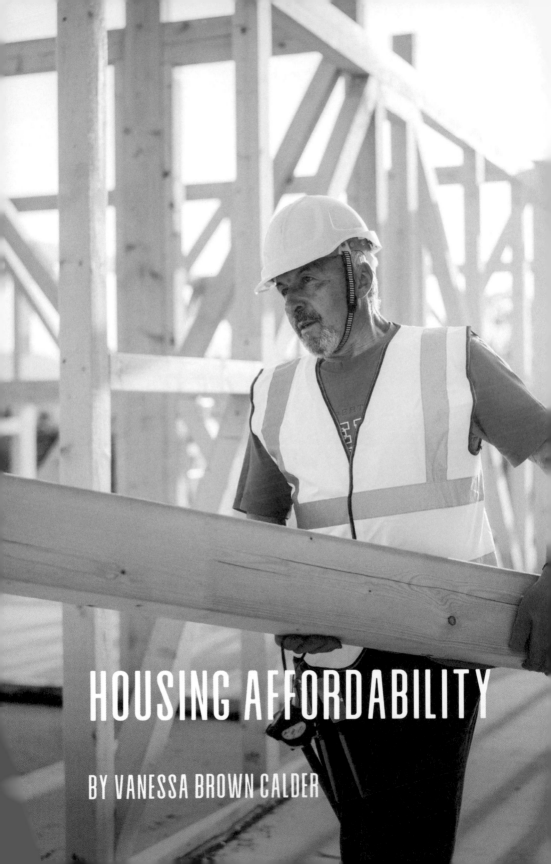

HOUSING AFFORDABILITY

BY VANESSA BROWN CALDER

THE ISSUE: FEDERAL AND STATE POLICIES CONTRIBUTE TO HIGH HOUSING PRICES, WHICH REDUCE AMERICAN WORKERS' MOBILITY, OPPORTUNITY, AND WEALTH

America has an acute housing imbalance. For many years, and in many places, housing supply has not met housing demand, resulting in high and rising prices in places such as New York City, San Francisco, and Washington, DC.

Housing supply challenges intensified during the pandemic. The number of "missing" housing units (i.e., the number of units required to keep up with household formation minus existing units) grew from approximately 2.8 million in 2018 to 3.8 million at the end of 2020—a 52 percent increase in just two years.[1]

As housing inventory dwindled, prices rose (see Figure 1). Prices for homes increased more than 20 percent from the beginning of the pandemic to the end of 2021, and rents increased more than 15 percent during the same period.[2] In markets with high levels of in-migration, including Sunbelt cities such as Tampa, Austin, Phoenix, and Las Vegas, price gains were even more extreme, with rents rising between 24 and 30 percent, year-over-year.[3]

Escalating prices reflect a demand-supply mismatch resulting from a variety of factors, including substantial migration to southern and western cities, outmigration from central cities to surrounding areas, pandemic labor shortages, supply chain delays, and rising prices for construction materials such as lumber and steel, which combine to limit the supply of new and existing homes.[4]

Several of these factors, however, are worsened by federal policy. For example, tariffs have increased the cost of a wide variety of construction materials and other essential home goods.[5] Even worse, the scope of these tariffs has expanded substantially over the last decade, with the federal government during that period applying new "trade remedy" (antidumping or countervailing duty) measures or other import taxes on softwood lumber; plywood; nails; shelving units; kitchen racks; steel sinks; cabinets and vanities; wood moulding and other millwork products; quartz countertops; ceramic tile; washing machines; solar panels; and a wide array of aluminum and steel products used to build housing (e.g., rebar).[6] Duty rates on many of these products are high, if not prohibitive, and a recent economic analysis found that U.S. tariff actions cause domestic construction material prices to increase significantly up to 18 months after implementation.[7]

Federal tax deductions for property and mortgage interest also increase home prices, particularly in metropolitan areas with relatively inelastic housing supply. These tax deductions make houses more valuable and increase people's willingness to pay, thereby making it harder for first-time homebuyers to afford a down payment.[8] Although these deductions were limited by the 2017 Tax Cut and Jobs Act (TCJA), existing policy terminates the act's limitations on itemized deductions after 2025 and retains a portion of both mortgage interest and state and local tax deductions.[9]

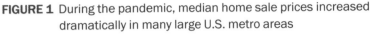

FIGURE 1 During the pandemic, median home sale prices increased dramatically in many large U.S. metro areas

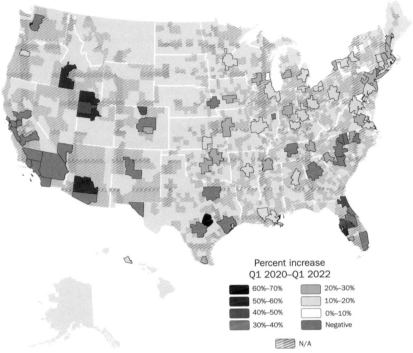

Percent increase
Q1 2020–Q1 2022

- 60%–70%
- 50%–60%
- 40%–50%
- 30%–40%
- 20%–30%
- 10%–20%
- 0%–10%
- Negative
- N/A

Source: "List and Sale Prices: Median Sale Price (Raw, All Homes, Monthly)," Zillow Research, https://www.zillow.com/research/data/.

Federal tax law also affects housing in other ways. Current policy, for example, requires developers to write off the construction costs for new apartments over decades, which, due to inflation and the time-value of money, raises the cost of development substantially. This feature of the tax code also has the unfortunate consequence of making non-real-estate investments with more favorable tax treatment more attractive than housing development, even when additional housing development is desperately needed. As a result, low-cost housing suffers as developers focus on luxury units that have higher profit margins and are more easily able to absorb the additional cost.[10]

Federal policy also reduces the supply of land available for housing. In western and southwestern states with high in-migration, the federal government owns a large amount of land, making it unavailable for development of any kind, including housing development (see Figure 2). For example, in Nevada, Utah, and Idaho, the federal government respectively owns 80 percent, 63 percent, and 60 percent of the land.[11] In other states, including Oregon, Wyoming, New Mexico, and Montana, the federal government owns around one-third to one-half of the available land.

In fast-growing states, these federal lands frequently touch urban or suburban areas, and thus they act as a hard barrier to localities' expansion. For example, Geomancer Inc., a company that analyzes real estate data, estimates that there are 217,000 acres of U.S. Forest Service (USFS) and Bureau of Land Management (BLM) lands within Utah city boundaries, and 650,000 acres of USFS and BLM lands within one mile of city borders.[12] As remote work and other factors increase demand for housing in areas bordering—and thus constrained by—federal lands, prices are sure to rise.

Finally, federal policy and industry lobbyists have put low-cost manufactured housing at a disadvantage. Specifically, low-interest-rate mortgages provided under the now-obsolete Section 235 program of the National Housing Act were limited to traditional stick-built homes, and the Department of Housing and Urban Development's (HUD) national building code has made it difficult for manufactured housing to compete with their stick-built counterparts.[13] Although the Section 235 program is no longer in effect, HUD still requires manufactured housing to be attached to a permanent chassis, or metal base frame, that allows transportability. This allows local governments to regulate manufactured homes more restrictively, as if they were mobile homes.[14] Such restrictions deny American workers more affordable manufactured housing options.

FIGURE 2 The federal government owns large amounts of land in western states with high in-migration

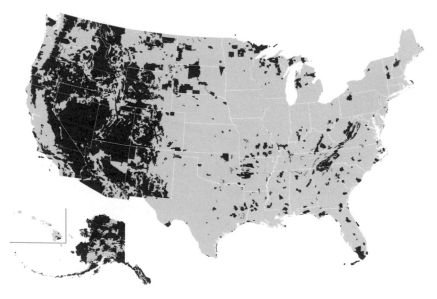

Source: "USA Federal Lands," ArcGIS layer, Esri, updated May 23, 2022, https://www.arcgis.com/home/item.html?id=5e92f2e0930848faa40480bcb4fdc44e.

Other federal laws and regulations, such as immigration restrictions and the Department of Energy's appliance and equipment efficiency standards, may also raise the cost of housing. Restrictions on immigration likely contribute to labor-market tightness and, given immigrants' prominent role in the construction industry, constitute a supply-side restriction in the housing sector. Indeed, a 2022 Federal Reserve Bank of St. Louis study found that pandemic-era declines in immigration were a major contributor to labor shortages and higher costs for the U.S. construction industry.[15] Immigration restrictions' final impact on housing prices is uncertain, however, because additional increased immigration would also boost housing demand.

Arguably more important than any policy at the federal level, however, are ever-increasing state and local regulatory constraints. Land-use regulation continues to limit housing supply by increasing development costs, creating uncertainty, and producing delays.[16] These regulations determine the height, width, architectural features, and use of a given property, and they subject development to lengthy review processes with many veto points. Together, these zoning regulations effectively freeze preexisting development patterns in place, which makes it difficult to build homes or accommodate new residents.

Many research papers tie land-use regulations to increased housing prices. Glaeser et al. (2003) found, for example, that zoning regulations pushed up the cost of apartments by around 50 percent in Manhattan, San Francisco, and San Jose.[17] This figure has likely only grown as regulatory constraints and demand have increased in recent years. Indeed, Gyourko and Kimmel (2021) examined 24 metropolitan areas and calculated a massive "zoning tax" (up to $500,000 per quarter-acre) in cities with restrictive land-use regimes but much lower zoning taxes in less-regulated places.[18]

In addition to the increasing regulatory obstacles, developer impact fees have grown over time. An impact fee is paid to the municipality by a developer to cover the cost of infrastructure or public facilities, act as a substitute for property tax increases, or otherwise supplement local government funds. One survey of 37 major metro areas found that the fees had increased by 45 percent between 2005 and 2016, and that the average impact fee was $21,000. These fees ostensibly land hardest on starter homes, whose would-be residents are less able to absorb the costs.[19]

Meanwhile, local building codes, which include structural, plumbing, mechanical, electrical, accessibility, and energy-related requirements, also raise the cost of housing. While their original purpose was to protect public health and safety, building codes have strayed from that goal and are used to achieve other objectives, with costly consequences. For example, stricter state building codes aimed at conserving energy have been observed to *increase* energy use per square foot and to reduce the square footage of homes at the lowest end of the income distribution.[20]

Current regulations not only reduce traditional housing development, but they also limit innovative ideas meant to act as an alternative to more expensive single family homes or traditional apartments.[21] For example, factory-built modular homes cost significantly less per square foot than traditional homes, but their development is hampered by regulations that limit density, including rules that limit or prohibit accessory dwelling units. Similarly, co-living homes, which pair single-resident rooms with shared common space, are constrained by regulations like "density factor," which caps the maximum number of units per building. Finally, flexible and short-term apartment rentals are restricted by state and/or local regulations that require apartment owners, among other things, to be licensed, to register their homes, and to be present in the home to rent a unit out short term.

These policies and others that raise construction costs and restrict housing development are important to workers because housing availability and affordability continue to influence employment opportunities for the roughly three-quarters of workers who work onsite full or part time.[22] In the past, Ganong and Shoag (2015) found that less-skilled workers could not afford the higher housing costs in heavily regulated cities that have strong economic opportunities, and so these workers became stuck in lower-cost areas that had lesser job prospects.[23] Although remote work is changing the geography of work opportunities for many workers, particularly those in certain services, housing will undoubtedly continue to function as a de facto gateway for millions of Americans' economic, educational, and social opportunities for many years to come.[24]

THE POLICY SOLUTIONS: REVISE FEDERAL TRADE, TAX, LAND, HOUSING, AND IMMIGRATION POLICIES; AND REFORM LOCAL LAND-USE REGULATIONS AND BUILDING CODES

Although migration patterns, supply chain delays, and inflation will continue to put pressure on housing prices, smart policy reforms can serve as an essential release valve for American workers and their families.

One increasingly popular policy that should be avoided, on the other hand, is rent control, which has been repeatedly found to perpetuate the very problems (housing shortages and higher prices) that it is ostensibly intended to solve.[25] In particular, artificially reducing or capping rents (and thus potential returns on investment) discourages landlords, builders, and investors from supplying rentable properties in a local market, while simultaneously boosting demand for rental housing in that same area. With less supply of—and more demand for—rental housing, high prices, shortages, and other problems inevitably ensue.

For example, the Diamond et al. (2018) research on San Francisco's rent regulation found that the policy reduced housing supply by 15 percent, reduced the

probability of renters moving by 20 percent, and raised rents by more than
5 percent city-wide.[26] Meanwhile, the Ahern and Giacoletti (2022) review of St.
Paul, Minnesota's, new rent control law found that tenants with higher incomes
benefited, while tenants with lower incomes lost under the policy.[27] Reports indicate that the St. Paul policy is causing developers to pull the plug on large-scale
housing projects and that it has already led to declining building permitting.[28]
Although the idea of rent control continues to tempt policymakers, serious proponents of housing affordability should avoid it—especially at the state or national
level (which cannot account for vast local differences).

Policymakers should instead pursue market-oriented reforms that will increase
residential construction and housing supply, and thereby lower prices for all
Americans. Research has repeatedly shown, in fact, that boosting the private construction of market-rate housing benefits not only residents of those new units but
also those living in lower-cost or lower-quality housing—far more broadly than
various "affordable housing" programs can.[29]

At the federal level, trade policy should be reformed to reduce the cost of housing materials. Although U.S. trade remedy laws' various substantive and procedural requirements make antidumping and countervailing duty measures difficult
to eliminate quickly, the administration should work with Congress to reform
the process that led to these tariffs in the first place. For example, Congress could
allow administering agencies to consider proposed duties' potential harms to
American consumers and others, as well as to the economy more broadly.

The administration also can and should unilaterally eliminate Section 232
tariffs on steel and aluminum imports (created in the name of national security),
as well as Section 301 tariffs on Chinese imports of various building materials
and appliances (applied to encourage China to eliminate various "unfair" trade
practices). As Cato Institute scholars have explained, these tariffs were imposed
on dubious legal, economic, and factual grounds; have not achieved their primary
policy aims (e.g., changing Chinese economic behavior); have fostered cronyism
and political dysfunction; and could be lawfully terminated by executive order.[30]
The administration also should relax or eliminate federal appliance and equipment efficiency standards that add to the expense of housing.

Congress can also play an important role in improving housing supply and
affordability. For example, Congress should make the limits that the Tax Cut and
Jobs Act placed on state and local tax deductions and the mortgage interest deduction permanent, and over the long term work to further reduce and eliminate
these deductions. To encourage housing development, Congress should reform
the tax treatment of development by allowing more rapid—ideally immediate—
expensing of structures.[31] According to Tax Foundation estimates, a more neutral
tax approach would reduce construction costs by around 11 percent, which would
make low-income units both more affordable and more likely to be built. To further aid housing construction, Congress should reform immigration restrictions

that prevent American companies from hiring foreign workers. (Research shows, for example, that immigrants accounted for roughly one-quarter of the United States' pre-pandemic construction workforce and even higher shares of certain building trades.[32])

Congress should also increase the amount of land available for housing and development in western and southwestern states experiencing high levels of in-migration. To that end, Congress could pass a law that requires the federal government to return some of the federal government's 640 million acres of federally owned land to state and local governments or private owners. Such a law could apply to non-specially designated and nonsensitive lands (lands that are not national monuments, critical areas, national recreation areas, etc.).

The Southern Nevada Public Land Management Act is an example of an existing program that returns federal land to private hands, and this program could be used as a template. This program makes federal public land in Clark County, Nevada, home to Las Vegas, available for auction.[33] Under this act, the revenue resulting from the sale of federal lands is divided among the secretary of the interior (for environmental conservation and projects), the state of Nevada (for educational purposes), and the Southern Nevada Water Authority. As a result, many interested stakeholders benefit from the sale of federal public lands.

Although zoning reform is mostly a state and local issue, some policymakers and analysts have suggested federal reforms to encourage states and localities to deregulate more comprehensively. Federal housing subsidies are concentrated in the states with the most restrictive zoning and land-use regulation, which means that states and cities that actively make houses less affordable are rewarded for doing so (see Figure 3).

To better align incentives, affordability subsidies should be the exclusive purview of state and local governments. But if we must take federal subsidies for housing affordability as a given, states and cities could be required to relax restrictive zoning measures to qualify for HUD subsidies. This would short-circuit the existing dysfunctional relationship between local regulatory policy and federal housing policy.[34] Likewise, although state and local building codes are frequently adopted from international and national building codes, federal policy could require state and local governments to reform the most egregious code requirements to qualify for federal subsidies.

Finally, governments should remove disparate regulatory burdens on manufactured housing. The Biden administration's Housing Supply Action Plan indicates its intent to update the HUD code regulating manufactured housing "to allow manufacturers to modernize and expand their production lines," among other reforms.[35] This proposal appears well-intentioned, but its scope and timing are unclear. Thus, Congress should take action to eliminate requirements mandating that manufactured housing be attached to an unnecessary, permanent chassis. It

FIGURE 3 Federal housing affordability subsidies are largest in the most-regulated states

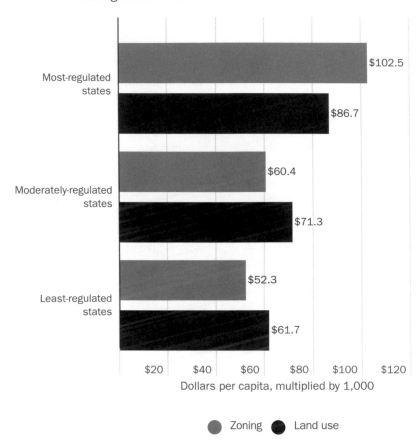

Dollars per capita, multiplied by 1,000

● Zoning ● Land use

Source: Vanessa Brown Calder, "Zoning, Land-Use Planning, and Housing Affordability," Cato Institute Policy Analysis no. 823, October 18, 2017.

should also revise HUD's national building code, which unfairly targets and regulates manufactured housing. Meanwhile, local governments should review and overhaul relevant regulations to ensure that manufactured housing is treated the same way as other housing types.

At the state and local levels, policymakers must continue to find ways to relax zoning and building requirements and reduce permitting costs. In recent years, some states and cities, including California, Connecticut, and Minneapolis, have up-zoned areas from low to moderate density, relaxed regulations such as parking requirements, and legalized accessory dwelling units (colloquially known as "granny flats") to increase housing supply and reduce costs.

While policymakers work to reform zoning to accommodate traditional housing, they should also pay close attention to existing barriers to housing innovation and work to identify and eliminate them. These barriers include limits on density (minimum lot size requirements, limits on the number of housing units in a building, and limits on square footage for a given lot size) for modular and co-living homes, as well as rules around licensing, registration, and renting of flexible apartment properties. Because any given zoning regulation exists within a broader context of many and varied restrictions on building height, size, and design, a comprehensive approach to state and local regulatory reform is necessary for success.

ACTION PLAN

Housing is a necessity that affects the lives of all American workers, and government policy has contributed to high and rising home prices in numerous ways. To moderate future home price increases and improve workers' economic opportunity and geographic mobility, governments at all levels should reform these policies to lower construction costs, increase housing supply, and correct current demand distortions.

In particular, the Executive Branch should

- eliminate Section 232 tariffs on steel and aluminum and Section 301 tariffs on Chinese imports via executive order to reduce the cost of construction materials and related products; and
- abandon recent Department of Commerce policy changes that ensure punitive trade remedy (antidumping and countervailing duty) restrictions on imports, including construction materials.[36]

Congress should

- reform the antidumping and countervailing duty laws, which led to tariffs on key building inputs (lumber, cement, steel rebar, appliances, etc.). Adding a "public interest" check prior to duties' implementation, for example, could prevent shortages of critical building materials;
- increase housing affordability and supply by making permanent the 2017 reforms to mortgage interest and state and local tax deductions and by eliminating these deductions long-term;
- revise depreciation schedules to allow for more rapid or immediate expensing of structures to encourage housing development;
- along with implementing immigration reforms that will help the U.S. labor market generally (e.g., clearing the 1.5-million-person employment authorization backlog and allowing dependents of H-2 (seasonal) workers to work), create a guest worker program specifically for construction and related year-round jobs. Currently, all lesser-skilled work visas are reserved for seasonal jobs;
- pass legislation similar to the proposed Helping Open Underutilized Space

to Ensure Shelter (HOUSES) Act so that non-specially designated federal lands can be returned to state and local governments and used for new housing development;[37]

- consider passing a law so that cities applying for HUD housing subsidies or subsidies that affect housing affordability, like Community Development Block Grants, are required to relax restrictive zoning to qualify. Measuring the restrictiveness of zoning to determine subsidy eligibility can be difficult, but one option is to require states and local municipalities to compute and report their local "zoning tax" using public and private data—that is, the difference between the market price of housing and housing construction costs. If a state or city's zoning tax declined or remained at zero over the previous period then cities could qualify for existing HUD subsidies.[38] Subsidy eligibility could likewise be reduced for states and cities with building code requirements that drift beyond health and safety objectives;
- relax the definition of manufactured housing as outlined in the National Manufactured Housing Construction and Safety Standards Act of 1974[39]— the new definition should allow manufactured housing to be constructed without a permanent chassis;
- eliminate HUD's Manufactured Home Construction and Safety Standards (HUD Code), which unfairly target manufactured housing for federal regulation; and
- relax the Department of Energy's appliance and equipment standards to allow state and local governments to set their own standards.[40]

State and local governments should
- reduce and eliminate zoning regulations and reduce permitting fees;
- identify and eliminate barriers to housing innovation, including density regulations that discourage the development of modular housing and co-living homes, and licensing and registration requirements that limit flexible apartment rentals; and
- establish an annual review of housing permitting and new construction figures to measure the effectiveness of state and local reforms.

Finally, local governments should
- Overhaul local regulation to ensure fair and equal treatment of manufactured housing alongside traditional stick-built housing.

NOTES

1. Sam Khater, Len Kiefer, and Venkataramana Yanamandra, "Housing Supply: A Growing Deficit," Freddie Mac Economic and Housing Research Note, May 2021.

2. "Median Sales Price of Houses Sold for the United States," U.S. Census Bureau and U.S. Department of Housing and Urban Development, Federal Reserve Economic Data, Federal Reserve Bank of St. Louis, April 26, 2022.

3. Jeff Tucker, "Inventory Down 40% from Pre-COVID Level as Price Growth Intensifies," Zillow, January 20, 2022.

4. Arjun Ramani and Nicholas Bloom, "The Donut Effect of COVID-19 on Cities," National Bureau of Economic Research Working Paper no. 28876, May 2021.

5. Scott Lincicome, "How U.S. Trade Policy Helped Construction Materials Costs Go through the Roof," *Cato at Liberty* (blog), Cato Institute, March 18, 2021.

6. Lincicome, "How U.S. Trade Policy Helped Construction Materials Costs Go through the Roof."

7. Scott Lincicome, "Dumping on American Builders and Homebuyers," *Cato at Liberty* (blog), Cato Institute, February 9, 2022.

8. "Priced Out: Why Federal Tax Deductions Miss the Mark on Family Affordability," Joint Economic Committee Republicans, May 18, 2020.

9. For example, the reformed mortgage interest deduction applies to $750,000 in mortgage debt for loans, which is a change from its former configuration, where the deduction applied to $1.1 million in mortgage debt. Similarly, the reformed state and local tax deduction is capped at $10,000; prior to the Tax Cut and Jobs Act, there was no limit on this deduction.

10. Scott Lincicome, "Why (Some of) the Rents Are Too Damn High," *The Dispatch,* December 22, 2020.

11. Carol H. Vincent, Laura A. Hanson, and Lucas F. Bermejo, "Federal Land Ownership: Overview and Data," Congressional Research Service, R42346, February 21, 2020.

12. Ryan Freeman, letter to Sen. Lincoln Fillmore and Rep. Keven Stratton, May 18, 2020.

13. James A. Schmitz, Jr., "Solving the Housing Crisis Will Require Fighting Monopolies in Construction," Federal Reserve Bank of Minneapolis Working Paper no.773, December 11, 2020.

14. Schmitz, "Solving the Housing Crisis Will Require Fighting Monopolies in Construction"; and "Manufactured Housing and Standards—Frequently Asked Questions," U.S. Department of Housing and Urban Development, Office of Manufactured Housing Programs.

15. Nathan Jefferson, Devin Werner, and Elisabeth Harding, "Demographics, COVID-19 Leave Construction with Tight Labor Supply," Federal Reserve Bank of St. Louis, April 20, 2022; see also Nicole Narea, "Immigrants Could Fix the US Labor Shortage," *Vox,* October 26, 2021.

16. Vanessa Brown Calder, "Zoning, Land-Use Planning, and Housing Affordability," Cato Institute Policy Analysis no. 823, October 18, 2017.

17. Edward L. Glaeser, Joseph Gyourko, and Raven Saks, "Why Is Manhattan So Expensive? Regulation and the Rise in House Prices," National Bureau of Economic Research Working Paper no. 10124, November 2003.

18. Joseph Gyourko and Jacob Krimmel, "The Impact of Local Residential Land Use Restrictions on Land Values Across and Within Single Family Housing Markets," National Bureau of Economic Research Working Paper no. 28993, July 2021.

19. Nick Timiraos, "'Impact Fees' Pinch Starter Homes," *Wall Street Journal,* May 5, 2016.

20. Christopher D. Bruegge, Tatyana Deryugina, and Erica Myers, "The Distributional Effects of Building Energy Codes," National Bureau of Economic Research Working Paper no. 24211, January 2018.

21. Vanessa Brown Calder, "Housing Innovation Faces Many Barriers," *Cato at Liberty* (blog), Cato Institute, September 1, 2022.

22. Lydia Saad and Ben Wigert, "Remote Work Persisting and Trending Permanent," Gallup, October 13, 2021.

23. Peter Ganong and Daniel Shoag, "Why Has Regional Income Convergence in the U.S. Declined?," Harvard University, John F. Kennedy School of Government, January 2015.

24. Lydia Saad and Jeffrey M. Jones, "Seven in 10 U.S. White-Collar Workers Still Working Remotely," Gallup, May 17, 2021.

25. Ryan Bourne, "The Folly of Bernie Sanders' National Rent Control Proposal," *Cato at Liberty* (blog), Cato Institute, January 27, 2020.

26. Rebecca Diamond, Timothy McQuade, and Franklin Qian, "The Effects of Rent Control Expansion on Tenants, Landlords, and Inequality: Evidence from San Francisco," National Bureau of Economic Research Working Paper no. 24181, January 2018.

27. Kenneth R. Ahern and Marco Giacoletti, "Robbing Peter to Pay Paul? The Redistribution of Wealth Caused by Rent Control," National Bureau of Economic Research Working Paper no. 30083, May 2022.

28. Christian Britschgi, "Is the Nation's Harshest Rent Control Law Unconstitutional, or Just Counterproductive?," Reason, June 23, 2022.

29. Emily Badger, "The Poor Are Better Off When We Build More Housing for the Rich," *Washington Post,* February 15, 2016; Evan Mast, "JUE Insight: The Effect of New Market-Rate Housing Construction on the Low-Income Housing Market," *Journal of Urban Economics* (2021): 103383; and Shaun Kho, "New Round of Studies Underscore Benefits of Building More Housing," *The Urbanist*, June 2, 2021.

30. Scott Lincicome and Inu Manak, "Protectionism or National Security? The Use and Abuse of Section 232," Cato Institute Policy Analysis no. 912, March 9, 2021; and Scott Lincicome, Inu Manak, and Alfredo Carrillo Obregon, "Unfair Trade or Unfair Protection? The Evolution and Abuse of Section 301," Cato Institute Policy Analysis no. 930, June 14, 2022.

31. Scott Hodge, "Better Cost Recovery of Apartments Can Assist Affordable Housing Crisis," *The Hill,* June 29, 2020.

32. "Building America: Immigrants in Construction and Infrastructure-Related Industries," New American Economy Research Fund, September 3, 2020.

33. "Implementation of the Southern Nevada Public Land Management Act (SNPLMA) Bureau of Land Management," U.S. Department of the Interior, Office of the Inspector General, September 2003.

34. Peter Van Doren and Vanessa Brown Calder, "A Public Comment on HUD's Affirmatively Furthering Fair Housing: Streamlining and Enhancements (Docket No. FR-6123-A-01)," Cato Institute, October 15, 2018.

35. "President Biden Announces New Actions to Ease the Burden of Housing Costs," press release, White House, May 16, 2022.

36. Simon Lester and Scott Lincicome, "Some New Data on U.S. Anti-Dumping Abuse," *Cato at Liberty* (blog), Cato Institute, April 9, 2021.

37. Helping Open Underutilized Space to Ensure Shelter Act of 2022, S. 4062, 117th Cong. (2022).

38. Van Doren and Calder, "A Public Comment on HUD's Affirmatively Furthering Fair Housing."

39. HUD claims that "any decision to remove the permanent chassis requirement [for manufactured housing] would be a legislative issue for Congress to address." See "FAQs—The 2000 Act," U.S. Department of Housing and Urban Development, Office of Manufactured Housing Programs.

40. For more information on this program see "Appliance and Equipment Standards Program," U.S. Department of Energy, Office of Energy Efficiency and Renewable Energy.

HOMEOWNERSHIP

BY NORBERT MICHEL

THE ISSUE: THE FEDERAL GOVERNMENT'S INVOLVEMENT IN HOUSING FINANCE HAS CAUSED AMERICAN WORKERS TO TAKE ON MORE DEBT WHILE NOT INCREASING HOMEOWNERSHIP

The U.S. government has become increasingly involved in housing finance since the 1930s. While the perceived success of this involvement has helped create the belief that the private housing market cannot properly function without extensive federal involvement, the historical record demonstrates the opposite. Robust mortgage financing exists in virtually every developed nation of the world without the degree of government involvement found in the United States. Yet, as shown in Figure 1, the U.S. homeownership rate remains below average among developed nations: 64.2 percent in the United States versus 71.1 percent for Organisation for Economic Co-operation and Development (OECD) countries.[1]

FIGURE 1 The U.S. homeownership rate is in the bottom half of OECD countries

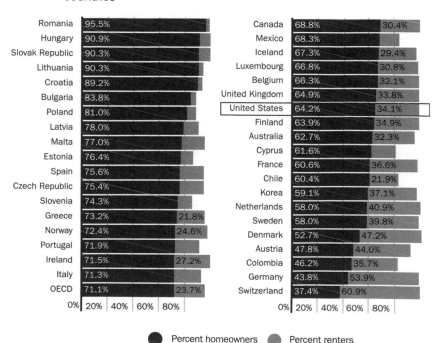

	Percent homeowners	Percent renters
Romania	95.5%	
Hungary	90.9%	
Slovak Republic	90.3%	
Lithuania	90.3%	
Croatia	89.2%	
Bulgaria	83.8%	
Poland	81.0%	
Latvia	78.0%	
Malta	77.0%	
Estonia	76.4%	
Spain	75.6%	
Czech Republic	75.4%	
Slovenia	74.3%	
Greece	73.2%	21.8%
Norway	72.4%	24.6%
Portugal	71.9%	
Ireland	71.5%	27.2%
Italy	71.3%	
OECD	71.1%	23.7%
Canada	68.8%	30.4%
Mexico	68.3%	
Iceland	67.3%	29.4%
Luxembourg	66.8%	30.8%
Belgium	66.3%	32.1%
United Kingdom	64.9%	33.8%
United States	64.2%	34.1%
Finland	63.9%	34.9%
Australia	62.7%	32.3%
Cyprus	61.6%	
France	60.6%	36.6%
Chile	60.4%	21.9%
Korea	59.1%	37.1%
Netherlands	58.0%	40.9%
Sweden	58.0%	39.8%
Denmark	52.7%	47.2%
Austria	47.8%	44.0%
Colombia	46.2%	35.7%
Germany	43.8%	53.9%
Switzerland	37.4%	60.9%

Source: Organisation for Economic Co-operation and Development.
Note: Homeownership rates include those with a mortgage. Data are from 2019 or latest available data. Those who are not renters or homeowners are categorized by the OECD as "other."

Furthermore, even though the U.S. ownership rate has changed little since the 1960s, volatility of American home prices and construction were among the highest in the industrialized world from 1998 to 2009.[2]

The United States is the only major country in the world with a federal government mortgage insurer, government guarantees of mortgage securities, *and* government-sponsored enterprises (GSEs) in housing finance. As of 2010, comparing the United States with 11 other industrialized countries, only two have a government mortgage insurer (Netherlands and Canada); two have government security guarantees (Canada and Japan); and two have GSEs (Japan and Korea).[3] Denmark even maintains a prepayable fixed-rate 30-year mortgage without the need for GSEs or other government support, and at a lower cost to borrowers than in the United States.[4]

Most federal intervention in housing finance boosts demand, typically by making it easier to obtain a home mortgage. Federal policies encourage borrowing by supporting the operations of Fannie Mae, Freddie Mac, Ginnie Mae, and the Federal Home Loan Banks and by providing loan insurance through the Federal Housing Administration (FHA), the Veterans Affairs (VA) home-lending program, and the U.S. Department of Agriculture's Rural Development Program. Prior to the 2008 financial crisis, the federal government controlled a dominant share of the housing finance system, and that share has since expanded. The operations of Fannie and Freddie (the two main GSEs) and the FHA account for the bulk of this federal intervention.

As of December 31, 2020, Fannie and Freddie had combined total assets of $6.6 trillion, representing approximately 42 percent of the nation's outstanding mortgage debt.[5] From 2008 to 2019, the FHA's annual market share of purchase loans ranged from 16.5 percent to 32.6 percent.[6] From 2009 to 2020, Fannie and Freddie's annual share of the total mortgage-backed security (MBS) market averaged 70 percent. Including Ginnie Mae securities, those that are backed by FHA mortgages, the federal share of the mortgage-backed security market averaged 92 percent per year.[7]

Rather than increase homeownership, the FHA has accelerated it for individuals who would otherwise obtain home loans later in the conventional market. Similarly, Fannie and Freddie have cost federal taxpayers billions of dollars and done little to measurably increase homeownership rates. The GSEs have, however, helped to enrich the politically connected and to increase both consumer debt and housing prices, putting sustainable homeownership out of reach for many lower-income households. The wedge between wage gains and home price appreciation, driven largely by government-induced leverage in housing markets, has been especially large for lower-priced homes (see Figures 2 and 3.) After the GSEs imploded in 2008, triggering a major recession and financial crisis, Congress could have shut them down. Instead, Congress chose to prop up the companies indefinitely, and now they remain under government conservatorship.

Broadly, federal policy should not prioritize owning a home. Even where homeownership has been shown to correlate with positive spillover effects, such as lower crime and better schools, it has not been shown to cause those spillovers. Regardless, even if homeownership *did* cause such spillovers, it would not follow that everyone should own a home. Buying a home—even without a mortgage—is risky for anyone with variable income or job prospects, and it imposes costs, such as taxes, insurance, and maintenance, that renters would otherwise not incur. Homeownership also can inhibit geographic mobility, especially for people with significant mortgage debt or living in struggling localities. Analyzing data from the Netherlands, Bernstein and Struyven (2022) suggested, in fact, that having a mortgage can be a serious impediment to geographic mobility when a loan exceeds a home's value (known as "negative equity," which often occurs during economic downturns).[8] Moreover, even in the absence of the FHA, the GSEs, and other federal programs, there would be no "correct" level of homeownership to target.

FIGURE 2 The cheapest U.S. homes have appreciated the most

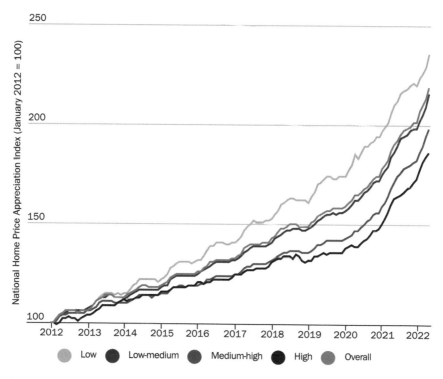

Source: American Enterprise Institute Housing Center.
Note: Data are for the entire country. April 2022 data are preliminary.

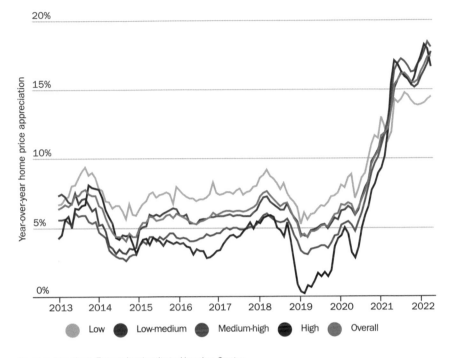

FIGURE 3 The cheapest U.S. homes typically experience the highest appreciation

Legend: Low · Low-medium · Medium-high · High · Overall

Source: American Enterprise Institute Housing Center.
Note: Data are for the entire country. April 2022 data are preliminary.

Nevertheless, countless government efforts to boost homeownership have not been successful and have instead tended to increase only *mortgage* ownership. Even as federal intervention in housing finance has steadily increased, the overall rate of homeownership has remained nearly constant over the past 50 years.[9] According to the Census Bureau, the homeownership rate was 64 percent in 1970. That is basically where it hovered for most of the 1980s and 1990s, higher than where it bottomed out in 2016, and almost exactly where it stood in the middle of 2019.[10] At the same time, the level of residential mortgage debt has increased more than fivefold—Federal Reserve data show that inflation-adjusted mortgage debt increased from about $3 trillion in 1970 (two years after Fannie Mae became a GSE) to $15.8 trillion in 2019.

THE POLICY SOLUTIONS: GET THE FEDERAL GOVERNMENT OUT OF HOUSING FINANCE

Federal policies have caused American workers to take on more long-term fixed-debt obligations while not increasing their net homeownership. This arrangement endangers workers' ability to build wealth and accumulate assets, especially in turbulent labor markets. Workers have also been paying more for housing because the increased use of long-term debt at lower interest rates has caused home prices—even those that are used for rental homes—to rise more than they would have otherwise. Evidence also suggests that these federal housing policies have created additional incentives for workers to remain in a particular geographic location—a "lock-in effect"—rather than relocate to adapt to changing job markets.[11]

Thus, the ideal solution would be to remove the federal government entirely from the housing finance industry. Many foreign governments are minimally involved in housing finance, and there is no "market failure" in this industry that necessitates government intervention. Should policymakers nevertheless insist on some level of federal involvement in the market, several discrete reforms are recommended in the following section. These reforms would help American workers by reducing home price growth and rental rates, lowering total consumer debt and increasing consumers' net worth, and providing more flexibility to move as job market conditions change.

ACTION PLAN

Multiple agency-level reforms can help reduce federal involvement in housing finance to the benefit of American workers. Ultimately, though, major reductions in the level of federal involvement will require Congress to act.

Thus, Congress should

- limit the FHA's single-family insurance portfolio to first-time homebuyers, without any refinance eligibility over the tenure of the loans in force. Additionally, the value of loan limits eligible for FHA single-family mortgage insurance should decrease to (at most) the first quartile of home prices in a given locality;
- end FHA multifamily mortgage insurance;
- at a minimum, reduce the FHA's level of loan coverage in the single-family mortgage insurance program from the current level (approximately 100 percent of the loan) to the private industry standard of 20 percent;
- eliminate any semblance of affordable housing goals for all financial institutions;
- eliminate the ability-to-repay standard, the qualified mortgage standard,

and all the mortgage servicing rules imposed by the Dodd–Frank Act; and

- shut down Fannie Mae and Freddie Mac and all their subsidiaries. Any legislation to close Fannie and Freddie should avoid creating a smaller version of the GSEs under a new name.

While the GSEs continue to exist, the Federal Housing Finance Agency should

- raise Fannie and Freddie's mortgage guarantee fees; and
- eliminate the geographic price differentials for the GSEs' conforming loan limits, narrow the GSEs' focus to the financing of primary homes, and gradually reduce conforming loan limits. (The GSEs should no longer support financing for second homes, vacation homes, investment properties, or cash-out refinancing.)

NOTES

1. These figures represent the combined ownership rate for people who own their home outright and those who own a mortgage, for both the United States and all Organisation for Economic Co-operation and Development (OECD) countries, using 2019 data, as reported in the OECD Affordable Housing Database, October 15, 2021.

2. Dwight M. Jaffee, "Reforming the U.S. Mortgage Market through Private Market Incentives," in Satya Thallam, ed., *House of Cards: Reforming America's Housing Finance System* (Arlington, VA: Mercatus Center at George Mason University, 2012), pp. 23–25.

3. Michael Lea, *International Comparison of Mortgage Product Offerings* (Washington: Research Institute for Housing America, September 2010).

4. Jesper Berg, Morten Bækmand Nielsen, and James Vickery, "Peas in a Pod? Comparing the U.S. and Danish Mortgage Finance Systems," *Economic Policy Review* 24, no. 3 (December 2018): 63–87; Frances Schwartzkopff, "World's Cheapest Mortgage May Be around the Corner in Denmark," *Bloomberg*, March 21, 2019; and Frances Schwartzkopff, "20-Year Mortgages Hit Zero for First Time in Danish Rate History," *Bloomberg*, August 7, 2019.

5. For the fiscal year ending December 31, 2020, Fannie Mae reported $4 trillion in total assets, while Freddie Mac reported $2.6 trillion. See "Fannie Mae 2020 Form 10-K," Fannie Mae, February 12, 2021, p. 61; and "2020 Annual Report on Form 10K, Fourth Quarter 2020 and Full Year Financial Results," Freddie Mac, February 11, 2021, p. 34. The 42 percent figure is the author's estimate using the Federal Reserve's (now discontinued) 2019 reported total for mortgage debt outstanding ($15.8 trillion). See Board of Governors of the Federal Reserve System, "Mortgage Debt Outstanding, All Holders (DISCONTINUED) [(MDOAH])," Federal Reserve Economic Data (FRED), Federal Reserve Bank of St. Louis, October 15, 2021.

6. See Office of Risk Management and Regulatory Affairs, Office of Evaluation, Reporting and Analysis Division, *FHA Single Family Market Share, 2020 Q1* (Washington: Department of Housing and Urban Development, 2020), p. 4.

7. These figures include both single-family and multifamily mortgage-backed securities. See Securities Industry and Financial Markets Association, "US MBS Securities: Issuance, Trading Volume, Outstanding," October 13, 2021; and Ginnie Mae, *Issuance Summary,* March 2021.

8. Asaf Bernstein and Daan Struyven, "Housing Lock: Dutch Evidence on the Impact of Negative Home Equity on Household Mobility," *American Economic Journal: Economic Policy* 14, no. 3 (August 2022): 1–32.

9. For more information on U.S. homeownership rates between 1940 and 1960 (which increased from 44 percent to 62 percent), see *How Private Equity Landlords are Changing the Housing Market, Before the United States Senate Committee on Banking, Housing, and Urban Affairs Hearing,* 117th Cong. 1st Sess. (October 21, 2021)(statement of Norbert J. Michel).

10. U.S. Census Bureau, "Homeownership Rate in the United States [RHORUSQ156N]," FRED, Federal Reserve Bank of St. Louis, October 15, 2021.

11. For examples, see Jennifer Brown and David Matsa, "Locked in by Leverage: Job Search during the Housing Crisis," *Journal of Financial Economics* 136, no. 3 (June 2020): 623–48; Sewin Chan, "Spatial Lock-in: Do Falling House Prices Constrain Residential Mobility?," *Journal of Urban Economics* 49, no. 3 (May 2001): 567–86; and Fernando Ferreira, Joseph Gyourko, and Joseph Tracy, "Housing Busts and Household Mobility: An Update," *Federal Reserve Bank of New York Economic Policy Review* 18, no. 3 (November 2012): 1–15.

ESSENTIAL GOODS

BY GABRIELLA BEAUMONT-SMITH

THE ISSUE: GOVERNMENT POLICIES ARTIFICIALLY INFLATE THE PRICES OF EVERYDAY ESSENTIALS, THUS SHRINKING AMERICAN WORKERS' REAL INCOMES AND LOWERING THEIR LIVING STANDARDS

Washington policymakers tend to forget an immutable truth: all American workers are also American consumers, spending a significant portion of their paychecks on essential goods such as clothing, food, shelter, and energy. Yet our elected officials frequently implement policies—even ones alleged to be "pro-worker"—that intentionally raise the prices of these necessities, thus reducing workers' real (consumption-adjusted) household incomes and living standards.

Necessities generally constitute a larger share of lower-income workers' total compensation, inclusive of taxes and government transfers. As shown in Table 1, for example, shelter, food, transport, utilities, and clothes accounted for approximately 68 percent of the poorest U.S. households' annual expenditures, but only 52 percent of the richest households' spending.[1] The essential nature of these items also means that Americans tend to consume roughly the same amounts of them each month, regardless of whether prices fall or rise (though differences across households surely exist).

Increasing prices of necessities are particularly painful for single-parent families, which spend the largest share of their incomes on basic goods. In 2019, for example, single-parent households devoted almost 5 percent of their annual spending to clothes, shoes, linens, and other miscellaneous houseware, totaling around $2,400 per family. By contrast, wealthy households spent much more on these same items (more than $5,100), but their purchases constituted a much lower share (just 3.5 percent) of their annual incomes.[2]

Thus, rising prices of basic necessities are typically a regressive tax on American households, disproportionately hurting workers at the lower end of the wage scale and larger families that consume more, especially ones led by a single parent. Costlier essentials also undermine government welfare and labor (e.g., food assistance or minimum wage) policies designed to help these same groups.

Unfortunately, numerous government policies inflate the prices of essential goods, to the detriment of most American workers and their families.

As discussed in the Transportation chapter, for example, tariffs, fuel economy regulations, taxes, maritime restrictions (the Merchant Marine Act of 1920, aka the "Jones Act"), and other policies significantly increase automobile and fuel prices in the United States, thus harming the almost 85 percent of Americans who drove to work prior to the pandemic.[3] These transportation taxes are unsurprisingly regressive: the Tax Foundation has estimated, for example, that

TABLE 1 Poorer Americans spend more on necessities

Expense type	Poorest quintile	Richest quintile	Single-parent family	Whole population
Shelter	24.5%	17.7%	21.3%	19.3%
Transport	16.0%	15.8%	17.5%	17.0%
Food	15.3%	11.5%	14.9%	13.0%
Health care	10.0%	6.9%	5.4%	8.2%
Utilities	8.8%	4.8%	7.4%	6.4%
Other	5.9%	21.5%	13.0%	16.0%
Entertainment	3.9%	5.6%	4.3%	4.9%
Household operations and supplies	3.7%	3.8%	4.1%	3.7%
Furniture	3.3%	3.5%	2.9%	3.3%
Apparel	2.9%	2.9%	4.4%	3.0%
Reading and education	2.9%	3.4%	2.2%	2.4%
Personal care	1.3%	1.2%	1.6%	1.2%
Tobacco	1.0%	0.2%	0.5%	0.5%
Alcohol	0.7%	1.0%	0.7%	0.9%

Source: "Table 1101. Quintiles of Income before Taxes: Annual Expenditure Means, Shares, Standard Errors, and Coefficients of Variation, Consumer Expenditure Survey, 2019," Bureau of Labor Statistics, 2019, https://www.bls.gov/cex/tables/calendar-year/mean-item-share-average-standard-error/cu-income-quintiles-before-taxes-2019.pdf; and "Table 1502. Composition of Consumer Unit: Annual Expenditure Means, Shares, Standard Errors, and Coefficients of Variation, Consumer Expenditure Survey, 2019," Bureau of Labor Statistics, 2019, https://www.bls.gov/cex/tables/calendar-year/mean-item-share-average-standard-error/cu-composition-2019.pdf.

a hypothetical 25 percent tariff on imported automobiles would decrease the average after-tax incomes of all taxpayers by 0.47 percent, with those in the top 1 percent facing the lightest (0.39 percent) burden.[4]

The Housing Affordability chapter, meanwhile, shows that federal, state, and local policies substantially increase construction costs, home prices, and rents—especially in many of the country's most attractive labor markets. Lower-income workers are again disproportionately harmed. By increasing developers' construction costs, for example, materials tariffs and federal tax policy encourage them to focus on luxury units with higher profit margins.[5] At the same time, high housing prices in heavily regulated cities with hot labor markets prevent lower-income workers in distressed areas from moving to the cities and improving their job prospects and lifetime earnings.[6]

Government policies also increase the price of food, on which the poorest quintile households spent $4,099 in 2020 (14.3 percent of their total spending, again the highest proportion of any income group). This includes—

- For dairy products (1.1 percent of bottom-quintile household expenditures), the Agricultural Marketing Agreement Act of 1937 artificially raises milk, cheese, and other dairy prices and imposes prohibitive tariffs and nontariff barriers on imports of these products. These policies not only raise prices but also insulate dairy farmers from market signals, encouraging them to produce dairy products almost regardless of market demand. The programs can also lead to shortages, as occurred when tariff-rate quotas and Food and Drug Administration (FDA) regulations effectively walled off the U.S. infant formula market from foreign competition and thereby contributed to empty store shelves for much of 2022.[7]

- The federal government essentially cartelizes the domestic sugar market. The U.S. Department of Agriculture (USDA) facilitates loans to sugar processors using collateral in the form of raw sugarcane and refined beet sugar to create a price floor for the sugar price.[8] To encourage repayment of these loans, the government restricts the supply of domestic sugar, increases demand for sugar through governmental purchases, and finally, restricts imports of sugar. These policies increase sugar prices—the USDA reported that the U.S. raw sugar price was 33.55 cents per pound in 2021, compared to 17.85 cents per pound at the world price—harming American consumers, as well as workers in sugar-consuming industries such as baking and candy-making.[9]

- Beyond dairy and sugar, the United States imposes high (greater than 10 percent) tariffs and tariff rate quotas on numerous food products—such as peanuts, tuna, cantaloupes, apricots, various meats, sardines, spinach, soybean oil, watermelons, carrots, celery, okra, artichokes, sweet corn, Brussels sprouts, cut cauliflower, and so on—costing American importers billions of dollars per year.[10] Also, countervailing duties (i.e., taxes on imports that have been allegedly subsidized by the governments of the origin countries) on imports of fertilizer are paid by U.S. farmers and, by contributing to lower yields and thus reducing food supply, put further upward pressure on domestic food prices.[11]

- Produce marketing orders allow fruit, nut, and vegetable farmers to dictate their commodity's requirements for sale on the fresh food market. Minimum prices, rigid inspection rules, and other terms of sale can insulate farmers from foreign competition, stymie entrepreneurship, increase domestic prices, and distort economic activity—all to American consumers' detriment.[12] For example, the South Texas onions marketing order implicitly creates quantity restrictions by mandating the quality and size of onions that farmers legally sell in this region. These barriers reduce competition and innovation by preventing farmers with other varieties from accessing the market, and they reduce onion supplies and thus inflate prices.[13] Marketing orders can even encourage collusion among farmers in a particular region, creating cartels that further boost prices.[14]

- The Renewable Fuel Standard (RFS) mandates the amount of biofuels blended into transportation fuel, thus increasing demand for corn-based ethanol. This can raise the prices of not only corn and corn-based products such as animal feed, but also other crops that policy does not encourage. The Congressional Budget Office and other organizations estimate that artificial demand for ethanol raises Americans' total food spending by between 0.8 and 2 percent.[15]

Government policies also increase the cost of energy, beyond just gasoline, and thus reduce Americans' real incomes and wealth. For example, state energy codes regulating a home's carbon footprint can reduce home values for low-income households by 8 to 12 percent, likely because these regulations end up reducing the number of bedrooms and square footage of homes in these lowest-income households.[16] Evidence also shows that this loss of wealth has not been offset by reduced energy use (and thus lower energy bills).[17] The Jones Act, meanwhile, increases the cost of both building offshore wind power facilities and shipping petroleum products between American ports (effectively prohibiting liquified natural gas shipments due to a lack of ships).[18] Federal energy projects, including those subsidized by the 2022 Inflation Reduction Act, are routinely larded down with costly Buy America rules that require the projects to use domestic materials.[19] And onerous state and federal environmental regulations, such as the National Environmental Policy Act (NEPA), have blocked or delayed *dozens* of hydropower, solar, wind, and geothermal projects across the country.[20] (See the Transportation chapter for more on the Jones Act, as well as NEPA and its state-level equivalents.)

The United States also applies trade remedy (antidumping, countervailing duty, and safeguard) restrictions on imports of numerous energy-related products, such as solar panels, wind turbines, electrical transformers, and oil and gas pipes, further increasing the cost of producing and distributing energy in the United States. Indeed, a 2022 trade remedies investigation of solar panels from several Southeast Asian nations so threatened the U.S. energy market that President Biden was forced to issue a legally dubious "emergency" declaration, pausing any potential duties, to ensure that "the United States has access to a sufficient supply of solar modules to assist in meeting our electricity generation needs."[21] Yet this sword of Damocles still hangs over the U.S. solar industry, potentially depressing domestic investment while leaving many other, similarly damaging duties on imported energy products in place.

American workers also pay more for clothing and footwear because of U.S. policy. Most notably, imports of these necessities face average tariffs of about 11 percent—some of the highest in the tariff code—thanks to the Smoot-Hawley Tariff Act of 1930. As a result, American companies and consumers have paid more than $300 billion in tariffs since the infamous law was enacted.[22] Adding insult to this injury, the tariff code systematically subjects lower-value versions of these essential goods to higher tariffs than their more expensive counterparts.[23] As shown in Table 2, for example, a cashmere sweater is subject to a 4 percent tariff, compared to 17 percent and 32 percent for wool and polyester sweaters, respectively. Cheap children's shoes, meanwhile, face a whopping 48 percent tariff, while designer men's loafers pay only 8.5 percent. Given that children's shoes and clothing must be purchased more often as kids grow, these tariffs are a particularly onerous burden for large, lower-income American families—and especially damaging, given the near-total absence of an apparel and footwear industry in the United States.[24]

Women's clothes and footwear also tend to be subject to higher tariffs than men's versions of these same items.[25]

TABLE 2 Tariffs are higher on mass-market products than luxury goods

Product	Luxury good	Medium-end good	Mass-market good
Shoes	8.5% (men's leather dress shoes)	20.0% (running shoes)	48.0% (valued at $3 or less)
Sweaters	4.0% (cashmere)	16.0% (wool)	32.0% (acrylic)
Men's shirts	0.9% (silk)	19.7% (cotton)	32.0% (polyester)
Handbags	5.3% (snakeskin)	10.0% (leather valued at $20 or less)	16.0% (canvas)
Pillowcases	4.5% (silk)	11.9% (cotton)	14.9% (polyester)
Necklaces	5.0% (gold)	6.3% (silver)	13.5% (silver jewelry valued at $1.50 or less)
Scarves	1.5% (silk)	9.6% (wool)	11.3% (polyester)
Blankets	0.0% (wool)	8.4% (cotton)	8.5% (polyester)

Source: U.S. International Trade Commission Tariff Database, https://dataweb.usitc.gov/tariff/database.
Note: The tariff codes for these products are: 64035960, 64029142, 64029160, 61101210, 61101100, 61103030, 61059040, 61051000, 61052020, 42022130, 42022160, 42022215, 63022900, 63022130, 63022210, 71131921, 71131110, 71131120, 61171040, 61171010, 61171020, 63012000, 63013000, and 63014000.

Even "free trade" agreements (FTAs) contain restrictions on footwear and apparel imports. Beyond simply keeping many high tariffs in place or delaying their phase-out for years, bilateral and regional trade agreements also impose convoluted "yarn forward" rules conditioning lower apparel tariffs on, among other things, the goods' use of American textile inputs.[26] As a result, foreign apparel producers pay more for U.S. materials or simply ignore the yarn forward rule and pay the higher, non-FTA tariff. Either way, American consumers lose.[27]

Federal trade policy similarly raises the price of homewares, such as small appliances and other household goods, on which poorer Americans again spend more of their incomes than do wealthier ones. (For example, low-income families spend almost 2 percent of their expenditures on these goods.) Silverware, plates and cups, and drinking glasses are subject to an average tariff of 11 percent, which is almost 16 times the average tariff for all other goods.[28] In fact, tariffs on a small set of home consumer goods made up well over half of all tariff revenue ($144 billion out of $2.33 trillion) as of 2017, even though these goods only make up 6 percent of total imports.[29] Even school supplies are more expensive because of U.S. trade policy. Ballpoint pens and notebooks, for example, are each subject to tariffs of about 10 percent; backpacks and gym bags face 28 percent tariffs.[30] Indeed, as annually documented by the National Taxpayers Union (NTU), when you combine these tariffs with the ones on shoes and clothing, almost everything an American student needs for school is subject to some sort of import tax.[31] Given that parents must buy their kids new or different supplies almost every school year (if not even more frequently), these tariffs constitute another significant and regular burden on working families.

Finally, federal immigration policy—quotas, processing delays, wage floors, and endless paperwork—could further inflate the cost of many essential goods by restricting the available supply of workers in related industries, especially ones employing a disproportionate share of immigrants. As noted in the Housing Affordability chapter, for example, immigration restrictions have contributed to labor market tightness in the construction industry, which relies heavily on foreign-born workers. Other industries, such as agriculture, food service, transportation, and warehousing, have faced similar hiring challenges during the pandemic.[32] Given that immigrants also consume essential goods, the precise effect of immigration restrictions on the prices of housing, food, clothing, and other necessities is uncertain. But the last two years have repeatedly demonstrated that these policies prevent the efficient functioning of several essential industries.

THE POLICY SOLUTIONS: LOWER THE COSTS OF FOOD, CLOTHING, AND OTHER ESSENTIAL GOODS BY REFORMING TARIFFS AND OTHER GOVERNMENT SUPPLY-SIDE RESTRICTIONS

Instead of trying to subsidize workers and families through a complex and distortionary system of tax credits, vouchers, and wage controls, governments should work to increase Americans' real incomes by lowering the costs of food, clothing, and other essential goods. Toward this end, the federal government should reform or repeal existing laws and regulations that raise the price of these necessities, to all workers' detriment.

To lower food prices in the United States, the federal government should enact several supply-side reforms—

- First, Congress should eliminate the U.S. dairy program either immediately or as part of broader reform of the Farm Bill, which is set to expire in 2023. Doing so would allow prices to reflect supply and demand for domestic dairy products and should free up tax dollars. To maximize competition in the dairy sector, Congress also should remove all tariffs and tariff-rate quotas on dairy products so that Americans can import cheaper varieties of milk, butter, cheese, and infant formula.[33] Congress took a small step toward liberalization with the 2022 Fixing Our Regulatory Mayhem Upsetting Little Americans, or FORMULA Act, by temporarily suspending tariffs on infant formula imports in response to largescale national shortages. However, for consumers to fully benefit, Congress should permanently remove these and other dairy tariffs while also directing the FDA to admit imported dairy and other food products that have already been approved by a competent regulatory body abroad (e.g., the European Food Safety Authority).

- Second, Congress should repeal all aspects of the U.S. sugar program, which distorts the domestic sugar market and enriches wealthy sugar companies at American consumers' expense. Doing so would lower the domestic price of sugar to more closely match the world price, providing particular benefits for workers in sugar-consuming industries and large, low-income households that tend to consume more processed foods.

- Third, Congress should repeal all remaining tariffs on imported foods, which raise domestic prices and needlessly protect and enrich a globally dominant U.S. agricultural industry. According to a 2021 report by the USDA, the elimination of agricultural tariffs would increase consumer well-being by $3.5 billion.[34]

- Fourth, Congress should reform the Agricultural Marketing Agreement of 1937, which authorizes the imposition of produce marketing orders that do not address food safety and instead simply raise prices and restrict competition and innovation. By eliminating the legal authority to impose these orders, Congress would help American consumers enjoy more and cheaper produce, improving both their budgets and health.
- Fifth, Congress should repeal the Renewable Fuel Standard to reduce demand for corn, thus putting downward pressure on corn prices and freeing up land for alternative crops. Since corn is often used as feed by dairy and meat farmers, they would also benefit from lower corn prices, likely passing on some of these savings via lower dairy and meat prices. Processed food products that use corn (e.g., cereal) would similarly benefit.

On energy, state governments should repeal energy codes that increase energy prices and decrease housing affordability. To further increase domestic energy supplies and lower prices, Congress should repeal the Jones Act, which needlessly restricts energy shipments between U.S. ports and makes offshore wind projects more costly; reform environmental regulations that have blocked or delayed numerous energy projects; and repeal energy-related subsidies and related localization mandates (e.g., Buy America rules) that distort the domestic energy markets and increase costs.

Furthermore, Congress should reform trade remedies to allow administering agencies (i.e., the Department of Commerce and International Trade Commission) to consider potential duties' effects on the broader public interest, including the energy market and American households. Where duties would compromise U.S. energy security or impose an unbearably high cost on American households, the agencies would decline to impose them. Congress should also give producers in import-consuming industries (e.g., solar panel installers or U.S. oil companies) legal standing to participate fully in trade remedy proceedings, and allow agencies to suspend duties in times of national emergency or to impose lower duties where doing so would achieve the laws' remedial objectives.

For apparel and footwear, Congress should eliminate all tariffs, yarn forward rules, and other restrictions on imported textiles, apparel, and footwear, which raise clothing and shoe prices yet protect few (if any) jobs. Given that Americans have paid hundreds of billions of dollars in apparel and footwear tariffs alone over the past 90-plus years, removing all import restraints on these goods would generate substantial consumer savings, especially for larger and poorer households that need to stretch their budgets.

Congress also should eliminate all tariffs on home goods and school products to alleviate the tax burden on parents' wallets so that they can allocate financial resources to other things, such as funds for home improvement or their children's education.

More broadly, the federal government should liberalize immigration to ease current labor pressures in agriculture, food services, transportation and warehousing, construction, and other industries that supply essential goods and disproportionately rely on immigrants. In particular, Congress should streamline the onerous employer-sponsored processes for H-2B visas, H-2A visas, J-1 visas, and green cards. Current caps on admissions should be eliminated, or at least drastically increased to accommodate employers' needs. The entire bureaucratic process also should be reformed to take no more than 30 days and to require a single application. It should be easier for the average American household to directly hire a foreign worker (e.g., as a housekeeper, landscaper, or au pair).

Furthermore, temporary visas should not be limited only to short-term jobs and should be renewable for as long as the worker is employed. Finally, the market should set wages, and foreign workers should be able to change jobs if the initial wage offer is at a below-market rate. If government continues to set wages, and no American worker accepts the higher wage offer, the employer should be able to pay the foreign worker any agreed-upon wage. Market wages would increase access to jobs and lower prices for household help, food, and other necessities.

Finally, Congress and state governments should pursue the reforms discussed in the Housing Affordability, Transportation, Child Care, and Health Care chapters to lower prices of these essential goods and services.

Individually, these and other current policies might only cost American households a few extra dollars per year. Collectively, however, the burdens can be significant—especially for large, low-income families—and reforming them would thus provide a tangible improvement in American workers' living standards. Consider, for example, recent International Trade Commission estimates finding that U.S. restrictions on imported food and clothing significantly increase the prices of these goods (see Table 3). Restrictions on butter and cheese, in particular, increase prices of these products by 20.8 percent and 15.3 percent, respectively—thus forcing Americans in the bottom quintile to pay an estimated $71.48 more per year (if they consumed only imported butter and cheese).[35] Given the wide array of restrictions on imports of other necessities and tariffs' inflationary effect on similar domestically produced goods, eliminating all of these import taxes would likely save American households hundreds of dollars per year.

TABLE 3 Trade restrictions make food, clothing, and manufactured goods more expensive

Sector	U.S. tariff rate	U.S. tariff-rate quota	Total
Refined sugar	1.6%	55.0%	56.6%
Raw cane sugar	1.3%	28.0%	29.3%
Butter	5.8%	15.0%	20.8%
Cheese	7.3%	8.0%	15.3%
Apparel	12.8%	0.0%	12.8%
Canned tuna	12.3%	0.0%	12.3%
Leather and allied product manufacturing (including footwear)	10.1%	0.0%	10.1%
Costume jewelry and novelties	7.5%	0.0%	7.5%
Carpets and rugs	6.3%	0.0%	6.3%
Other textile products	5.5%	0.0%	5.5%
Fiber, yarn, and threads	5.2%	0.0%	5.2%
Fabrics	5.0%	0.0%	5.0%
Beef	1.0%	0.0%	1.0%

Source: U.S. International Trade Commission, "The Economic Effects of Significant U.S. Import Restraints, Special Topic: Effects of Tariffs and of Customs and Border Procedures on Global Supply Chains," Investigation no. 332-325, Publication 4726, September 2017, p. 14, https://www.usitc.gov/publications/332/pub4726.pdf.

Note: Tariff is an ad valorem equivalent share of the cost, insurance, and freight (c.i.f.) value of imports. Tariff-rate quota is measured as an export tax equivalent—that is, the degree to which it increases the "export price" of a commodity (defined as the price before entry into the United States).

ACTION PLAN

While it may seem intuitive to help workers by trying to directly subsidize their nominal incomes, these policies generate numerous distortions and unintended consequences—including higher prices for the very goods and services that these policies target. Embracing market-oriented reforms to reduce the costs of basic necessities is a better approach to improving the real incomes of all American workers, while giving them more control over their expenditures in the process.

Congress should therefore

- unilaterally remove tariffs and duties on necessities including food, clothing, shoes, automobiles, auto parts, homewares, school supplies, and construction materials, including tariffs imposed under Section 232 on steel and aluminum, and Section 301 tariffs on Chinese imports;
- repeal the Jones Act, or, at the very least, exempt energy shipments from the law and repeal its U.S.-built requirement that dramatically raises the cost of purchasing new vessels, including tankers;
- include in the next Farm Bill provisions cutting the dairy and sugar programs, or at least removing tariff-rate quotas on imports of dairy and sugar products;
- require the FDA to admit imported infant formula and other dairy products already approved by competent regulatory bodies abroad, such as those in Europe and New Zealand;
- reform the Agricultural Marketing Agreement of 1937 to repeal all agricultural marketing orders;
- repeal the Renewable Fuel Standard to free up land for alternative uses and to lower food prices;
- eliminate subsidies for all energy products and eliminate all localization mandates (Buy America rules) tied to U.S. energy and transportation projects;
- reform antidumping and countervailing duty laws to account for downstream impact and to give downstream stakeholders legal standing in proceedings; and
- remove caps on H-2B and J-1 visas; base wages for H-2B and H-2A visas on skill level; and create a guest worker program specifically for construction and related year-round jobs.

The executive branch should

- form an agreement with Canada to remove the export quota and tax on Canadian exports of infant formula stipulated in the United States-Mexico-Canada Agreement.

State and local governments should

- repeal energy codes.

NOTES

1. "Table 1101. Quintiles of Income before Taxes: Annual Expenditure Means, Shares, Standard Errors, and Coefficients of Variation, Consumer Expenditure Survey, 2019," Bureau of Labor Statistics, 2019.

2. Ed Gresser, "Trade Policy, Equity, and the Working Poor: United States MFN Tariffs Are Regressive Taxes Which Help Few Workers and Harm Many," Progressive Policy Institute, April 2022.

3. Michael Burrows et al., "Commuting by Public Transportation in the United States: 2019," Census Bureau, April 2021.

4. Erica York, "Automobile Tariffs Offset Half the TCJA Gains for Low-Income Households," Tax Foundation, June 4, 2018.

5. Scott Lincicome, "Why (Some of) the Rents Are Too Damn High," *Cato at Liberty* (blog), Cato Institute, December 22, 2020.

6. Peter Ganon and Daniel Shoag, "Why Has Regional Income Convergence in the U.S. Declined?," Harvard University, January 2015.

7. Agricultural Marketing Agreement Act of 1937, 7 U.S.C. §§ 601–674 (1937); and Jessica DiNapoli, "Baby Formula Makers Raced for FDA Approval. They May Be Waiting a While," Reuters, June 15, 2022.

8. Colin Grabow, "Candy-Coated Cartel: Time to Kill the U.S. Sugar Program," Cato Institute Policy Analysis no. 837, April 10, 2018.

9. "Sugar and Sweeteners Yearbook Tables," Economic Research Service, Department of Agriculture, August 19, 2022.

10. See, for instance, Scott Lincicome, "Promoting Free Trade in Agriculture," Heritage Foundation, July 11, 2016.

11. Scott Lincicome, "Countervailing Calamity: How to Stop the Global Subsidies Race," Cato Institute Policy Analysis no. 710, October 9, 2021; Daniel J. Ikenson, "Tariffs by Fiat: The Widening Chasm between U.S. Antidumping Policy and the Rule of Law," Cato Institute Policy Analysis no. 896, July 16, 2020; Jon Emot and Jenny Carolina Gonzalez, "'Farms Are Failing' as Fertilizer Prices Drive Up Cost of Food," *Wall Street Journal,* January 21, 2022; and Patrick Thomas and Kirk Maltais, "Surging Fertilizer Costs Push Farmers to Shift Planting Plans, Raise Prices," *Wall Street Journal*, December 15, 2021.

12. Cynthia David, "Grape Expectations—Suppliers Talk Varieties, Packaging, Season," *The Packer,* May 18, 2020.

13. Gabriella Beaumont-Smith, "The Produce Cartels," *Cato at Liberty* (blog), Cato Institute, December 21, 2021.

14. Darren Filson et al., "Market Power and Cartel Formation: Theory and an Empirical Test," *Journal of Law & Economics* 44, no. 2 (October 2001): 2000–31.

15. "The Impact of Ethanol Use on Food Prices and Greenhouse-Gas Emissions," Congressional Budget Office Publication no. 3155, April 2009, pp. 8–10; and Richard K. Perrin, "Ethanol and Food Prices—Preliminary Assessment," University of Nebraska–Lincoln, Faculty Publications: *Agricultural Economics* 49, May 9, 2008.

16. Vanessa Brown Calder, "When Environmental Regulations Harms the Poor," *Cato at Liberty* (blog), Cato Institute, January 31, 2018.

17. Christopher D. Bruegge et al., "The Distributional Effects of Building Energy Codes," National Bureau of Economic Research Working Paper no. 24211, January 2018.

18. Colin Grabow, "Jones Act Inflicts Costly Burden on US Offshore Wind," *Cato at Liberty* (blog), Cato Institute, August 2, 2021; and Michael Ratner et al., "U.S. Liquefied Natural Gas (LNG) Exports: Prospects for the Caribbean," Congressional Research Service, R45006, November 1, 2017.

19. See, for instance, Scott Lincicome, "... But We Won't Do That," *The Dispatch*, August 10, 2022.

20. Adam Millsap, "Energy Abundance Is Possible and Europe Shows Us Why It Is Necessary," *Forbes*, March 3, 2022.

21. Jeffrey A. Chester et al., "Biden Uses Emergency Powers to Pause New Solar Import Tariffs—Frequently Asked Question," Greenberg Traurig, June 10, 2022.

22. Not adjusted for inflation; based on "USFIA Speaks Out on 90th Anniversary of the Smoot-Hawley Tariff Act," press release, U.S. Fashion Industry Association, June 19, 2020; and Matt Priest and Julia K. Hughes, "Why the 90-Year-Old Tariff Act Needs a 21st-Century Makeover," *Sourcing Journal*, June 29, 2020.

23. Miguel Acosta and Lydia Cox, "The Regressive Nature of the U.S. Tariff Code: Origins and Implications," Harvard University, April 2, 2022.

24. In 2020, American apparel and footwear production accounted for 3.5 percent and 2.3 percent of the U.S. market, respectively. See Sheng Lu, "AAFA Released New Statistics Showing the Economic Impacts of the US Apparel and Footwear Industry," FASH455 Global Apparel and Textile Trade and Sourcing, University of Delaware, August 31, 2021.

25. Miranda Hatch, "Is Trade Sexist? How 'Pink' Tariff Policies' Harmful Effects Can Be Curtailed through Litigation and Legislation," *BYU Law Review* 47, no. 2 (October 15, 2022): 651–84.

26. Vivian C. Jones and Liana Wong, "Rules of Origin," Congressional Research Service, IF10754, February 17, 2021.

27. Michaela D. Platzer, "Renegotiating NAFTA and U.S. Textile Manufacturing," Congressional Research Service, R44998, October 30, 2017.

28. Ed Gresser, "PPI's Trade Fact of the Week: the U.S. Tariff System Is Biased against Poor Families," Progressive Policy Institute, March 23, 2022.

29. Gresser, "Trade Policy, Equity, and the Working Poor."

30. Coalition for GSP, "GSP Expiration Makes High 'Back to School' Tariffs Even Worse."

31. Bryan Riley, "Back to School Season Highlights High Cost of Import Taxes," National Taxpayers Union, August 26, 2022.

32. Nicola Nara, "Immigrants Could Fix the US Labor Shortage," *Vox*, October 26, 2021.

33. Sallie James, "Milking the Customers: The High Cost of U.S. Dairy Policies," Cato Institute Policy Brief no. 24, November 9, 2006; Gabriella Beaumont-Smith, "Rock-A-Bye Trade Restrictions on Baby Formula," *Cato at Liberty* (blog), Cato Institute, May 10, 2022; and Scott Lincicome, "America's Infant Formula Crisis and the 'Resiliency' Mirage," *The Dispatch*, May 11, 2022.

34. Jayson Beckman and Sara Scott, "How the Removal of Tariffs Would Impact Agricultural Trade," Economic Research Service, Department of Agriculture.

35. Calculations by author; "The Economic Effects of Significant U.S. Import Restraints, Special Topic: Effects of Tariffs and of Customs and Border Procedures on Global Supply Chains," International Trade Commission, Investigation no. 332-325, Publication 4726, September 2017, p. 14; and "Table 1101 Quintiles of Income before Taxes: Annual Expenditure Means, Shares, Standard Errors, and Coefficients of Variation, Consumer Expenditure Surveys, 2020," Bureau of Labor Statistics, 2020.

CONCLUSION

BY SCOTT LINCICOME

Partisans today routinely insist that free markets can no longer address the needs of American workers and, in fact, often undermine them. Thus, the story goes: we need new government interventions—wage subsidies, child allowances, paid leave mandates, tariffs, industrial subsidies, contract restrictions, etc.—to rescue drowning American workers and their families.

This prevalent view, however, suffers from obvious flaws.

For starters, there never has been a Golden Age when everything was perfect for American workers and their families. Tradeoffs in work, life, and family have always existed and always will. Government cannot change this reality. No one can.

In many important ways, moreover, Americans have it much better today— even after a global pandemic and rampant inflation—than they did just a few decades ago.[1] An American born in 1976, for example, has experienced significant long-term improvements, not merely in consumer goods and technology, but also in incomes, poverty, life expectancy, infant mortality, education, environmental quality, and more.[2] And, while the pandemic was surely terrible for most Americans, it would have been far *worse*—more death, more misery, etc.—if it had occurred just 20 years earlier.[3]

Perhaps most importantly, and as documented throughout this book, the claim that markets have failed American workers ignores the panoply of federal, state, and local policies that distort markets and thereby raise the cost of health care, childcare, housing, and other necessities; lower workers' total compensation; inhibit their employment, personal improvement, and mobility; and deny them the lives and careers that they actually want (as opposed to the ones DC policy-makers think they should want).

Indeed, just as technology, globalization, recessions, and then the pandemic were increasingly disrupting our world and workplaces, governments—through licensing, zoning, criminal justice, benefits, education, and myriad other policies— were making it increasingly difficult for Americans to adjust and prosper, often under the guise of "pro-worker" policy.

In truth, it's *policymakers* who have failed American workers over the last several decades, not some mythical "free market."

These realities argue for a new approach to policy targeting today's American worker—one that all but the most hardened of skeptics should embrace:

- First, reform the anti-market policies that economic experts of all stripes have shown to lower most Americans' living standards and to inhibit employment and mobility. Doing so is particularly important for low-income and low-skill workers, who suffer reduced living standards and increased financial distress in high-cost, heavily regulated cities like New York than they do in more affordable ones like Houston.[4] Yet current federal, state, and local policies not only increase less-skilled workers' economic burdens in expensive American cities but also discourage them from moving to cheaper ones.

- Second, implement commonsense, market-based policies—regarding education, remote work, independent work, employee benefits, and others—to better reflect our modern workforce and economy and what the New American Worker actually wants. Surveys show, for example, that we increasingly value flexibility over wages and independence over employment security. Yet many in Washington think of the American worker as helpless and in need of government protection from cradle to grave, despite the long-term harms that such policies inflict on these very same workers and the economy more broadly. By contrast, pro-market policies that respect the individual agency and ability of all workers would allow them to pursue their unique hopes and dreams in a more dynamic, diverse, and high-wage economy—and to adjust to whatever comes next.
- Third, policymakers should consider new pro-worker government interventions in the economy only after the aforementioned reforms are undertaken and real but rare market failures (not those actually caused by government) are demonstrated. Any proposed policy solutions, moreover, should be crafted to minimize drags on labor productivity and economic growth. Simply throwing more money at an existing program or creating yet another new program to address the challenges facing today's American workers promises to create higher costs and more distortions, not alleviate the concerns that are today mistakenly blamed on the free market. It also denies American workers the freedom and responsibility they deserve.

Of course, even if governments were to adopt this book's recommendations in their entirety, a labor utopia would not magically appear. Nevertheless, the policies proposed herein offer a better way forward than the anti-market labor agendas now popular on the left and the right. Time and again, including during the pandemic, we have seen that freer markets can best deliver vital goods and services, often in new and once-unimaginable ways. We've seen that protected, subsidized, and over-regulated markets, by contrast, produce higher prices, fewer choices, and even shortages when problems inevitably arise. And we've seen that American workers can, through their own initiatives, not merely survive our disruptive and messy modern world but eventually thrive therein—if governments will let them.

NOTES

1. Scott Lincicome, "Giving Thanks," *The Dispatch*, November 24, 2021.

2. See "Explore How Much the World Has Changed Since You Were Born," HumanProgress; Andrew McAfee, "The Economy Keeps Growing, but Americans Are Using Less Steel, Paper, Fertilizer, and Energy," Reason, October 9, 2019; Zeke Hausfather, "Absolute Decoupling of Economic Growth and Emissions in 32 Countries," Breakthrough Institute, April 6, 2021; and Marian L. Tupy and Gale L. Pooley, *Superabundance: The Story of Population Growth, Innovation, and Human Flourishing on an Infinitely Bountiful Planet* (Washington: Cato Institute, 2022).

3. Megan McArdle, "The Pandemic Has Been Awful. But Imagine It Had Struck 20 Years Ago," *Washington Post,* April 21, 2021.

4. Rebecca Diamond and Enrico Moretti, "Geographical Differences in Standard of Living across US Cities," *VoxEU*, March 17, 2022.

ACKNOWLEDGMENTS

Writing and editing a book, I've recently discovered, sounds a lot easier than it actually is—*especially* when it has multiple contributors and lots of charts. I'm therefore indebted to my Cato Institute colleagues who donated their valuable time and efforts this year to help make my half-baked ideas a serious reality. This includes not only the chapter authors, each of whom kindly agreed to distill their ample expertise into a few thousand words, but also all the support staff—researchers, art and data viz wizards, copyeditors, proofreaders, publication managers, and so on—who helped produce the book you're now reading. I'd especially like to thank my research assistants, Ilana Blumsack and Alfredo Carrillo Obregon, for their essential (and surely grueling at times) research and administrative work. I'm also grateful to the numerous outside experts whose research, support, and advice I utilized to supplement my and my fellow Catoites' already-strong work. And finally, I'd be remiss not to thank my family, especially my wife Elizabeth, for enduring my endless kvetching about "the book" this year. I promise it's over—until the next one.

—Scott Lincicome

ABOUT THE EDITOR

Scott Lincicome is the director of general economics and the Herbert A. Stiefel Center for Trade Policy Studies at the Cato Institute. He is also a senior visiting lecturer at Duke University Law School and columnist for *The Dispatch*. Lincicome has written on numerous economic issues, including international trade; subsidies and industrial policy; manufacturing and global supply chains; economic dynamism; and regulation.

Prior to joining Cato, Lincicome spent two decades practicing international trade law. He holds a BA in political science from the University of Virginia and a JD from the University of Virginia School of Law.

ABOUT THE CONTRIBUTORS

Pedro Aldighieri is originally from Brazil and holds a BA and MA in economics from the Pontifical Catholic University of Rio de Janeiro. He is currently pursuing a PhD in economics at Northwestern University.

Gabriella Beaumont-Smith is a policy analyst at the Cato Institute's Herbert A. Stiefel Center for Trade Policy Studies, where her research focuses on the economics of U.S. trade policy. Previously, she was a Senior Policy Analyst in Trade and Macroeconomics at the Heritage Foundation. She holds an MA in economics from George Mason University and a BA in economics from the University of Connecticut.

Ilana Blumsack is a research associate in economics at the Cato Institute, where she assists in research on fiscal and labor policy and on economic dynamism. She received a BA in economics and political science from the Hebrew University in Israel.

Ryan Bourne holds the R. Evan Scharf Chair for the Public Understanding of Economics at the Cato Institute and is the author of the recent book *Economics in One Virus*. He has written on numerous economic issues, including fiscal policy, inequality, the cost of living, and rent control. Previously, Bourne was head of public policy at the Institute of Economic Affairs in London. He holds a BA and MPhil in economics from the University of Cambridge in the United Kingdom.

Vanessa Brown Calder is the director of opportunity and family policy studies at the Cato Institute, where she focuses on polices that support family and increase opportunity. Previously, she was executive director and staff director at the U.S. Congress Joint Economic Committee under Sen. Mike Lee of Utah. Calder holds a master's degree in public policy from Harvard's John F. Kennedy School of Government and a BS in urban planning from the University of Utah.

Michael F. Cannon is "an influential health-care wonk" (*Washington Post*), "the most famous libertarian health care scholar" (*Washington Examiner*), and the Cato Institute's director of health policy studies. *Washingtonian* named Cannon one of Washington's "Most Influential People" in both 2021 and 2022. He is the coauthor of "Drug Reformation: End Government's Power to Require Prescriptions" and "Would 'Medicare for All' Mean Quality for All? How Public-Option Principles Could Reverse Medicare's Negative Impact on Quality" (*Quinnipiac Health Law Journal*). He holds an MA in economics and a JM in law and economics from George Mason University and a BA in American government from the University of Virginia.

Chris Edwards holds the Kilts Family Chair in Fiscal Studies at the Cato Institute and is the editor of DownsizingGovernment.org. He has testified to Congress on fiscal issues many times, and his articles on tax and budget policies have appeared in the *Washington Post, Wall Street Journal,* and other major media outlets. He is also the author of *Downsizing the Federal Government* and coauthor of *Global Tax Revolution*. Edwards holds a BA in economics from the University of Waterloo and an MA in economics from George Mason University.

Colin Grabow is a research fellow at the Cato Institute's Herbert A. Stiefel Center for Trade Policy Studies where his research focuses on domestic forms of trade protectionism such as the Jones Act and the U.S. sugar program. Grabow holds a BA in international affairs from James Madison University and an MA in international trade and investment policy from George Washington University.

Neal McCluskey is the director of the Cato Institute's Center for Educational Freedom. He is the author of *The Fractured Schoolhouse: Reexamining Education for a Free, Equal, and Harmonious Society* and is coeditor of several volumes, including *School Choice Myths: Setting the Record Straight on Education Freedom* and *Unprofitable Schooling: Examining Causes of, and Fixes for, America's Broken Ivory Tower*. McCluskey holds a PhD in public policy from George Mason University.

Norbert Michel is vice president and director of the Cato Institute's Center for Monetary and Financial Alternatives, where he specializes in issues pertaining to financial markets and monetary policy. Previously, he was the director for data analysis at the Heritage Foundation, and he has also taught economics, finance, and statistics at Nicholls State University in Louisiana. He is the author of *Why Shadow Banking Didn't Cause the Financial Crisis and Why Regulating Contagion Won't Help*. Michel holds a PhD in financial economics from the University of New Orleans.

Jeffrey Miron is vice president for research at the Cato Institute and the director of graduate and undergraduate studies in the Department of Economics at Harvard University. He is an expert on the economics of libertarianism and is the author of *Drug War Crimes: The Consequences of Prohibition and Libertarianism, from A to Z*, in addition to numerous op-eds and journal articles. Miron received his PhD in economics from the Massachusetts Institute of Technology in 1984.

Jeffrey Singer is a senior fellow in health studies at the Cato Institute. He is the founder of Valley Surgical Clinics Ltd., the largest and oldest group private surgical practice in Arizona, and has been in private practice as a general surgeon for more than 35 years. He is also on the Board of Scientific Advisors of the American Council on Science and Health and is a fellow of the American College of Surgeons. Singer received his MD from the New York Medical College.

Brad Subramaniam is a former research associate in economics at the Cato Institute. His research covered numerous economic topics, including price controls and antitrust regulation. He holds a BA in economics from the University of Chicago, where he specialized in empirical methods. Subramaniam currently attends the University of Virginia School of Law.

Michael D. Tanner is a senior fellow at the Cato Institute, where his research focuses on poverty and welfare policy, entitlements, and Social Security. He is the author of numerous books, including *The Inclusive Economy: How to Bring Wealth to America's Poor, Going for Broke: Deficits, Debt, and the Entitlement Crisis*, and *Leviathan on the Right: How Big-Government Conservatism Brought Down the Republican Revolution*.

ABOUT THE CATO INSTITUTE

Founded in 1977, the Cato Institute is a public policy research foundation dedicated to broadening the parameters of policy debate to allow consideration of more options that are consistent with the principles of limited government, individual liberty, and peace. To that end, the Institute strives to achieve greater involvement of the intelligent, concerned lay public in questions of policy and the proper role of government.

The Institute is named for *Cato's Letters,* libertarian pamphlets that were widely read in the American Colonies in the early 18th century and played a major role in laying the philosophical foundation for the American Revolution.

Despite the achievement of the nation's Founders, today virtually no aspect of life is free from government encroachment. A pervasive intolerance for individual rights is shown by government's arbitrary intrusions into private economic trans-actions and its disregard for civil liberties. And while freedom around the globe has notably increased in the past several decades, many countries have moved in the opposite direction, and most governments still do not respect or safeguard the wide range of civil and economic liberties.

To address those issues, the Cato Institute undertakes an extensive publications program on the complete spectrum of policy issues. Books, monographs, and shorter studies are commissioned to examine the federal budget, Social Security, regulation, military spending, international trade, and myriad other issues.

To maintain its independence, the Cato Institute accepts no government fund-ing. Contributions are received from foundations, corporations, and individu-als, and other revenue is generated from the sale of publications. The Institute is a nonprofit, tax-exempt, educational foundation under Section 501(c)3 of the Internal Revenue Code.

CATO INSTITUTE
1000 Massachusetts Ave. NW
Washington, DC 20001
www.cato.org